another country
Writings by and about
HENRY KREISEL

Edited by Shirley Neuman

Volume VII
NeWest Literary Documents Series

NeWest Press
Edmonton

First edition

Canadian Cataloguing in Publication Data

Kreisel, Henry, 1922-
Another country

(Western Canadian literary documents; 7)
ISBN 0-920316-87-5 (bound). — ISBN 0-920316-85-9 (paper).

1. Kreisel, Henry, 1922- - Criticism and interpretation.
I. Neuman, S.C. (Shirley C.) II. Title. III. Series.
PS8521.R43A6 1985 C813'.54 C85-091223-7 PR9199.3.K73A6 1985

Acknowledgments

Publisher: Jack Lewis
Cover design: Norman Yates
Book production: Susan Colberg
Typesetting: June Charter
Assistance with proofreading and indexing: Stephen Scott
Printing and binding: Friesen Printers, Manitoba
Financial Assistance: Alberta Culture, Canada Council
    Multiculturalism Program: Government of Canada

NeWest Publishers Limited
Suite 204, 8631 - 109 Street
Edmonton, Alberta
Canada   T6G 1E8

For Kurt and Gus,
who were with me in the beginning,

and for Salka,
who rescued me. (H.K.)

For Marguerite,
who has taught me more
than I have taught her

With best wishes

Henry Kissel

Contents

A Preface

Perhaps only Henry Kreisel himself was surprised when the 1974
printing of the diary he had kept during his internment quickly sold
out—and sold out to historians and archives as well as to the general
reader. For the diary proved to be a rare record of a sparsely docu-
mented event: the British internment as 'enemy aliens' of Austrian
and German refugees in 1940. Those seeking information about the
actual physical removals of these 'prisoners' from one camp to
another and from England to Canada, about the conditions of their
lives in camp, about their psychological responses and adaptations to
exile and internment, and about the circumstances leading to their
eventual release found it in the notes kept by the young Henry Kreisel.

This collection is an outgrowth of that first publication of the
internment diary. It makes the diary available to readers again and
supplements it with selections from his poems and fiction written
during internment, writing which shows the emotional responses,
the philosophical and psychological adaptations the boy was
making to his experiences as refugee and internee. Later retrospective
letters, reminiscences and interviews in which Henry Kreisel recalls
his Viennese family, his internment, his choice of a vocation, his
release and his adaptation to another country offer an indication of
the life his flight and internment had disrupted, and of that other life
into which they propelled him.

That these experiences would become central to Henry Kreisel's
life and to his writing could hardly be otherwise. It is not so much
that they enter into the specific plots of his fiction, although they
sometimes do that, as that they are what he **writes out of** in a
philosophical or spiritual sense. They determine that generous
humanity that marks his relation to the world and to all its men and
women, and especially to the powerless. (The source of Henry
Kreisel's writing, these early experiences are, paradoxically, also
germane to his periods of not writing: generating in him as they did
an anxiousness to participate as fully as possible in the life of his new
country, to mark by action his gratitude to it, they also led him, as an
early story would have it, to tell the voice of the 'urge to write' to go
away while he dealt with the more cacophonous tones—some plati-
tudinous, some genuinely urgent—of university administrators for
many years at a time.)

The remainder of this collection reflects the writer that, struggling in an internment camp to express himself in English, the young Henry Kreisel willed himself to become. Several of his letters and interviews offer information about his own work. Personal essays, written for various occasions, record what it meant for him to become a **Canadian** writer. To the body of his work is added the text of a radio play not previously published and two short stories written since the publication of The Almost Meeting and Other Stories. A final section gathers several reviews and critical articles which amplify his own understanding of his work with that of his readers.

April 1985

england
and internment

On July 22nd 1938, Henry Kreisel landed at Dover. He had just turned sixteen and was seeking refuge from the Nazi takeover in Austria. By Christmas that year, his permit to stay had been extended until April 22nd 1939 'for training' at Montague Burton Ltd., a Leeds clothing factory. While working there, he began to write in English. Further extensions followed until, on October 6th 1939, he was granted an exemption from internment on the grounds that he was a 'Refugee from Nazi oppression.' But the exemption was not long honoured and, on May 16th 1940, he was interned with other 'German' refugees from the Nazi regime as an 'Enemy Alien.' He recorded the event in the first entry of a new diary.

After he was released from internment in November 1941 Henry Kreisel stored the diary in an old suitcase where he found it in 1973. He spoke about it to Sheila Watson who was then one of the editors of white pelican. *She persuaded him to let her transcribe and publish it (*white pelican, *4, 3 [Summer 1974], 5-35). With it appeared the first chapter of* Miguel Amore, *a novel Henry Kreisel had worked on in the internment camp during the summer of 1940 and a poem, 'Herschel Grynspan (Thought when hearing of his deportation to Germany),' dated '30.9.1940.' The diary was preceded by an 'Introduction' by Henry Kreisel and by a note by Sheila Watson. Her note read: 'The following diary is an exact transcription from the copy book in which Henry Kreisel recorded what happened after he was called to the main office of the Montague Burton Company in Leeds at 12:30 p.m. on May 16, 1940, then taken away by the "two men in raincoats".' The 'Introduction' and the 'Diary' are reprinted here. The translations of letters and the sign in German have been provided by Henry Kreisel for this printing.*

Nº 669979

Aliens Order, 1920.

CERTIFICATE OF REGISTRATION

You must produce this certificate if required to do so by any Police Officer, Immigration Officer, or member of His Majesty's forces acting in the course of his duty.

(C33488—3) 200,000 6/39

ENEMY ALIEN

REGISTRATION CERTIFICATE No. 669949.

ISSUED AT LEEDS CITY

ON 5ᵗ August 1938.

NAME (*Surname first in Roman Capitals*)

KREISEL Heinrich

ALIAS

Left Thumb Print
(*if unable to sign name
in English Characters*)

PHOTOGRAPH

Signature
of Holder } Heinrich Kreisel

2

ENDORSEMENTS AND REMARKS.

Permitted to land at Dover on 22ⁿᵈ July. 1938, on condition the Holder registers at once with the Police; does not remain in the U.K. longer than TWELVE MONTHS ↄ does not enter any employment, paid or unpaid, while in the United Kingdom. (Authority. H.O. K11422)

F. Swaby.

Chief Constable.

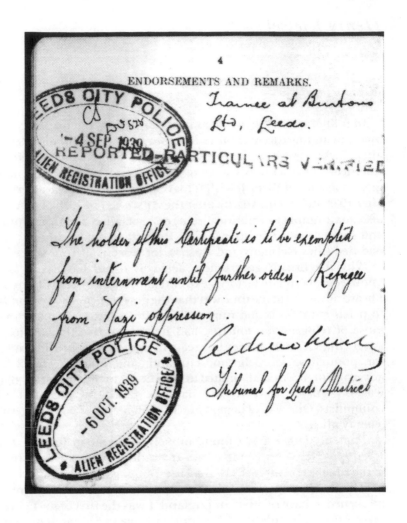

4

ENDORSEMENTS AND REMARKS.

Trainee at Burtons Ltd, Leeds.

REPORTED PARTICULARS VERIFIED

The holder of this Certificate is to be exempted from internment until further orders. Refugee from Nazi oppression.

Tribunal for Leeds District

Henry Kreisel
Diary of an Internment

Introduction

In mid-May of 1940, while France was falling, the British government, in an unexpected and sudden move, interned all male 'enemy
aliens' who were over sixteen years of age. Some women were also
interned. The 'enemy aliens' were German and Austrian citizens, the
great majority of them Jewish refugees who had fled Nazi Germany
after 1933 and, later, Austria after the *Anschluss* in 1938. There were
also a fair number of political refugees, Socialists and Communists,
and some devout Christians, both Protestants and Catholics, who
had fled from Germany and Austria for reasons of conscience.

Why the British government acted as it did has never, to my
knowledge, been satisfactorily explained.[1] The most plausible reason
I heard advanced at the time was that the government was responding
to persistent reports and rumors that fifth columnists, many in the
guise of refugees and tourists, had helped to pave the way for the
advancing German armies by creating panic and confusion among
the population of Belgium, Holland, and France. The British
government, it was said, wanted to reassure its own population that it
was on guard, alert to the dangers posed by potential fifth
columnists. One way of demonstrating this alertness was to intern all
'enemy aliens.'

Thus my father and I found ourselves caught in the net. I was
seventeen. Neither my mother nor my brother, who was only fifteen
at the time, were interned. We had been among the very few fortunate
families because we were able to escape after the *Anschluss*, since we
happened to have relatives in England. I was the first of my family to
leave Austria, in July 1938. My brother came to England in January
1939, and my parents not until August 1939, only a month before the
outbreak of war, and after some harrowing experiences, including
detention in concentration camps.

In May 1940 we were wholly unprepared for what was about to
happen to us. I was working as an apprentice cutter in the large
clothing factory of the Montague Burton Company in Leeds, when,
at 12:30 p.m. on May 16, 1940, I was called to the main office. This
was so unusual an occurrence as to cause something of a sensation
among my fellow workers. What could I possibly have done to be

summoned so peremptorily to the main office? Apprentices, when summoned at all, to be reprimanded or fired, were only called to the little cubby-hole office of the foreman on the floor. Never to the main office, where the real bosses were. One of my co-workers asked me to let him have my log so that, if I didn't come back, he could claim the work I had done.

My knees shaking, I followed the man who had been sent to fetch me, and was taken upstairs to the office of the assistant general manager. Two men in raincoats were waiting. The assistant general manager stood behind his desk. He had a sombre look, but I remember him speaking kindly. These gentlemen, he said, were detectives who had come to fetch me. The room began to sway. I could not find my voice. My throat seemed parched. What had I done? Then one of the detectives said that all aliens were being interned for a brief period. But there was nothing to be afraid of. It would all be sorted out quickly. My record was clean. I would soon be sent back. His manner was reassuring. I felt safer. It was likely, he added, that I would be detained for a day or two. Therefore they would drive me home so that I could get some pyjamas and a toothbrush. That was ominous. But I accepted his word at face value. The man was so obviously sincere. The assistant general manager shook my hand and said to be sure and come to see him when I got back to the factory. I said I would. Then I walked out of the office, between the two detectives, a kind of prisoner.

I don't remember whether we talked in the car. Another car was parked outside the house where we lived. My father had been fetched from the store where he was working. He was shaking and nervous and was packing a small suitcase, with a detective watching. Not to worry, this detective kept saying, not to worry. We'd be back in a day or so. Just take a toothbrush and some pyjamas. They said nothing about a razor, only about a toothbrush.

Could I take some books? Certainly, certainly. I had bought *The Brothers Karamazov* and a volume of poems by Keats and Shelley a few days before at a second-hand bookstore and I quickly put them into my little suitcase.

Then we drove off, my father and I, in separate cars. I must have been more dangerous than he, for two detectives escorted me, only one escorted him. We met again at Leeds Town Hall. A large crowd of people had gathered there to see the enemy aliens, potential fifth columnists, being rounded up. Photographers snapped pictures which would appear in the papers that night and next morning. All England would see that the government was alert, was on guard.

So began what was to be an internment lasting more than a year and a half. It was to take me to Canada, a country that I barely knew by name and that was only a large red stretch on the school maps we had used in Vienna in our geography lessons. It was a silent, mysterious land for me, known by all refugees as the country whose doors were most tightly shut. Virtually no one could get in. Ironically, then, it was to this country that we were ultimately taken, without passports, without papers. And when we got to Canada, we were in Canada, and yet not in Canada, for the internment camps were regarded, *de jure*, as territory leased to Great Britain for the duration of the war.

So I left England, and was not to see the country again, nor my mother and my brother, until, by a commodius vicus of recirculation, I returned to Leeds for a visit with my Canadian wife exactly nine years later, in May 1949.

Loss of freedom is a shocking experience. It was all the more so for us because we felt ourselves to be allies of Great Britain. We regarded Britain as the country that had rescued us from Nazi tyranny. To be then incarcerated by our friends seemed almost incomprehensible, a kind of betrayal. Certain passages in the diary reflect this feeling.

When we arrived in Canada, there was consternation among the Canadian officers in the camps. They had expected German prisoners of war, for that was the agreement Britain had made with Canada. But at the time the British army had simply not taken enough prisoners of war to fill the camps, and so the authorities sent civilian internees instead. For some time we were officially classed as prisoners of war, a status we persistently and bitterly fought. The diary records the day on which that status was finally changed, although on the surface nothing seemed to have happened, as I record cynically. Yet I was wrong. The change in our legal status made it possible for organizations and individuals who were working on our behalf—the Canadian Jewish Congress, the Society of Friends, and some other groups as well as influential Canadians who had heard of our plight—to bring pressure on the Canadian government to admit us into the country as landed immigrants.

In the beginning there was no hope at all, and we did not even consider release in Canada as being remotely possible. There seemed more of a chance that the United States might admit those (and there were quite a few) who had relatives there. Then, during the second year of our internment, the possibility of release in Canada seemed suddenly real. The most fantastic rumors circulated. Hopes were raised, then dashed.

The diary records the coming and going of various committees and individuals. Weeks passed and nothing happened, and a mood of despondency settled over the camp. Then reports began to circulate that efforts were being made by various organizations to find sponsors for those of us who had had to interrupt their schooling so that they might continue their studies in Canada. All those who might be eligible were asked to prepare a *curriculum vitae.* I was extremely sceptical about the whole thing, but thought nothing would be lost if I complied. I'd never prepared such a document before, and I suppose I must have thought that what was wanted was something very high-flown, and I produced the *curriculum* that is preserved in the diary. I obviously tried to make things look as impressive as possible. I felt myself on the defensive, since I had chosen not to register as a student with the camp authorities, thereby signifying that I wished to prepare myself for writing junior matriculation examinations by following the official high school curriculum. I had instead chosen to concentrate all my intellectual efforts on my own writing, and on reading books I was able to borrow from other internees. In this way I had read most of the major novels of Tolstoy and Dostoevsky, virtually all of Thomas Mann's works, a good deal of Heinrich Mann, the major novels of Kafka, Hemingway, and Steinbeck, the poetry of Goethe and Schiller, a good deal of Milton, Keats, and Shelley, twelve plays by Shaw, and virtually all of Shakespeare's plays. In addition to these writers, whom I read in some depth, I read single novels and plays by dozens of other writers. My major disappointment, on re-reading the diary, is that I made virtually no comment on what I was reading and on what I thought about it. I obviously thought that what I was writing was vastly more important.

In a way it was. For some of the manuscripts I had sent out of the camp with one of the visitors found their way into the hands of the Mendel family in Toronto. They saw some promise in these writings and sponsored my release and subsequent studies at the University of Toronto. (When I published *The Rich Man* in 1948, I dedicated the book to my parents and to Omama Toni Mendel.)

Very early on during my internment I decided that I would write in English. I had known the language for less than two years, a fact quite apparent in curious idiomatic usages here and there, but I felt it absolutely essential that I embrace English, since I knew that I would never return to Austria and wanted to free myself from the linguistic and psychological dependence on German. I had learned English quickly once I was in England, had gone to night school in Leeds for a short time, and had read a good deal. Still, I was aware of the magnitude of the task I had set myself. I remember asking someone during the first days of internment whether it was possible for someone to write in a language other than his mother tongue. Yes, he answered, and mentioned Conrad. From that moment Conrad, one or two of whose stories I had read in German translations, became a kind of patron saint for me, though I could not get a Conrad novel in any of the camps. No one seemed to have brought one. Conrad was not, at that time, fashionable. Still, his example gave me courage, and once launched, I never wavered.

I did write in German to my mother, and some of the letters I wrote to her must obviously have seemed so important to me that I copied them into my diary. These letters now seem to me somewhat extravagant, but they were deeply-felt and meant a great deal to both of us. I had always been very close to my mother, and I was keenly aware how hard things were for her. The letters not only express my deep devotion for her, but were also designed to give her courage during a very difficult period.

The diary entries stop very abruptly on October 1 and 2, 1941, on a despondent note. There is first a now mysterious entry about 'the cobbler Reif' who 'went mad last week' and was taken to an asylum. I say 'now mysterious' because I cannot recall the event and have no recollection whatever about Reif. On the very next day (Yom Kippur) there is the last entry, in which I record that my mother's application for our release had been rejected.

Yet only a few weeks later I was in fact to be released. The news came suddenly, in a letter from Mrs. Mendel. I was stunned, for I had given up all hope. But I was in fact among the first group of internees to be released. I spent two days in Montreal with the family of the Mr. Robinson who had visited the camp with his wife the previous August, and then went to Toronto, to meet for the first time the members of the family that had sponsored my entry into Canada, and who continued to give me their support during my undergraduate years at the University of Toronto.

At the end of November 1941 I entered Harbord Collegiate in Toronto to prepare for the senior matriculation examinations which I sat in June 1942. In the fall I began my studies in English Language and Literature at the University of Toronto.

Once the first break had been made, the internment camps began to empty, though the process was slow. It took more than a year for the camps to be emptied. The internees were either released in Canada or returned to England. Once I had been released, it seemed easier for my mother to secure the release of my father. In February or March he returned to England.

I was allowed to visit him before he left Camp I, and travelled from Toronto to Montreal and from there to the internment camp, on the Richelieu River, to bid him farewell. It was a strange journey and a very strange experience. Many of my friends were still interned, and I was now free, so that I felt as if I had entered a dream that was being slowly replayed.

In many ways the internment camp experience is central to my own development. Suspended in a kind of no man's land for more than eighteen months, I could look back at the horrendous events of the 1930s and see them in some kind of perspective, and I could prepare myself intellectually for the tasks I wanted to undertake in the future.

Our treatment in the camps was, on the whole, humane. Certainly those internees who had known Nazi concentration camps could testify to that fact. As a group, the internees formed a quite remarkable society. Many of the older internees had had distinguished careers as artists and musicians, as professors and lawyers, as doctors and scientists, as rabbis and priests, and many of the younger ones were to have distinguished careers in later years. A very partial list of names, recalled at random, and set out in no particular order would include Max Stern, founder of the Dominion Gallery in Montreal, and one of the pioneers in the promotion of Canadian art; Peter Oberlander, Head of the Department of Town Planning at the University of British Columbia; Ernst Deutsch, professor of geophysics at Memorial University in Newfoundland; the late Oscar Cahen, one of the founders of the post-war movement of Toronto painters; Gregory Baum, professor of systematic theology at St. Michael's College, and one of the leading members of the world ecumenical movement; Walter Hitschfeld, Dean of Graduate Studies at McGill University; F. D. Hoeniger, professor of English at Victoria College and former Head of the Department; Helmut Blume, Dean of Music at McGill; the late Kaspar Naegele, former Dean of Arts at the University of British Columbia; Emil Fackenheim, professor of philosophy at the University of Toronto; John Newmark, pianist and world-renowned accompanist; Ernest Reinhold, professor of German and former Head of the Department at the University of Alberta; Walter Kohn, professor of mathematics and former Head of the Department at the University of California at La Jolla; Eric Koch, writer and C.B.C. executive; Henry Fliess, architect; Helmut Kalman, musicologist and Director of the Music Division of the National Library. The list could go on and on. Certainly Canada was not the loser when the government allowed that group to enter the country.

Intellectual and creative activity was greatly encouraged in the camps, in spite of the very limited opportunities and resources available. What was available in the long, long evenings was time. There were endless discussions and debates on art and music, on politics and religion. The great *Kulturkampf* of late 19th century Germany was fought out every day between the theologians and the secularists. The great political struggles of the left were fought out, and the struggles between liberal capitalism and socialism. I am sorry that I did not record my impressions of these debates, always lively, often passionate, sometimes violent. I suppose I took them for granted. But I learned and absorbed a lot. It was not until many years later that I finally realized that I had had a liberal education in many ways more remarkable than the article available in universities.

Edmonton, May 1974

May 16. 1940. Leeds. At 12:30 I am called away from work and told that I would have to be interned. Town Hall in Leeds for 5 hours. Then *Pontefract* (Yorkshire). Barracks full of dirt and dust. We sleep on the floor. Food very good. We are allowed to receive visitors. My mother comes to visit us, and I write a poem about it. For two hours we are taken out into the fresh air every day. We have variety and sometimes classical concerts. Our own people entertain us of course. There is an excellent violinist amongst us who plays every night after lights out. We do not see him, we just hear the sound of the violin. Really marvellous. Hygenical conditions are not too good, there are only two lavatories for 150 men. Food, however, is excellent. On the 20th of May I start to write a novel which I think I will call "Miguel Amore" when it is finished. It is going to be quite long, about 300 pages, I think. I have had the idea quite a long time, about one year.

30.May 1940. at 13:30 we are told to be ready in half an hour as we are going to be moved. We hope it will be the Isle of Man, we land however in *HUYTON*. We sleep in new-built but unfurnished houses on the floor. Health conditions much better than in Pontefract but food scarcely. I am often hungry. Post-supply is bad as well. First we dont get letters at all, later it grows better. We make music across the barbed wire. Soldiers stand on one side, we on the other. We sing and play, they sing back. We grow very intimate with them. This is stopped after a few days by the officers. There are so many professors and lecturers among the internees that a camp university is opened. One of us has a gramophone and records, including the fifth symphonie, by Beethoven, and the Unfinished by Schubert.

After two weeks it is announced that all internees would be transferred to the Isle of Man. During the two weeks stay in Huyton two chapters of Miguel Amore are written. I feel, however, dissatisfied with them and angry I throw it aside, deciding either not to write any more at all, or at least to rewrite.

15.June 1940. Arrival in Douglas, Isle of Man.

Hygenical conditions excellent. We sleep in beds again. Food is not enough, though. We are allowed to bathe in the sea, and are taken for walks. We live fairly peaceful and undisturbed for some 10 days, when it is announced that all unmarried men between the ages of 16 and 40 are going to be moved. There are rumours to Canada, but we do not know. They ask for volunteers, so my father volunteers. During the whole stay in Douglas I did not write a single line.

4. July 1940. We are taken to Glasgow where a liner is waiting for us. Sobiesky. We had nothing to eat all day. Although they had asked for volunteers 200 have to be turned back. We get to know later that they have been sent to Australia. 1500 passengers on a boat that can hold about 500. Nevertheless we feel happy. The first day I feel sick, but the rest of the yourney is very nice indeed. We sail in convoy. Food excellent. We come into fog.

12. July 1940. In the morning we land in St. John, Newfoundland. The harbour is beautiful but the town itself seems very primitive. At dinnertime the anchor is lifted and we sail again.
On the 14.th of July we reach the Laurencebay, later Laurenzriver, and on the 15. July 1940 at 6 o'clock in the morning we land in Quebeck. At dinnertime we leave the boat, heavily guarded, enter a train, leaving for Trois Riveres (Three Rivers).

15. July 1940. 7 O'clock in the evening we reach Trois Riveres. Nazis are there and there is trouble at once. We have to sleep in a big hall that is full of dust and dirt. We all feel depressed. We are stationed in an exhibition-building, and the big hall has been used for horses. Few days later the Nazis leave. — — We get letters marked "Prisoner of War Mail. — We protest, but in vain. We try again and again to convince the Military authorities that we are Refugees. Yes, on the way from the station to the "Camp" the streets were flanked with people. The whole population of "Three Rivers" seemed to have come, and the children, having seen us pass, ran in front to see us again. The language spoken is French. The people actually believe that we are parachutists and Fifth columnists.
We have now the quarters of the Nazis. They are clean and comfortable. Opposite is a Base-ballstadium and from the dining hall windows we can watch the games. We are told that we will leave soon.
On the 15th of August we leave, and after 24 hours yourney we reach Camp "B" in New-Brunswick near Fredericton. It looks terrible at first sight. The barracks are not ready yet. We are surrounded by woods. There is possibility to work. We can go out and cut trees. As there are usually not enough workers raids are frequent.
Sometimes soldiers come with bayonets.
There is an internal crisis when "Prisoner of War" clothes arrive, blue jackets with big red circles on the back. Some want to take them, others are against it. Say that if we accept them, we declare ourselves to be Prisoners of War. At last we do take them. We now get writing-paper that does not bear the Prisoner of War mark.

CENTRAL INTERNMENT CAMP DOUGLAS I.O.M.

This to certify that papers belonging to :-

Mr....*KREISEL Howard*

born on....*5. 6. 22.*....at....*Vienna*...

are impounded and are at present being held in this office and that the particulars following hereafter are correctly copied from the said papers :-

1.
...*Austrian*....Passport. No....*B 7/84*

Issued on....*29 Juni 38*.....at....*Vienna*.

Expires on....*31. Dec. 38*.........

2.
Registration Book No....*66 979*...........

Issued on....*5. Aug. 38*.........at....*Leeds City*

3.
Identity Card No.................

4.
Signature....*Heinrich Kreisel*

....................................Captain,
For Camp Commander.

[Here there are one and a half blank pages and the diary starts again.]

i.1. 1941. New-Year. A rather sad New-Year. Is it our New-Year at all? Should Jews celebrate New-Year twice a year? There are discussions in our group about it. In the afternoon I signed a refusal paper to go back to England. Reason: Immigration to the United States. I hope it will be possible. Our future is like a dark, impenetrable wall. I said I should give something if I knew where I will be next year at the same time.
1938 Vienna, 1939-1940 England, 1941 Canada. 1942 - where?

2.1.1941. I go out to work in the woods. It is beautiful. We are three, and work by ourselves without a guard. One almost feels free. Free! Freedom! What words! I can hardly imagine how it will feel, being free again, being able to go where you like, talking again to people, not always to the same, having girls again! I have forgotten what a woman looks like. I felled one tree only, the other time I spend discussing with my friend H.A. Lissauer about writing. I think of writing a new short novel, but the theme has got to develop itself within myself. I receive a letter from America which I answer, also write to Gustl Gewürz. In the evening I go to an evening of sonatas, played by Kander (violin) - Neumark (piano). I enjoy myself tremendously.

3.1.1941. I went out to work again. We were just two and worked by ourselves quite a distance away from everybody else. I went for a walk until I reached a little brook that was quite frozen and over which a wooden bridge was laid covered with brushwood. The ice was as clear as glass and beneath it the water could be seen flowing and its perpetual, monotonous gluck-gluck could be heard. I broke the ice with my axe and drank some water. We had to walk about twenty minutes back to the camp. The farther away from it the better you feel. I thought how it would be if a girl would walk past us. It did not happen, though.

At supper there was an interesting conversation at our table which I think is worth being recorded. An elderly gentleman complained to my father about the most terrible behaviour and quite impossible manners of the young boys of sixteen or eighteen, or even twenty. He said the worst of all was that the young boys did not show any respect toward the older ones. I did not say anything at the time but I will write something now. First of all I want to make it clear that I do not want to take the part of the younger generation of whom I am one myself, and whose behaviour and manners, and disrespect towards

"CHESTERFIELD"
4, Mona Drive,
DOUGLAS.

Menu

MONDAY

DINNER AT 12,30 p.m.

Reis - Suppe

Lamm - Braten
y Sauce

Kartoffelauflauf

Salat

Rhabarben - Compot

Tee

"Golden Shred" the most palatable
and easily digested marmalade

On the Isle of Man internees were quartered in hotels that had been hastily commandeered by the military authorities. Some blank menus had been left behind. Among the internees were some professional chefs. They did the best they could with the meagre rations supplied and always posted a dinner menu, in part as an ironic commentary on what they served and in part to make the meal appear better than it was.

older "gentlemen" is really beyond all critic, but I do want to give some explanation as to the latter. If you are outside, living under normal circumstances you see your elders, at least those whom you respect, always wrapped up in a mantle of etiquette, of manners and of dignity. You never get the idea into your head that those same persons would ever use bad language, would throw themselves over food and grasp as much as they can, would start fights over an apple or over onespoonfull of porridge. Here that mantle of dignity is thrown aside and you see men as they really are, literally speaking naked. Outside you do not live so close together with your elders, you keep yourself or are kept at a respectful distance. Here you live with them, body on body, and if you see how brutal some of them are, how selfish, if you find out that those whom you thought to be of excellent character are really low subjects and despiteful, if you see how intolerant most of them are, except matters concerning themselves, then it is only too easy, and by all means natural, that you should lose all respect that ever you may have had.

4.1.1941. It is Saturday, and I did not go out to work. It is very cold, and at about 5 o'clock a snowstorm breaks loose accompanied by an icy wind. In the afternoon I heard a broadcast from the Metropolitan Opera. It was a performance of Tannhäuser by Wagner. A very good cast. Lauriz Melchior (Tannhäuser), Kirstin Flagstad (Elizabeth), Kerstin Thorborg whom I saw many times in Vienna (Venus), Herbert Janssen (Eschenbach) I saw Janssen at the Vienna Opera in Dec. 1937 singing the same part. Emanuel Liszt (Markgraf). At night I sign the paylist for December (1 Dollar, 60 cents).

5.1.1941. It snowed nearly the whole day. At 7 o'clock the fall of Bardia is reported. I do hope the war will end victorious for the Allies.

6.1.1941. A very beautiful day. We worked directly at the little brook still farther away from the camp. When we entered the camp it reminded me of animals being let into a big cage. I received two letters, one from auntie Rosa and one from Gustl, both of Dec. 18th. I answered Gustl immediately.

7.1.1941. I went to the dentist and did not go to work. Wrote a letter to Rosenzweig, and wrote a short story called "The two poppies".

8.1.1941. Went to work. Beautiful day.

12.1.1941. For the first time I read some novels publicly. I had great success. Best liked was the novel "Ginger" which I wrote on the same day. Somebody said that Ginger could have been written by the hand of a well-known writer.

19.1.1941. The group 5 is dissolved and I take up new "residence" in group 15 (Kitchengroup) It is very quiet there.

24.1.1941. I met Shalom Nagler, a very talented sculptor. I read something to him. At night he introduces my work to Mr. Mayer, who is in charge of the post-office and in close connection with the officers. He promises to help me to make it possible for me to send some of my novels out to papers.

31.1.1941. Jonnie Neumark, the pianist who has produced "Androcles and the Lion" in the camp, asks me if I could write a play for him.

2.2.1941. I start to write a play. "The Road to Evil," and complete it by Monday nine o'clock in the morning. It was not satisfactory, but it does not matter. I will try again.

12.2.1941. We have a skatingring. I go to work sometimes, but most of the time I write. I have decided to re-write "Miguel Amore" completely and to give it a new title. I heard a Wagner concert conducted by the masterful baton of Toscanini. Too beautiful for words.
I wrote a letter to mother some time ago, here it is.

Meine teuerste Mutter,
   Ich habe soeben durch Tante Rosa Deinen Brief erhalten, leider war er mit keinem Datum versehen. Ich schreibe den Brief ganz allein, ohne ihm irgendwem zu zeigen, denn er soll ganz allein für Dich sein. Es scheint mir doch etwas an der Idee der Gedankenübertragung wahr zu sein, denn wie sonst könntest Du, Teuerste, viele viele Meilen weg von mir, fühlen wie sehr ich mich nach Dir sehne und wie weiss ich hier, dass Du es tust? Aber gerade weil wir uns so sehr nacheinander sehnen, müssen wir aufrechten Hauptes durch diese schwere Zeit schreiten, und der feste Glaube, dass wir bald wieder beisammen sein werden, wird uns zusammenbringen. Glaub'mir das, Mutter. Je länger ich von Dir weg bin, Mutter, umso mehr sehe ich wie ich Dir ähnle, in der Sprache, in den Bewegungen, in allem und jedem, von den schärfsten, markantesten Charakterzügen bis hinab zu den kleinsten, unbedeutsamsten. Kurt fragte ob ich viel schreibe. O, ja, sehr viel. Ich habe

sehr viele Kurzgeschichten geschrieben und arbeite jetzt an einem Roman. Ich schreibe alles in Englisch. Es wird Dich freuen zu hören dass ich schon oft vorgelesen habe und sehr viel Erfolg gehabt habe. Ich habe viel für Dich geschrieben, Mutter, und hoffe Dir bald vorlesen zu können. Küsse diesen Brief, Mutter, und ich werde hier fühlen, dass Du mich geküsst hast.[2] Dein Dich liebender Sohn Heini.

28.2.1941. I wrote to mother.

Meine teuerste Mutter, Ich habe heute einen Brief von Dir erhalten, der vom 20. Jan. war. Ich bin so froh zu hören, das soweit alles in Ordnung ist. Ich beantworte diesen Brief wieder allein, dieses ewige "Wie geht es Dir, mir geht es gut," das ich immer schreiben muss, wenn der Papa dabei ist, ekelt mich schon an. Für Gedanken, die sich ins philosophische verlieren, hat er ja kein Interesse. In einem der letzten Briefe schreibst Du, Du wolltest mir einen Brief schreiben aber Kurt sagte er wäre zu sentimental. Musst Du denn Deine Briefe jedem zeigen? Zu sentimental, zu traurig? Gibt es denn etwas, dass noch trauriger sein könnte als die Welt von heute? Schreibe, was Du am Herzen hast, schreib' es wie immer Du willst. Was vom Herzen kommt, geht zum Herzen, wie auch immer die Ortographie sein mag. Wenn Du mit mir Dich sonst immer unterhieltest über Deine Probleme, und über meine, hast Du da jemanden gefragt, ob Du mit mir sprechen sollst? Schreibe, was auf Deinem Herzen liegt. Alles, was Du denkst schreib' auf. Du kannst schreiben, ich weiss es, denn sonst könnte ich es nicht. Du hast nur die äussere Form nicht gelernt, die Ortographie und den Stil, und mir hast Du geholfen, es zu lernen. Alles was ich kann, kann ich durch Dich. Die vielen Stunden, die Du mit mir verbracht hast während ich die Elementarbegriffe des Schreibens und Lesens erlernte, sind nicht spurlos an mir vorübergegangen. Du hast gesäet und Du wirst ernten, ich verspreche Dir das. Ich werde einmal zu der Welt sagen: "Schau' her, das ist meine Mutter, alles was ich bin und kann ist ihr Verdienst." Einmal, wann, das weiss ich nicht, aber einmal wird es sein. Ich küsse Dich, Dein Sohn Heini.[3]

21.III. I published a story in the camp-magazine called "Die andere Seite." The story was called "Mummy who are they?"

24.III. I wrote a letter to the Colonel asking whether it is allowed to send stories to magazines.

25.III. I sat in our improvised café, and opposite me there sat two boys. They read my story which I had signed H.K. After they had finished reading, one said to the other: "A fine story. Very well done. I wonder who the author is." "H.K." said the other. "Who can it be?" I bent across to them and asked: "Have you finished with it?" "Yes," they said, looking at me, and then they gave me it. I was highly amused.

The letter I wrote yesterday came back today, rejected. It said an official of the camp, Dr. Rosenberg who is in charge of Education will have to see about the matter first. I am not going to have my stories read and censured and criticized three or four times before they actually reach the desk of an editor.

And so in the further sense of the word, my stories have been rejected without having been read, and without having reached the desk of an editor at all. I must have patience and wait till I am free. There is no other possibility. Patience is a precious thing, but sometimes it's damned hard to be patient. Meanwhile I am piling manuscript on manuscript, and I'd long to see them in print. I have a feeling, though that it will be a long time yet. Patience, patience, patience, that's the only thing that can help me. I'll stand it!

There is nothing in all the world that could change my mind of becoming a writer. I'll fight to the last minute, and I'll gain recognition. The only time I'll give up will be when I'm dead.

10.4 Dr. Rosenberg came to me, asking me to let him read some of my work, and I couldn't say no. He liked what he read, and he sent a letter to the colonel, speaking very highly of me.

Pessach. We had a very nice Seder. I had Seder once with the Chassidim. It made me think that I was at a Seder taking place many years ago. The old Chassidim must have celebrated Seder like that. The man who gave the Seder dressed in a white "Kittel," sat at the end of the table, flanked by two Rabbis, and the others sitting on long tables.

12.4.1941. There is a crisis in the camp, owing to the fact that work, which has been paid at the rate of 20 cents per day, will now have to be done free. What's to be the outcome is uncertain yet.

The war situation is again very dark for the allies. Bardia, the Germans claim, has been recaptured. The Jugoslavs and Greeks are putting up a nice show, fighting well. I am still optimistic. The Allies must win. I do believe that they will win in the end.

I heard an all Wagner concert to-day, relayed from Carnegie-Hall. What a master Wagner was! Tristan and Isolde impresses me more and more. A great, a very great work of music.

18.4.1941. For the first time we have talking-pictures. But it was terrible. Some picture about Red Indians. The picture broke a few times.

29.4.1941. I am ill and have temperature. I am in the camp hospital.

5.5.1941. I am still ill. I still have a temperature.

10.5.1941. There is again the matter of fatigues. They ask for 55 men each day. We decide not to send them.

12.5.1941. The 55 men do not go out to work. Some of us are now interned one year, others will "celebrate" the anniversary in 4 days. I am still in the hospital though I have nearly fully recovered. There are demonstrations in the camp and it is decided not to go to work the next day and not to eat. Hungerstrike for one day.

13.5.1941. The plan is put into action. At 8.15 soldiers with bayonets fixed come into the compound, go into the huts. They call the names of the 55 men supposed to do fatigue work. They all refuse to work save five. The fifty men are put into jail. We have tried to send a telegram to the Home Office, saying that we have gone on hunger-strike because we have been unjustly interned, and nothing is being done about it. The commandant, however, said he would not send it, that it would do us harm if he did. Well, the day went by we had to stay in our huts till evening. I was still at the hospital. I am quite well again. The 50 men are released. We will have to do fatigue. Of course it was clear that we could not win, but it seems to have had effect. The commandant is very eager that nothing should be heard about our strike in Ottawa or other official quarters. So in a way we have been successful, showing that we can take a lot but if it goes too far we can give a bit, too.

14.5.1941. The soldiers are very friendly, never have they been so friendly before.

15.5.1941. Rabbi Kraus comes from Fredericton, makes a speech telling us that we must not grumble at being interned, that Canadians are interned in Germany (what a silly, idiotic comparison!), that we must never go on strike again (here he is interrupted with shouts). I don't blame him, he had to do it; it was obvious. But it only shows how much afraid the commander is that nothing should be heard about our strike. The roll-call that for a day has been kept in the open air takes place in the usual way (at six o'clock in the morning and at 7 o'clock at night we line up in front of our beds to be counted.

16.5.1941. I write to mother.

Teuerste Mutter. Ich habe Deinen Brief vom 14.April. Ich kann viel ausdrücken mit Worten, aber die Freude ausdrücken über diesen Brief das kann ich nicht. Ich habe ihn gelesen und wieder gelesen, dann unter meine Hefte gelegt, und wenn ich eines nehme um zu arbeiten, dann seh' ich den Brief, dann nehm ich ihn wohl, les' ihn und leg ihn zurück. Ein Gruss von der Mutter. Ein Jahr wars vorige Woche, das sie mich holten. Traurig ist die Welt, wohl wahr ist's. Wie hast Du gesagt im Brief? "Der Mensch muss streben!" Ja, Mutter, streben muss er, streben nach Geist, nach Wissen, um zu verstehen, dass es mehr gibt im Leben als Essen und Schlafen. Wenn er das versteht, ist es soviel leichter die Schwierigkeiten des Lebens zu tragen. Da ist Musik! A, herrliche Musik! Beethoven und Wagner! Wir haben ein Radio und können die Symphonien hören. Ich habe Tristan gehört und Symphonien. Was für ein Grosser unter den Grossen war doch dieser Beethoven. Was fühl ich nicht alles wenn er zu mir spricht durch seine Musik! Wie er weint über die Welt, wie er jubelt in heller Freude, und betrübt ist, und liegt und weint und weint. Höre die 5. Symphonie. Wie er jubelt zum Leben, wie er "JA" sagt zum Leben, mit Fanfaren und Trompeten in diesem letzten Satz der grossen Symphonie. Er, der taub war! Würden doch die Menschen leben in diesem Geist. Lerne Musik verstehen, Mutter, sie wird es Dir soviel leichter machen, das Leben zu tragen.[4]

June 5th.1941. It's my birthday. And just today I've got to do fatigue-work. It's like being a slave. We were driven to work and have to work for nothing. All day I wove nice dreams for a better future and a more peaceful life. But after all, it's only dreams, reality is far, far different.

June 14. A list comes out bearing the names of 61 men to be returned to England. Everybody longs to be on this list, everybody is sick of internment. We want freedom, even if there are bombs in England and none here. Internment bears heavy on my nerves, the barbed wire seems to be coming nearer and nearer, almost choking me. Freedom, freedom!

June 18. The boys leave for England. They stand in the space between the two gates and wave back to us. We stand in the compound, longing to be in civilian clothes like they, going back to the old country. Then the gate is opened, they go out, into the trucks and they are gone. Everybody is in a bad mood, as always when boys are going back to ordinary life. American emigration is an impossibility. It was a crime almost that Mr. Patterson and Mr. Goldner told us beautiful things although they knew reality was quite different. If they had told us straight how the matter stood, many would have gladly gone back to England. In the afternoon the Sergeant-Major comes round telling us that we, too, would be moved to other camps though not to freedom, and have to be ready within 24 hours. I have written to mother to make an application for our release.

June 20. We leave Camp "B" for Camp "I". Camp "B" in Fredericton, New-Brunswick, was a Paradise almost compared with Camp I. Camp B was very big, four big sleepinghuts, very comfortable, a large recreation hut, and all possible accomodities. We travel 30 hours and are guarded like very dangerous criminals. As I watch the people through the windows, I must think that they can not be less dangerous or more innocent than I and many more. Yet we are treated like this. It is enough to make anybody lose faith in the world and in mankind. In Edmunston we can see the U.S. borderhouse about 200 yards away, just across a river that runs parallel with the train. What an irony! The land of liberty and freedom so near and yet so far.

June 21st. We arrive at St.Valentin. Nearly all the population has come to see us get off the train. They think we are the most dangerous enemies and look very grim. We march about an hour until we reach a pier. Still more people staring at us. A little boy of seventeen who looks like fifteen and marches just in front of me gets a lot of attention. They probably think: "So young and already a prisoner. He probably committed a great crime." The camp is on an island: Ile aux noix. We are taken there by boat and as we arrive we undress and go for a swim naked. Boats pass us with girls but somehow I don't get excited and am not ashamed to be seen in the nude. So far everything seems all-right and and we think this Camp I is great. Then we enter— and one more illusion is gone. It is an old fortress and the people sleep in catacombs. It used to be a museum. The men already there make a very bad impression. Nearly all have been in the Kitchener Camp in England and before in a German concentrationcamp; they have thus spent three years in camps. They have the real camp attitude. The camp is terrible. All much stricter than in Camp B. In the centre, written with black letters on a white board, are the following words in bad German:

Wichtige Bekanntmachung. Streng verboten. Das Gebiet zwischen den
Stackeldraght Zaun der das Innere des Lagers umkreist und dem mittleren
Zaun, sowohl als wie das äussere Gebiet, ist für alle (Kriegs) gefangene des
Konzentrationslagers streng verbotene Zone. Die Wachen werden ohne
Warnung auf jeglichen Gefangenen in diesem verbotenen Gebiet schiessen.
Auf Befehl des Kommandanten.

KONZENTRATIONSLAGER I.[5]

There is very little room in our sleeping quarters. We sleep in the
recreation hut. It is remarkable that most of us don't say: I wish I were
free again, but most say: O, were we back in Camp B. The only thing
that's good about the fort is that one can go swimming. The name of
the fort is LENNOX. The island was the first piece of land which the
English occupied when they fought the French in 1812. Now we
don't even see a passing motor-car. The space in which one can move
is not half as big as in Camp B. Immediately you get to the barbed
wire. I have never hated anything so much as barbed-wire.

June 24th. I work on a farm here. Really gardening. Pulling grass
away from vegetables. The swimming is marvellous There is a fellow
here, they call him Franzl. He is half-nuts. But a type worth
remembering. Tall with a shaved head. He asks everybody whether
he'll get his camera back which he handed in on the Isle of Man. He
has been in the Pioneer-Corps already but after a month they
discharged him. I think it is a terrible injustice to intern him afterwards. Hayes and Goldner came. But by all means I don't know why.
They told us nothing new.

The barbed wire is to fall after the first of July when our status is
officially changed.

July 1st. The status is changed. Practically everything is the same.
When we went out to work this morning the Sargeant asked some
boys why they are not wearing the redpatched shirt. —— I receive a
letter from my brother. I will answer it tomorrow. At night it is so hot
in the quarters, I think I am in a Russian bath.

July 2nd. I answer my brother.

Dearest Kurt

I got your letter of May 27th. It was a very inspiring letter and I enjoyed
reading it. There can be no doubt: you are making progress. As the days grow

long, you write, you find yourself trying to penetrate into the deep secrets of nature. Meaning into the secrets of man. Because man is the creature most worthy of study because he has advanced most of all the mammals that walk the earth and swim the seas. The story of man is the most simple and yet the most difficult of all stories. We both want to be writers, we both have chosen out of our own free will to tell the story of man to his fellow-man. Whether you tell the story of love or of hate, it is always the story of man. And one thing is certain: Man is eternal. Always there comes up one question: Who am I? And the answer is: I am Man. Who made me? Man. To whom will I give life? To man. Thus the circle is completed. Our grandparents never died, because they gave life to our parents, and our parents will never die because their life is in us. And we likewise will never die. To know this means to have mastered the greatest secret of nature. And one more thing it means: One cannot be afraid of death. Because I am Man and you are Man and Man can never die for he is eternal.

9th July 1941. Letter to Mother.

Meine vielgeliebte Mutter, Ich danke Dir für Deinen wunderschönen Brief, den Du mir zum Geburtstag geschrieben. Ich bin durchdrungen von der Überzeugung, dass wir bald wieder beisammen sein werden. Auch ich denk so oft an die Tage zurück, da ich noch auf Schule ging. Erinnerst Du Dich, wie Du neben mir zu sitzen pflegtest wenn ich meine Aufgaben machte? Und oft hab ich mich von meinem aufbraussenden Temperament fortreissen lassen und hab' begonnen zu schreien. Du hast mich immer beruhigt, denn Du allein weisst, dass ich es nicht bös meine. Ich bin heute noch so, und werde wohl immer so bleiben. Ich glaube, dass das was ich für Dich und über Dich geschrieben habe schön ist, nicht weil ich so denke sondern weil andere, die es gelesen haben, mir gesagt haben, dass es schön ist. Wenn man in jemandem nur Gutes sieht, kann man schön denken und schreiben. So schreibst Du mir, und natürlich ist es richtig! Natürlich weist Du's, denn in Deinem Herzen bist Du eine Dichterin. Erinnerst Du Dich wie Du mir immer Geschichten aus Deiner Kindheit erzähltest. Ich entsinne mich genau auf jede einzelne, und ich will darangehen sie niederzuschreiben. Tales my Mother told me will ich es nennen. Es freut mich, dass Du schon englische Bücher liest. Lies viel, denn durch das Lesen kann man eine Sprache am besten meistern. Aber wozu erzähl ich Dir das, Du weisst es ja, denn Du hast es mich ja gelehrt. Ich küsse Dich vielmals. Dein Sohn Heini.[6]

20th July. I went out to the Commander and presented him two manuscripts (A Child of Death, The Market and the Symphony No. 5 by Beethoven) as well as some poems, asking him for permission to send it to a magazine.

25th July. I go again to the Commander. He asks me again what I want to do with the manuscripts. Then searches amongst his papers and gives them back to me. Says he has no objection if I wish to send them off. I am positive he did not even read a single sentence. He is a major, very small and has X legs. He seems to be a very stupid fellow. (He was, as I got to know, an insurance agent before the war broke out). To think that I need the consent of such a fellow, who has, I am sure, not read twenty books in his whole life to judge by his appearance. I have no envelopes, so I cannot send the stories away. Always obstacles, always obstacles. I fear I will have a long and hard way to go yet. This seems to be a writer's fate. I am determined!

9th August. There comes to the Camp a certain Mr. Robinson, K.C. who is the chairman of the Committee (honourable, of course) and who makes an excellent impression on me. He looks like a very clever and intelligent man, a man of great knowledge. He is tall, has white hair and wears pince-nez. I decide to give him some manuscripts. I write a short letter, explaining everything to him with few words. When I come into the room where he is, I find him sitting in his shirt. I give him the manuscript. He exclaims: "O, a ganze megilleh." "No," I say, "these are stories." "Oh," he says, "stories." Then, looking at me, "Well, you better see my wife, she is outside. That's a thing for her."

The visitor hut is outside (we can receive visitors now). Women are not allowed into the compound. I go out. I find an elderly lady, who is still very handsome and must have been beautiful when she was young. She has white hair and wears glasses when she is writing. Her face is plain and wellformed. Her eyes are vivid. She is the first woman to whom I have spoken for over a year. If I remember rightly, she wore a white-and-blue dress and a black hat, which was a good contrast to her white hair. "I'm glad to see you," says she. "I'm pleased to meet you," I say. Then she asks my name. I speak a bit soft so she cannot understand me. Perhaps I tremble a bit. I show her my name on the letter I had written. She writes it down.
"I have something extraordinary," I say. "Please read the letter. It will tell you everything."
She reads the letter. "So you hope to become a writer once," she says, looking intently at me.
"I *am* a writer," I am about to say, but check myself, and just say: "Yes."

"You have chosen the hardest profession of all," she says with slight irony in her voice.
"I couldn't help it," I mumble, taken aback.
Again she says. "Any artist has a hard way to go."
"Perhaps that is just why I chose to be a writer," I answer.
"Do you want me to return the manuscript to you?"
"No. Perhaps you could send them to a paper."
"Well, we'll see what we can do."
"Perhaps you could let me know what you thought of them," I say.
"Yes," she says.
The stories I gave her are Farewell and A broken Form as well as poems.
>"Now go, products of my heart
>Go out into the world
>And tell them what I am."

I come back and tell my father. "You ought to have said writing is not your profession," he said, driving the blood to my head.
"But it *is* my profession," I answer.
"Oh," he laughs, "is that so? I didn't know. Well, let us hope."
I went away, in order not to have to quarrel.
My father shows little interest in my work, I am afraid. He has so far only once asked me to translate something to him and then it had been my suggestion. It was after I had read some of my work publicly in Camp "B" Since then he has never once asked: "What are you writing now?" Or anything like that, while other friends come constantly and ask me to show them something. The painter Heymann pressed me over a week to translate something to him, as he does not know English. It hurts me infinitely that my own father is so imaterial to what I am doing. But it is by no means strange to me. He never took interest in our studies (my brother's and mine) when we were in Vienna. All that and a lot of other things he did in Vienna stand out very clear and vivid in my mind and though I want I cannot forget them.

Aug. 10th. All last week, and some time before that, there is great talk about returning to England between me and my father. We have written and asked mother to make an application for our release. I don't know whether it would be the right thing to do to return to England. There might be a chance to be released here.
But my father has suddenly changed his mind, and as five months ago he called those who returned to England asses and argued heftily

with them, he now has turned completely. "Back, back!" That's his character. No consequence at all. No willpower whatsoever. I am not sure whether I should go back. Though I suppose if my father wishes it so much, I'll have no choice.

Meanwhile we must wait and see.

Sept. 7. Again many members of various committees come to the Camp. A Mr. Raphael makes a speech, speaks an excellent English, but fails to impress me with his empty phrases. A certain Mrs. Cowan has come with him. She is the first lady to enter the compound. She is small, about thirty years of age, has a doll's face, a very wellformed body. She wears a blue dress and blue shoes to match. I then go back to my work (making nets). Suddenly I am called to this Mrs. Cowan by Mr. Fischer, the camp leader. He asks her whether she can get a sponsor for me, so I might be released in Canada and she says yes. Then he mentions that I write, asks me to bring down some of my work. I gave her a copy of my poems, The letter of a young mother, Ginger, and The Market and the Symphony No. 5 by Beethoven. She said she'll have them published (From Mrs. Robinson I still have no answer). I told her that I have no typewriter and need one. She makes a note.

12.Sept. 1941.   Curriculum Vitae

I first opened my eyes to look into this Vale of Tears called the World, on the fifth day of June 1922 in Vienna. On the seventh day after my birth my parents gave me the name Heinrich, and thus my person was named Heinrich Kreisel.

The wheel of time turned and the years past. At the age of six I entered school. I was, I daresay, a good pupil, and distinguished myself in language and composition. I was never much good in mathematics. It is a subject I loathe. At an early age I began to form an interest for writing and literature, and whenever I had time I would make up a story or a poem.

I entered highschool and studied with good results. I was about fifteen when my first story was accepted by a newspaper and published. I reached the sixth grade of the Gymnasium, which is equivalent to the standard of Junior Matric, when one day in March 1938 Hitler marched into Austria.

I came to England on the 22nd of July. I could not go on with my studies and had to start work. In the evenings, however, I visited

Night-School and studied Journalism and Literature, still composing stories and poems and more the like.

During internment I have concentrated fully on writing, this being the reason why I did not go for matriculation in Canada. I have given tests of the writing I have done to Mrs. Robinson when she visited this camp and Mrs. Cowan. It would be a fulfillment of a dream if I could study literature.

Hoping you will accept this favourably, I am Sir

Yours thankfully

Oct. 1st The cobbler Reif went mad last week. They took him to an asylum today.

1st.
Oct. 2nd. It is Jom Kippur today. At night I get a letter from mother, saying that her application for release has been rejected. I can only return if I join the Pioneer-Corps.

---

[1]Since this introduction was written, two books have been published that shed more light on this episode, even though to this day researchers still find difficulty in obtaining documents vital to an understanding of what happened. The two books in question are Eric Koch, *Deemed Suspect: A Wartime Blunder* (Toronto: Methuen, 1980), and Peter and Leni Gillman, *'Collar the Lot!': How Britain Interned and Expelled its Wartime Refugees* (London: Quartet Books, 1980).

[2]My Dearest Mother,
    I have just now, through aunt Rosa, received your letter, but unfortunately it didn't have a date. I write this letter quite alone, without showing it to anyone, because it is intended entirely for you. I think there is some truth in the transmission of thoughts, because how else could you, my dearest, who are so many, many miles away from me, how could you feel how much I long for you, and how I know what you feel? But precisely because we yearn so for each other, we must go through this difficult time with our heads held high, and our firm faith that we shall soon be together again will bring us together. Believe me, mother. The longer I am away from you, mother, the more I realize how like you I am, in speech, in gestures, in everything, from the sharpest, most marked characteristics to the smallest and most insignificant. Kurt asked me if I write a lot. Yes, a great deal. I've written a lot of short stories

and am now working on a novel. I write everything in English. You will be pleased to hear that I have often read publicly, and that I have had a great deal of success. I have written a lot for you, mother, and I hope that I'll soon be able to read to you. Kiss this letter, mother, and I shall feel here that you have kissed me. Your loving son Heini.

[3]My Dearest Mother, I have today received your letter of January 20. I am pleased to hear that things are all right. I am responding to your letter again alone, because this eternal "How are you, I am all right," which is what I have to write when Papa writes a joint letter, makes me sick. He has no interest whatsoever in ideas that move towards the philosophical. In one of your last letters you wrote that you wanted to send a letter to me, but Kurt said it was too sentimental. Do you have to show your letters to everyone? Too sentimental, too sad? Can there be anything that could be sadder than today's world? Write what is in your heart, write whatever you want to write. Whatever comes from the heart goes to the heart, whatever the spelling may be. Whenever you talked to me about your problems, and about mine, did you then ask anyone if you should talk with me? Write whatever is in your heart. Write about everything that you think about. You can write, I know that, because otherwise I couldn't. It's just that you haven't learned the formal elements, orthography and style, and yet you have helped me to learn these things. Everything that I know, I know because of you. The many hours you spent with me while I learned the main principles of writing and reading have not been lost without trace. You have sown and you will reap, I promise you. I shall some time say to the world: "Look, that is my mother, everything I am and know is her doing." Some time, when, I do not know, but it will happen some time. I kiss you. Your son Heini.

[4]Dearest Mother. I received your letter of 14. April. I can express much in words, but I cannot express the joy your letter gave me. I have read and re-read it, then I put it among my notebooks, and when I reach for one in order to work, then I see your letter and pick it up and read it, and then put it back again. A greeting from the mother. It was a year ago last week that they came for me. A sad place is the world, that is certainly true. How did you put it in your letter? "A human being must strive!" Yes, mother, he must strive, strive after spirit, after knowledge, in order to understand that there is more to life than eating and sleeping. And when one understands that, then it's easier to bear the difficult burdens of life. There is music! Oh, wonderful music. Beethoven and Wagner! We have a radio here and can hear some symphonies. I have heard Tristan and symphonies. What a titan among titans was Beethoven. How much I feel when he speaks to me through his music! How

he sheds tears about the world, how he expresses pure joy, and how sad he is, and lies there, crying. Listen to the fifth symphony. How joyful he is about life, how he says "YES" to life, with trombones and trumpets, in this last movement of the great symphony. He, who was deaf! Would that human beings could live in this spirit. Learn to understand music, mother. Music will make it easier to bear the vicissitudes of life.

[5]Important announcement. Strictly forbidden. The area between the barbed wire that circles the inner space of the camp, and the middle area as well as the outer area is a strictly prohibited zone for all prisoners (of war). The guards will shoot all prisoners without warning in this prohibited area. By order of the commandant.

CONCENTRATION CAMP I.

[6]My deeply-loved Mother, I thank you for your beautiful letter which you wrote me on the occasion of my birthday. I am deeply convinced that we shall soon be together. I also think often about the days when I went to school. Do you remember how you used to sit beside me when I did my assignments? Often I allowed my impetuous temperament to carry me away and began to scream and shout. Then you calmed me down, because you knew that I did not mean any harm. I am still like this, and suppose will always remain so. I think that what I have written for you and about you is fine, not because I think so, but because others who have read it tell me that it is fine. When you see the good in someone, then you can think and write well. That's what you wrote to me, and it is certainly true. Certainly you know that, because in your heart you are a poet. Do you remember how you always told me stories about your childhood. I remember every one of them precisely, and I'll start to write them down. Tales my Mother told me. That's what I'll call it. I am really pleased that you are now reading English books. Read a lot, because it's through reading that one can master a language best. But why am I telling you this. You know it well, because you have taught it to me.
Many kisses. Your son Heini.

The following description of Henry Kreisel's internment is taken from a letter he wrote to Robert Weaver, March 27 1956. It responded to a request for information for a program Weaver wanted to do on the internment of 'aliens.' Such a program was finally made for television.

from a letter to Robert Weaver

. . . I was interned on May 16, 1940, at exactly 12.30 p.m. I was working in a factory at the time, and it was just about time for lunch when I, together with several refugees working in the same place, was called into the manager's office, and informed by two plain clothes policemen that I would have to be interned. I remember being stunned for a minute, but I recovered at once, and I remember thinking that I wouldn't have to show up at the plant the next morning, and feeling rather good about that. Internment itself was a possibility we had all been considering, and there had been rumors of other refugees having already been interned. They drove me in a car to our house, and there they picked up my father, too. We were each allowed to pack a suitcase. Then they drove us over to the townhall in Leeds, and there we waited in a little room for about five hours, while they gathered in the sheep for transport to the temporary internment quarters. More and more fellows kept arriving, some silently stunned, others voluble and angry. I wondered whether my mother and my brother would also be interned (they never were). Most of us there felt insulted, felt wronged, felt that the country that had given us refuge was now turning against us. I remember one man saying that we would all be sent back to Germany, and he talked gloomily of suicide. But the consensus of opinion was that Britain would never do such a thing.

When we were taken out to waiting buses, there were large crowds of people looking on. They stared in silence as soldiers with rifles and fixed bayonets escorted us to the buses. The fixed bayonets really annoyed me. I felt a sense of outrage, because I was so completely conscious of never having done anything, and I was acutely aware of my status as 'victim'—victim first of Nazi tyranny, and then, ironically, victim because by nationality I belonged to a nation with which Britain was at war, but with which I also felt myself at war. I therefore resented the appellation of 'enemy alien.' I had never before been so acutely aware of irony and paradox, and I think that the experience has left a lasting effect on the way I see things.

We were taken from Leeds to Pontefract, and there, in a large barrack hall, very dirty and dusty, we spent the first night. We got a good supper, and the Commandant, an elderly Colonel, talked to us and apologized about the dirt. That impressed us. Many of the refugees had been in Nazi concentration camps, and the humane attitude of the Commandant stood in striking contrast to their earlier experience. (Our treatment was always humane and decent, both in England and in Canada.) There were no beds or bunks, and we slept on the floor, everyone getting one blanket. I remember lying there in the darkness, trying to sort out the impressions of the day and trying to come to terms with them, when suddenly the sounds of a violin filled the dusty barracks. One of the fellows, an excellent professional violinist, unable to sleep, had got up (I could barely see his silhouette against the window) and was playing one of the partitas for unaccompanied violin by Bach. The effect was indescribably beautiful, and I have never forgotten it. The music brought order into the chaos of the present situation, and somehow gave it a kind of perspective. It acted, not as a means of escape, but as a means of clarification. Its effect was powerful on all who heard it, even on those, like my father, who had never listened to anything more complex than a Strauss waltz. (It became a nightly ritual. We stayed in Pontefract for sixteen days, and every night he played for us after 'lights out.') I fell asleep soon after. I woke up feeling pretty stiff, and my mouth was full of dust. There was a long line of fellows waiting to go to the can (there were two toilets for 150 people) and I joined the line-up. And I remember thinking that if I hadn't been interned I would be setting off for the factory in a half hour or so. And the fact that I didn't have to gave me immense satisfaction.

The first day was spent in intense speculation of what would happen to us. Uncertainty was the worst thing about internment in general. Uncertainty, often followed by periods of depression, because you had the feeling that you would never get out. Sometimes we used to say that it would be better to know exactly how long you would have to remain, even if it were, say, three years. Startling rumors would spring up. Somehow it would get round that we would all be released in a week, and there was a tremendous feeling of elation everywhere. And just as suddenly the mood changed, and then everybody would be gloomy. Well, there were a thousand rumors going about that first day. I listened to all, spread a few myself. In the afternoon I got hold of a book and read and felt wonderful. To be reading on a working day! All in all, I didn't feel too badly that first day. The thought that I would get time to read and study was exhilarating. Many of the other fellows were of course depressed, especially those who had been rudely torn from interesting and rewarding occupations, or married men who did not know how their families would get on without them.

We were shunted about England, spent time in various camps, ended up on the Isle of Man. And then, on the fourth of July, unmarried men under forty (with a few others, who had volunteered) were told to be ready for another move. We weren't told where we were to go, but there were wild rumors about. Some said we were going to Scotland, some said to Australia. (That was correct up to a point. A minority of internees ended up in Australia.) But the general view was that we were going to Canada. (The only hard bit of news was that someone had overheard an officer say something about Canada to another officer.) Canada it was. We landed, after a pleasant trip on the Polish ship Sobieski, in Quebec on July 15 at six o'clock in the morning. (Our trip was rather exceptional. Other fellows had a rough time.)

. . . I have a diary,[1] and in it are recorded reactions of the moment. Some of these reactions are understandably gloomy, but luckily one tends to forget gloomy moments. On the whole, camp life was anything but gloomy, and our treatment, as I said before, was humane and decent. My father, for instance, who had spent almost a year in Dachau, and had got to England just before the war broke out, always spoke of camp as a kind of rest cure. He worried about my mother naturally, but he had few complaints. Though he was over fifty, he loved to go out into the woods of New Brunswick to cut trees, although he had never done any hard manual labour before. Younger fellows, who had fiancées in England, or young fellows who had not, but could hardly wait to get out and get their hands on some women, were naturally less patient. Many also wanted to get into the war, and so there was constant agitation to have our cases re-examined. This agitation, helped powerfully by influential organizations outside, was eventually successful.

Looking back over the experience, I can say, pretty much without qualification, that the experience was beneficial to me. For one thing it enabled me to do a great deal of reading and writing. It was almost as if someone had offered me a block of time at the moment when I needed it most. When I got out of camp I had read more than most undergraduates have read by the time they graduate, and I had written about six hundred pages of stuff. (A novel, short stories, essays, none of them much good, but invaluable just the same.) When I got out I was a hell of a lot better prepared for the University than most kids are. . . .

It should be said that intellectually the camps here were very stimulating. Without exaggeration it can be said that there was more food for the mind to be found there than in most Canadian towns. The place was lousy with doctors of all sorts, doctors of medicine, of philosophy, of theology. At night the place (I am here speaking particularly of the camp near Fredericton in New Brunswick) became alive with argument. Sitting around one bunk, an orthodox rabbi would argue with a Neo-Thomist, and in another hut, around another bed, a Marxist philosopher was having it out with a Platonist. There was always a crowd around the beds on which the contestants sat, and sometimes the arguments grew violent. In this casual manner was I initiated into the world of ideas. There were also several psychiatrists around, two passionate Freudians, and one Adlerian, and they were always giving lectures and having debates, with each other and with everybody else. There were Zionists and anti-Zionists, Stalinists and Trotskyists, Socialists of all hues, Capitalists of all hues (from the little greengrocer to one of the most influential pre-Hitlerian bankers), and a sprinkling of anarchists. (One of them, a silent, bearded chap, had fought in Spain in an anarchist battalion, and I took a few lessons of Spanish from him, but then he was shifted to another camp and took his books, and so ended my Spanish lessons.) Talk about the market place of ideas! I have never since encountered it again in so concentrated a form. (I don't want to give the impression that there were nothing but intellectuals in camp. The majority played cards most of the time, I suppose, though all were vitally interested in the conduct of the war, and were always debating the issues, and after a German victory the camp was as gloomy as a graveyard at night. The point is that anyone who was interested in serious issues and serious ideas could have that interest satisfied.)

There was a good deal of music in camp, too; most memorable were the weekly concerts which John Newmark and Gerald Kander gave.

All in all, I learned a lot in camp. It was a valuable experience, too, because it brought me in contact with all sorts of people, all of them eager to tell of their experiences. We had depraved bastards with us. (One of the fellows had been a pimp, and I used to listen to him with avid interest.) Several of the rather shady characters used to come to me and ask me to write letters for them, because they had seen me writing a lot, and they couldn't write too well themselves. When you write letters for people you find out a great deal. (Vide Samuel Richardson.) When I lecture and talk to freshmen here, I am constantly amazed at their naivety. Well, when I was interned I was seventeen, and when I was released about a year and a half later, I had some ideas about what went on in the world, and I understood better what was happening in Europe and in Asia, because I had listened to so many arguments and read a lot, and I knew also more about what men do and how they behave and what drives them on, because I had listened to them pour out their experiences and had seen them in action, sometimes behaving nobly, but often like selfish bastards. The experience of internment, then, while I shouldn't like to have to go through it again, is nonetheless an experience which I am glad to have had.

Lastly, the experience benefitted me because it brought me to Canada. For that alone it would have been worth it. This may sound soupy and sentimental but it is a simple fact.

Henry Kreisel

---

[1] I knew I had the diary, and I remember looking for it at the time; but I couldn't find it. I did finally find it in 1973 (see p. 18). H.K.

Remembering his years in Vienna, Henry Kreisel finds his recollections of the personal circumstances and emotions of his childhood inextricably mixed with his ambivalence about the city which, having first richly nourished his imagination, then turned murderously on his people. He wrote 'Vienna Remembered' for this collection.

Henry Kreisel
Vienna Remembered

The death of parents opens the doors of memory. The past imposes itself upon the present and demands a reassessment. So I thought, as I stood by my father's grave, of how the early conflict between us had provided the fuel that powered my ambition. I early felt the need to express and so to release powerful emotions that, left unexpressed, would have been threatening. I also discovered early that the best way in which I could deal with such emotions was by distancing myself from them, and that the way to do this was to create fictional characters and let them act out strong dramatic situations. In this activity I had the unswerving support of my mother. She was always eager to hear what I had written, and I used to read my stories to her. Occasionally my father would also listen. But what he liked best was to hear me recite poems. His favourite poet was Schiller, and he was particularly impressed if I knew a long Schiller poem by heart. To read aloud always gave me great satisfaction. To tell stories conferred on the story-teller a kind of power. Literature was therefore akin to magic.

Ever since I can remember, I was a voracious reader. We didn't have many books at home, but there were good libraries in the neighbourhood and my mother always encouraged my brother and me to use them. We loved to go there and browse around and take books home.

Literature, and later the theatre, were both refuge and a source of understanding. Books and the theatre helped me to grope for explanations of human relationships, and helped me to bear, as I watched it, the difficult marriage of my parents.

The atmosphere in Vienna in the late 1920s and into the middle 1930s was conducive to the growth of one's literary and artistic consciousness, even if one lived, as we did, very much on the fringe of the artistic life of the city.

We lived in the Leopoldstadt, one of the outlying districts of the city. It was a lower middle class and working class area, and it housed a large number of people who had come to Vienna in the early part of the century and then during and immediately after the first world war, mostly from the eastern part of the old Habsburg empire, from places in Hungary, Bohemia, Poland, Rumania, Serbia, and Croatia. The district was thus a real melting-pot of religions and nationalities, with old animosities intact, and yet people lived together in reasonable harmony most of the time. Not until the Nazis took over Austria in 1938 was I ever afraid to walk in the streets at any time during the day or night. When I was growing up I felt a tremendous attachment to the district and could not imagine living anywhere else. There were tensions, but there was also a feeling of community.

To this part of Vienna my maternal grandparents came, in 1915 or 1916, with their three youngest and still unmarried daughters, Helene, Bertha, and Rosa, all in their early twenties. The family came to Vienna because my grandfather was afraid, as the war on the eastern front intensified and stories of soldiers raping young women began to spread to the small Polish towns and villages, that his daughters were at risk. Vienna, the capital of the empire, afforded a measure of safety. Besides, my grandparents' oldest daughter, my aunt Toni, had married and moved to Vienna some years earlier, and so there was someone there who could help them adjust to life in a great metropolis.

Toni's husband, Abraham, had a younger brother, Leo. Leo, who was to become my father, met one of the three sisters, Helene, who was of course his sister-in-law, and after a passionate courtship married her. Their first child, a boy, did not live. I was born in 1922 and my brother Kurt in 1924. A day or two after I was born, Toni's and Abraham's older daughter Salka married Jacob Zucker, who had settled in England a few years earlier, and moved there. For us it proved a blessing, since it was Salka who became our lifeline in 1938 and helped to rescue several members of our family. All my aunts and uncles and their families who had remained in Poland perished during the second world war, as did my aunt Bertha and her husband.

My grandfather had been reasonably well off in Poland, but never managed to find a secure financial footing in Vienna. My grandparents lived just around the corner from our apartment. My mother's family was very close-knit. Strong emotional ties bound

them together. Every Saturday my aunts Bertha and Rosa, who lived
further away, came to visit my grandparents with their children, and
my brother and I always looked forward to those occasions, when we
could play with our cousins. Every two or three years Salka and her
children came from England, and we could show off our English
cousins, rolling their exotic names dramatically off our tongues—
Ralph, Bessie, Blanche. And when we asked them to speak English to
our friends, we would bask in reflected glory. Once, around 1930, my
mother's youngest brother, Adolph, who had gone to the United
States right after the war, came to visit his now widowed mother and
his sisters. What an occasion that was! The memory of his arrival
found its way into *The Rich Man*, though the leading figure of that
novel, Jacob Grossman, has little in common with my uncle.

My father's family was more remote. His parents had gone to live
in then Turkish-ruled Jerusalem in the 1890s and I never knew them.
Apart from Abraham, two of my father's brothers, Julius and Philip,
also lived in Vienna, but we did not see them very often. I was very
fond of Philip, who was a bachelor and seemed a romantic, dashing
figure to me. It was always exciting when he came to visit us. He used
to tell droll stories that kept me spell-bound. I saw him for the last
time in July 1938, on the railway station in Brussels. I was on my way
to England, and he came to the station to see me for an hour or so,
until the train moved on again. Philip had escaped to Belgium after
the *Anschluss* and was hoping to get a visa so that he might go to the
United States. Alas, he didn't make it and was trapped by the German
sweep through Belgium in 1940, disappeared eventually into the
great maws of the Nazi concentration camps and was never heard
from again.

But when I was a child, and in spite of ominous signs, the horror of
the 1930s and 1940s was unimaginable. The extended family in
which we lived gave us a sense of security, a feeling of belonging. It
was the boat's anchor in turbulent waters.

Outside there was the great city, beckoning to us, waiting to be
explored. There were really several cities, all quite distinct, all with
their own unique characteristics. There was the immediate district,
with its polyglot population, hard-hit by the economic depression
after 1929, but also vibrant with street life and full of interesting
characters. Not far away the Danube (*die Donau*) flowed, a broad,
gray-brown river, full of dangerous eddies, but with some safe
stretches, too, where we often went swimming. There, too, under the
bridges, we used to see derelicts and hoboes eating scraps of food and

smoking cigarette butts or, in the evenings, sleeping, covered by threadbare bits of cloth. There were times when we ourselves were economically hard-hit, and then I used to frighten myself with the thought that I might end up sleeping under a bridge by the river.

A ten or fifteen minutes' walk in the other direction brought us to the Prater, the great amusement park area of Vienna, open all year round, a magnet that drew us several times a week. It was a place of endless fascination, its splendors inexhaustible. In the centre of the Prater was the great stadium, and there the important international soccer matches were played. We were rabid soccer fans, and of course played the game ourselves whenever there was an opportunity, mostly in the streets, much to the annoyance of mothers who were always complaining that we were ruining our shoes. We used to dream of one day getting proper soccer boots, but that dream was never realized. My brother was a particularly brilliant gymnast and a marvellous dare-devil of a goalkeeper, much in demand when sides were chosen.

An hour's walk, and a world away, there was *die innere Stadt*, the inner city, with its broad, tree-lined boulevards, the beautiful, elegant shops, the great cathedral, the *Burgtheater* and the opera house, the museums, and the magnificent squares and palaces of the Hofburg, all splendid reminders of imperial Habsburg grandeur. These monuments of a vanished empire were almost too overwhelming for us. They seemed remote, part of another world, almost another country.

But not the theatres and the opera house. For to go to the theatre or to the opera was a way of entering a world of magic. It was through school that we gained entrance into this world. It was possible to get very cheap standing-room tickets through the schools, and I started going regularly to the opera and the theatres when I was about twelve, in 1934. Most of the time I went with Gus. We had come to know each other in 1928, when we started school, and became close friends. We were inseparable. Gus eventually went to the United States, served in the army there, and later became a pediatrician. Our close friendship has endured to this day. Occasionally my brother came with us, but he was not yet ten when we first started to go to the *Burgtheater* and the opera, and he was not too interested. We saw and heard some of the greatest actors and singers of the time and became very knowledgeable and also highly critical, and we would sometimes refuse to applaud even very great singers like Beniamino Gigli, if they had an off-day and didn't reach the high standards we had come to expect.

I loved school, particularly the study of language and literature. Mathematics, however, was a terrible burden that had to be endured. But school and particularly the *Gymnasium*, where I started to study in 1932, opened the great world of art and literature, and everything else was secondary.

But there was a dark side. It was in 1934 that the smouldering conflicts that were eventually to tear Austria apart first broke into my consciousness, though I didn't yet fully comprehend the nature of the social and political forces that then came into open collision. For it was in February 1934 that the government, then led by Chancellor Engelbert Dollfuss, moved the army against their main political rivals, the Social-Democrats, and engaged them in battle. The government moved artillery to the banks of the Danube and began shelling the *Gemeindehäuser*, the workers' apartment blocks, where the main resistance was centred. Since these were not far away from where we lived, we could hear the pounding of the guns. For three days the battle raged. The streets were deserted, armed soldiers patrolled them. We were not allowed to go out, even during the day.

The aftermath of this brief, but bloody civil war was disastrous. The Social-Democratic Mayor of Vienna, Karl Seitz, was deposed. Several prominent Social-Democratic leaders were hanged, and others fled into exile. The country became a one-party state. But the unrest was now palpable, and I became aware for the first time of the murderous political games that were being played out.

In the summer of 1934 Chancellor Dollfuss was assassinated in an attempted coup by the underground Nazi party. The coup failed. 'Order' was restored. But everyone knew that Hitler's Germany was deeply implicated in the plot, even though Hitler repudiated any suggestion that he was involved in the affair. Yet all the pieces that were to lead to the annexation of Austria by Germany barely four years later were now in place.

In Vienna an uneasy calm settled over the city. But just underneath the surface, the cauldron was boiling, a poisonous brew was being concocted. It was this Vienna that I tried to evoke some ten years later when I started to make the first sketches for *The Rich Man*, and sent Jacob Grossman on his long-dreamed-of, but ultimately sad and tragic journey.

Anti-Semitism was endemic in Austria. It was even politically respectable. Some popular politicians, men like Karl Lueger, who was Mayor of Vienna from 1897 to 1910, used it shamelessly and demagogically. Yet the Jewish community was on the whole a flourishing one. It produced great writers like Hugo von

Hofmannsthal and Arthur Schnitzler, great composers like Gustav Mahler and Arnold Schönberg, and great singers like Richard Tauber. Sigmund Freud lived most of his life in the city, as did Theodore Herzl, the founder of modern Zionism. It was a tremendously creative community, and it surely contributed enormously to the cultural fabric of the city.

Certain professions were closed to Jews. They could not normally aspire to careers in the civil service or in the teaching profession unless they converted to Roman Catholicism. We learned to adjust to the social realities, as Jews have done for centuries, for though anti-Semitism was endemic and on occasion virulent, it was not yet murderous.

We realized, when we were in school, that we had to be exceptionally good to gain entrance to institutes of higher learning, and so we worked very hard. But scholarship has always occupied a high place of esteem in Jewish society. My parents, who had little formal education themselves, always recognized the importance of learning, and were prepared to make many sacrifices so that my brother and I could have the education that was denied to them.

In elementary school and later in the *Gymnasium,* Jewish students mingled easily with the other students, who were mostly Catholics, with a sprinkling of so-called *Evangelische,* that is, Protestants. In the Vienna I knew, Protestants were rather rare kinds of religious birds. I never knew exactly what they believed. Catholicism was of course ubiquitous. Its presence was everywhere apparent—in the streets where priests, nuns, and monks walked about in their habits, in the colourful processions we watched on the great religious holy days, and in the great churches we passed everywhere.

In the *Gymnasium,* advancement was by merit, and though some teachers had the reputation of being anti-Semitic, I don't remember that they ever let this influence their generally correct behaviour.

Everything changed of course after the German invasion on March 11, 1938. That event came as a tremendous shock, though it really was predictable, certainly since the beginning of the final crisis a month earlier, when the hapless Austrian Chancellor, Kurt von Schuschnigg, journeyed to meet Hitler at Berchtesgarden and was presented with what amounted to an ultimatum. When Schuschnigg decided to call a plebiscite on March 13 to demonstrate to Hitler that Austrians wanted to be independent, Hitler acted and sent his armies across the borders. We did not want to believe that the worst could happen, and when it did, we were shattered.

What was most shattering of all was to witness the jubilation with which the general population greeted the triumphant Nazi army, and how they assented so easily when, on March 13, Austria ceased to exist as an independent, sovereign state and became a province of the German Reich.

Not everyone had cause to rejoice, of course. Arrests of political and religious opponents of the Nazis, and of prominent Jews, began immediately. The Gestapo set up headquarters in the city. Everyone knew someone who had been arrested. Not until after the war did the actual figures emerge. In Vienna alone, writes Alan Bullock, some seventy-six thousand people were arrested.[1]

The schools remained closed for a few days, and when we returned, in some trepidation, everything was changed, changed utterly. Jewish students were immediately segregated, and had to sit in the rear benches of their classrooms. Some of our fellow students still tried to be civil, some even friendly, but most were now openly hostile. There were verbal taunts and then increasing physical violence. Most of the teachers, either out of fear or because they approved of what was going on, turned a blind eye to the increasing violence in the corridors and even in the classrooms. The Director of the *Gymnasium* sequestered himself in his office while his school was being taken over by barbarians.

Two teachers stood out in their decency—one was Father Ullmann, a priest who gave courses in religion for Catholic students, and the other was a man whose name was Zeitelberger and who taught mathematics. We had always thought of him as a bumbling, ineffectual teacher, though he was always kind. But now he emerged as a truly heroic figure for the Jewish students, for he attempted to protect us from violence, both verbal and physical, and he openly defied the bullies, even though they threatened him.

I don't know what became of Zeitelberger, but for me he has always remained a living presence, a symbol of all that is best in human beings, and I paid tribute to him in *The Betrayal*, when Theodore Stappler returns to Vienna after the war and encounters Zeitelberger, 'a man of great compassion and deep humanity.' It is Zeitelberger who urges Stappler to do something with his life, to teach and to heal. 'Teaching and healing—that was all he talked about in his rambling way.'

It became increasingly difficult for me to concentrate on my studies, though my mother encouraged me to finish the year. But after a particularly nasty and violent incident in May, I absolutely refused to go back to school and dropped out.

Vienna itself, the city I had loved with a great passion, had become a waste land city for me. Danger now lurked everywhere. We wanted desperately to flee, to find refuge somewhere. But this was not easily accomplished. Visas were extremely difficult to get.

In England, Salka Zucker began to make extraordinary efforts to get us out. She succeeded in the first instance to get visas for my cousin Henny and me, perhaps because we were the oldest of the children of the three sisters. We left Vienna at the end of July 1938. My parents and my brother did not get out until much later, after some harrowing experiences.

The last four months of my life in Vienna have tended to blot out much of the affection I had for the city, and to this day my feelings for Vienna have remained highly ambivalent. It is a city of light, but the light is always extinguished and darkness engulfs the city. It is a city of great music and dance, but the music becomes cacophonous and the dancers turn into grimacing and threatening figures. It is a city of elegant streets and smart shops, but suddenly the streets are full of frenzied, self-intoxicated crowds that turn murderous.

I returned to Vienna for the first time after the war in 1954 with my wife because I wanted to show her where I had spent my early years. The city was still under four-power occupation. The great opera house had been destroyed and was not yet rebuilt. The *Burgtheater* had been severely damaged and the damage had not yet been repaired. There was rubble everywhere. The city had a shabby, provincial look, all vitality drained out. We had planned on staying for about two weeks, but after four or five days I couldn't bear to remain in the city any longer. So we packed our suitcases and went to Italy.

We came once more to the city, in the spring of 1976. This time I felt better about the city. Austria was again an independent country, although I had the feeling that the country had not yet fully faced the disastrous events of the 1930s and 1940s.

Vienna had been lovingly rebuilt. But at the same time the city seemed like a gigantic museum, full of beautiful buildings and objects, but lacking the nervous and creative energy that it once had and that is the hallmark of a truly great metropolis, of New York, say, or London, or Paris. Vienna had that quality once, but it was now gone. That was particularly evident to me when we went to the *Burgtheater*, to see plays by Goethe, Schiller, and Lessing. After the excitement of the London stage, the Viennese stage seemed positively dowdy. The actors spoke beautifully, but their gestures and movements seemed oddly dated, as if they were trying to conjure up some glorious, romantic past in order to preserve it. But this was the last part of the 20th century, and nothing that I saw in the productions of *Faust*, *Don Carlos*, and *Nathan der Weise* gave me a sense that I was watching and listening to something that had to be urgently communicated.

Walking about the city, seeing plays, making trips into the *Wienerwald*, the famous Vienna Woods, going to Schönbrunn and the other great Habsburg palaces, gave me the feeling that the Viennese wanted to return to the great imperial past, when the Danube was blue and the birds were singing in the parks and the Kahlenberg beckoned in the distance.

Everywhere the far-away past was lovingly restored and lingered over, but the more immediate past was treated as if it did not really exist or was at any rate too painful to recall. And when the doors were opened and skeletons rattled, the doors were quickly shut again.

These were no doubt highly subjective reactions. Yet I could not deny the fact that the city still had some magic power, nor could I deny that it had put an indelible stamp on me. My aesthetic sensibility was largely shaped by it—my love for literature and my understanding of how literature is created, and my love for music and the lyric theatre, and my enduring passion for the dramatic stage. (My involvement with the graphic arts, only rudimentary in Vienna, would have to await the influence of my wife and the experience that London afforded me.)

But Vienna also was the place where I encountered the forces of evil in the world and looked into the heart of darkness.

I must be grateful to the city for what it gave me, though it will remain for me forever bitter-sweet, a place where exhilaration and agony are inextricably mingled.

---

[1]Alan Bullock, *Hitler: A Study in Tyranny* (N.Y.: Bantam Books, 1958), p. 198.

With Hitler's invasion came the dispersal of those closest to the young Henry Kreisel. While those who remained in Europe died in the camps, his grandmother went to Tel Aviv, his parents and brother escaped after him to England, and his best friend ended up in the United States. This new diaspora meant that Henry Kreisel's memories of his grandmother would be entirely Viennese; he would never see her again and could know her life after 1938 only through family legend.

Henry Kreisel recalled the end of that legend following the occasion on November 6 1980 when Professor Mervin Butovsky interviewed him. The interview was one of several Professor Butovsky conducted with Jewish-Canadian writers, seeking 'to record in the writers' own words their personal sense of living in two worlds.' (Much of the interview is printed further on in this collection of writings by and about Henry Kreisel.) Part of their conversation dwelt on the European family history of Henry Kreisel. After it had been completed, he sent to Professor Butovsky the following 'Postscript,' a genealogy, but also an account of one journey to a chosen land that had not yet become a homeland.

Henry Kreisel

Postscript to an Interview

Both my paternal grandparents and my maternal grandmother are buried in Israel.

My paternal grandfather, who lived in Rumania, where my father was born, was ultra-orthodox and decided, when he was in his fifties, to move to Jerusalem so that when his time came to die, he would die in the Holy City. So the family moved to Palestine, as it then was, around 1898 or 1899, when my father was about eight years old. My father went to school in Jerusalem, a sort of *yeshiva*, I suppose, but left when he was about eighteen to go to Vienna, where he had an older brother. There he met my mother and of course I was born there.

My paternal grandfather died either shortly before or after I was born in 1922. My grandmother died in the early 1930s. I remember my father coming home one day, telling us that his older brother had just had a telegram telling him of their mother's death. Then my father took off his shoes and sat *shiva* for his mother.

My maternal grandmother, Hinde Schreier, went to Tel Aviv after the Nazi invasion of Austria in 1938. One of her daughters, my aunt Toni, had gone there with her family around 1935. My grandmother died in Tel Aviv in 1944, I believe, and of course she is buried there. When my wife and I were in Israel in 1976, we visited her grave, and since she had been very close to me when I was a boy, it was a very moving moment for me to stand by her graveside.

My cousin, who lives in Tel Aviv, has been trying to locate the graves of our paternal grandparents in Jerusalem, but has been unsuccessful. It's possible that the graveyard where they were buried was destroyed in one of the battles that raged in and around Jerusalem in 1948 during Israel's war of independence, or that it was subsequently destroyed during the Jordanian occupation of part of Jerusalem.

One other little note of interest. Hinde Schreier, my maternal grandmother, died on a Friday and had to be buried on the Sabbath and of course the body could not be driven to the cemetery, but had to be carried. My cousin told me that it was a memorable occasion, because the coffin had to be carried for some ten or twelve miles, and every hundred yards or so the bearers changed. Total strangers, who happened to be walking by, stopped and helped to carry the coffin for a short distance and then others would take over. So hundreds of people carried her to her grave. It was, said my cousin, almost like a regal procession.

Henry Kreisel's parents

The two pieces which follow are taken from notes Henry Kreisel kept at the time of his father's funeral and during his mother's last illness. They pay tribute to the different characters and different strengths of his parents, and to the love he bore them.

Henry Kreisel

[Written on the death of my father]

Note: My father died in Leeds, in the north of England, at the end of January 1969. He had been ill, and was in hospital, but his death was sudden. My brother phoned me around 4 a.m. Edmonton time and told me. I managed to get a direct flight to London about noon the next day and arrived in Leeds in the afternoon. The death of my father was a shattering experience, more disturbing curiously than the death of my mother, two years later. I had been always closer to my mother, but my father's death threw me into greater emotional turmoil than hers.

I stayed in Leeds for the mourning period—a week—and some time during that week wrote the piece that follows.

'Do you want to see him?' asked the beadle.

I looked at my brother. We both nodded.

Chapeltown Synagogue. Old now. Run down. Once, with its dome, its solid stone structure had seemed imposing. I saw it first in 1938, a frightened, strange little refugee, barely sixteen years old, just arrived from what was then Nazi Austria. Most of the Leeds Jewish community lived in Chapeltown then, and the Great Synagogue was the symbol of their communal life. A man called Stern was the cantor of the synagogue—a smallish, beak-nosed man. He had a beautiful tenor voice and he came out of the great tradition of cantorial singing. Not that I went very often in the barely two years I spent in Leeds. But often enough, drawn mainly by his voice. So the voice is a living memory. The man, too, in a strange way. He had divorced his wife and married her sister—a kind of scandal people used to talk about. He died a few years ago and his widow wanted him to be buried in Jerusalem. Appealed for funds from the Leeds Jewish community to take his body there. My mother frowned on this. It was wrong, she thought, to take money for the dead when the living needed it so much more.

Now she stands there, slightly to the side, small-looking, gaunt, slightly shiverish, talking to someone.

The thirtieth of January 1969, a remarkably beautiful day. Only about four hours ago I arrived, flying from Edmonton where the temperature was about thirty below—January the coldest month in living memory. A scant forty-eight hours ago, when it was 4 a.m., my brother had phoned to say that my father had died. Not wholly unexpectedly, but not anticipated at that time. In the hospital for treatment of a bladder tumor, his heart suddenly stopped. So here I am, in Chapeltown Road, not having slept for more than twenty-four hours, somewhat disoriented after the transatlantic flight, not feeling really tired, but just suspended, neither time nor space having any real substance, propelled through time and space to land here among these strange, yet so familiar landmarks.

'Come with me,' said the beadle.

He was a short man, a parchment-like, wrinkled face looking out from under his broad-brimmed hat. When we arrived at the synagogue, he had taken my mother, my brother and me into the foyer, and there made deep cuts in one of our garments, a mark of the mourner, to be worn for the duration of the period of mourning.

We followed him, my brother and I, detached ourselves from the small group of people who had now gathered there—our cousins and some of their children, some friends, and Jacob Uri—Yankele—who had arrived from London only an hour or so earlier, to say good-bye to the friend of his youth when together they had celebrated the good and joyous life in post-Habsburgian Vienna. Yankele was a bachelor then, my father a married man, and so my mother, regarding Yankele as the rake, has still a somewhat ambiguous feeling for him, fifty years and more after all the merriment and all the joy—merriment and joy in which she did not participate. All now a memory. And she is grateful that he has come from London, loyal friend after all, not just a friend for good times. I look back at him standing there in a blue overcoat, in his sixties now, with a walking stick, mourning in a way his own lost youth in the death of the companion of his youthful celebrations.

We walk over cobbled stones, turn into an alley. We come to a small wooden building, what must have been a garage. The beadle unlocks the door. We enter.

The coffin sits on trestles. A plain wooden box, the Jewish custom. He opens the lid. My father lies there, white-enshrouded. His head deep in the coffin, the face turned slightly sidewards. Very peaceful. In a deep sleep. He was always a very heavy sleeper. Hard to waken. Now sleeps and will not wake again. Awesome in a way. I notice the white little bootees that have been tied neatly round his feet— touching in a way, like bootees on a small child.

I look at him. I look at my brother, I look back at my father, sleeping in his coffin. I have come thousands of miles to bid him farewell.

In his own way, he was an extraordinary man. I used to loathe him at times when I was a boy because he was always out on the town, gambling, womanizing, leaving us to lead our lives—my mother, my brother and me. Things change. I am more tolerant of his foibles and failings. In the last twenty years I've come to love him, perhaps because we haven't lived in close proximity, have seen each other only intermittently. But not really. I've come to understand his extraordinary zest for life. He was a sensuous, sensual man. A great raconteur, too. Not educated. Full of sure opinions. But full of life. My last memory of him when he and my mother were about to fly back to England from Edmonton in the late summer of 1967 and we were at the airport and he looked out at a plane just landing and said, 'What a smashing bird!' Now sleeps forever.

The beadle closes the coffin. Tears well up in me. I control myself. We walk out into the bright sunshine, back to where the others are standing, ready to drive out to the cemetery as soon as the coffin has been put on the hearse.

My mother will not go to the cemetery. She will go back to my brother's house. I take her arm.

'We went to look at him.'

'Did you? I'm glad. They say that sometimes there might be another body. By mistake from the hospital. But you saw him?'

'Yes. He looks very peaceful. You go back to Kurt's house.'

'Yes.'

Yankele joins us. 'I wish I had known you were going to see him. I would have come along. To see him.' The lost youth. A mournful look in his eyes.

The hearse now comes into view. My brother and I get into the first car, right behind the hearse, and sit down.

'I'm glad you've come,' he says again, for perhaps the tenth time since I've arrived, 'it's a great help. I would have felt so much more alone otherwise.'

I have always felt very close to him, but never closer than at this moment.

from Journal entries, December 1970 and January 1971

Dec. 23/70.   I write this in an Air-Canada plane somewhere over the Atlantic on my way to Leeds. Had a phone call yesterday afternoon from my brother who told me that my mother was critically ill and at death's door.

It was not unexpected news. On Nov. 25 or 26 Kurt phoned to tell me that my mother had fallen out of bed and had broken her femur and was now in hospital. Then she got pneumonia. But she had, he said, also lost the will to live. Still, how one is stunned when expected news of this kind actually comes. I was quite numb. I wish only, as I fly across the Atlantic, that her end may be peaceful and suffering not prolonged, and that I may yet see her alive.

She was an extraordinary woman, full of natural tact and very wise, too. She had, I became aware when I saw her during the last two or three years, the expected prejudices of a woman of her generation and background. And yet she also transcended these, and considering that she had a very limited formal education and moved hardly outside the circle of the immediate family, her sensitivity and understanding were quite remarkable. The portrait I did of her, many years ago, when I modelled Shaendl in *The Rich Man* on her, though idealized, nevertheless catches something of the essential and fundamental character of her. She was a great source of strength to me, as a spiritual presence, while I was interned and afterwards, when I began to make my way as a student, writer, professor.

In Esther I saw something of my mother, and they have been the two great women figures in my life—my anima.

I am now very calm, flying towards something that is both known and unknown, expected and yet mysterious.

Dec. 24-29.   A smooth landing, but too late to make the 8:10 to Leeds. I must wait till 10:00. Phone Kurt to tell him I have arrived. Mother still alive. Kurt waits for me at the airport with Frances and Debbie. Frances has grown into a gorgeous young girl of fifteen. Debbie, who's eleven, is a charming little girl, very loveable.

Since visiting hours are from 11:30 to 12 in the morning, we go at once to the hospital. St. James's. I once was there, almost exactly thirty-one years ago, in 1939, when I was supposed to have my appendix out. A huge, late Victorian complex of red brick buildings.

My mother is in the orthopaedic ward—a long ward, beds close together. Walls apple-green, peeling in the corridor, but clean. Streamers strung across the ceiling, a Xmas tree.

My mother sits in a chair, looking drawn and haggard, but not as bad as I had prepared myself for. She looks infinitely weary, like a wounded bird. I feel like taking her in my arms and stroking her.

Kurt says, 'Here's Heini. He's come to see you all the way from Canada.' She looks up and for a moment her eyes light up, fairly sparkle. Something registers—clearly. She speaks, but her words are slurred and I can't make them out. But she has recognized me, if only for an instant. Then her head falls forward and she closes her eyes.

I hold her hand. She looks up again. *'Wo ist Bertha?'* she asks. Where is Bertha? That's her sister, who perished in the war. Past and present are commingled. So it will be. Toni and Bertha, two of her sisters, are mentioned most frequently. She speaks in Yiddish, in German, in English. To the nurses always in English. So she differentiates. Every sentence is an enormous effort, summoned forth from some diminishing reservoir.

My mother suddenly asks, 'Does Esther like her job?' and nods when I say yes. I tell her about Philip. She is now far away. Her temperature is normal now, so the pneumonia seems for the time being conquered. She also suffered a mild stroke which has left her speech impaired.

I sleep when I get back to Kurt's place and go again to the hospital at 7 p.m. She is now in bed. I tell her I couldn't come in the afternoon because I was tired after the long journey. She looks puzzled. 'I've come from Canada,' I say. 'I have a son in Canada,' she says. 'I'm your son. I'm Heini. I came to see you.' She gives me a long, long look, smiles and closes her eyes. I don't know whether it is all real to her. Does she wake or does she sleep? She is in a twilight world, in and out.

So it will be for the five days I am in Leeds. They become one long day, really. To the hospital at 11:30, then at 3 p.m., then at 7 p.m. An hour each time.

I am grateful to Kurt and Phyllis on whom falls the whole responsibility. They are extraordinarily devoted and conscientious. Esther and I would do it, too, of course, but we are far away. I hope she won't have to suffer long. She is not in physical pain, but there is discomfort and she is **so** tired.

They make her sit up in a chair during the day and she longs to go to bed. She tells us to open the bed, so she can 'jump in.' She tried desperately to lift herself from the chair, but she can't move. She's as helpless as a baby.

One day (Sunday) she was really angry and her speech was better. She was desperate to be put to bed, but the nurses had their orders and wouldn't do it.

So she waits for death, aware of it, waiting. When we are with her, we wish she would get better, but then we realize the impossibility. She cannot recover the strength she lost and she won't ever walk again.

Let the agony not be too much prolonged. Let her end be peaceful. Yet though she is so infinitely weary, she has amazing tenaciousness.

The family comes to see her—Salka, Henny, Blanche, Cyril, Ralph, Shirley. She recognizes them, then we all fade off for her. Yet she wants people there.

On Monday night I stay behind. Stroke her hands and her hair. An awful moment, for I know that I shall now never see her again, and I envy Kurt that he will be allowed to be with her at the end, whenever it comes.

On Tuesday morning I leave. The 9:40 plane to London is cancelled and I have to take a train which gets me to London at 1:30. A dreary London day, gray and dull and foggy. I take a taxi from King's Cross across London to BOAC terminal, past the British Museum. How long it seems since I worked there every day. Past Whitehall, past Victoria Station, all the familiar landmarks. I thought the plane wouldn't be able to take off, it seemed so foggy. But we got away on time and now are past Greenland and in about four hours I shall be home.

Jan. 13/1971.   Mother passed away today. The phone call came from Kurt just as I walked into my office about 8:40. Her passing was peaceful. She had been moved into a nursing home in Harrowgate and that had been a very worthwhile thing. She had her own room and was very well taken care of. They didn't make her sit up. So she could sleep and wait for death and for peace.

On Sunday last she couldn't recognize anyone any more. So there must have been more strokes, as the young doctor in St. James's had anticipated. Then, on Monday, she began to moan, as if in pain. The doctor gave her morphine and said that she would now sleep away. So it proved.

When I spoke to Kurt, and he told me how it had been, I felt infinitely relieved. I hated to think of her so helpless, so weary. She did not want to live any more and I was afraid that the heart would tick on and the body machine would keep going for another six months or so. It was a dreadful prospect. So, for her sake, it is good that she is now at rest. Her spirit will live on, in me, in Kurt, in her grandchildren.

Solomon Schreier, her father, is after all a real presence in my life. And yet he died forty years ago or more.

But when I hung up, I felt suddenly desolate.

writings from internment

Much of his time in internment Henry Kreisel spent realizing his new ambition: to write in English. Although the writing is remarkably sure for an adolescent who had only recently begun to learn his chosen language, it is, of course, juvenilia; the stories are not accomplished, the poems even less so. Nonetheless, they are of interest to his readers, for they show unusual consistency between the boy trying to make sense of the upheaval he was living through and the mature novelist. Even in his earliest stories Henry Kreisel reveals himself as a writer for whom the impulse to formal experiment fades before the pressure of what he has to tell. What he has to tell in this apprentice-work falls into two themes with many variations: he writes (always desiring a better world) about injustice and hate, whether they manifest themselves in war or in the poverty of those who work (or sometimes cannot find work) that others indifferent to them may be wealthy; and he writes about the ways in which every life, that of the most modest greengrocer or the even poorer woman he serves, is replete with tragedy and joy. His themes are present in these first assays as is his humane and measured narrative voice; it is his literary skills which would change and develop as he settled into his new life in another country.

The biographical and historical interest of this early writing is also considerable. A form of expression alternative to and additional to the internment diary, it tells us much about the circumstances, emotions and adaptations of the writer-to-be as he came to terms with the traumas of Hitler's invasion of Austria and his own flight, of his separation from his mother to whom he was exceptionally close, and of the stigmatization of his internment.

The manuscripts Henry Kreisel has saved from that time include six large (8" x 11") notebooks, numbered 1 to 7 (notebook 4 is missing), and three smaller scribblers. In the first three of the large notebooks he has written close to three hundred pages of a novel titled The Torch of Hate. *(This is the novel referred to as* Miguel Amore *in the internment diary, a part of the first chapter of which was published under that title in* white pelican *in 1974.) It is divided into two sections, 'Love' and 'War,' and seems to have been written with the* bildungsroman *tradition in mind. The first section follows its protagonist, Miguel Amore, through his sexual and emotional initiation into love: lured by a prostitute into her room, he can only stare at her and flee in disgust; he then falls in love with a pretty and compassionate young woman only to leave her after two years for the forthright and unhappy, but intense and intelligent, sister of a close friend. A good deal of lyricism, of the sort one can imagine a youthful D.H. Lawrence writing had he been discreet, is expended on the contentments and complications of these affairs.*

But political unease hovers in the background even in the 'Love' section. Miguel's friend and second beloved are from a 'Northern' province whose disagreements with the 'South' intrude more and more on the young men's consciousness. Miguel at one point tells his friend a story he has read in a history book, one that is obvious allegory for German-Austrian political relations during the years following the 1934 civil war in Austria, but he cannot complete it because the pages have been torn out of the book. Henry Kreisel, writing this novel in 1940-41, must have had Miguel's same difficulty since the historical events on which he based his novel had certainly reached no resolution. At any rate, the manuscript stops with notebook 3; whether it was continued or even completed in the missing notebook 4 or whether other stories were recorded there, he can no longer remember.

The 'War' section moves forward with more urgency and melodrama, though it is not without a sense of the tedium as well as the tragedy of military life (military glory is alien to Henry Kreisel's sensibility even as a boy). Miguel is separated from both his friend and his fiancée (unknown to him, she is pregnant), who are now 'enemies' and must return home. He and his friend find themselves in opposing armies; his friend is shot and his fiancée, in despair at the loneliness of a life with neither brother nor lover near, drowns herself. If it is difficult to imagine the author extricating himself from this plot, it nonetheless does reveal a conviction evident in all his fiction that the actual force of historical cataclysm can be measured only in its effects on individual lives.

Also evident in this early work is the symbolic method Henry Kreisel would later use with considerable effectiveness with props like Tassigny's painting. The opening chapter of the novel uses symbolic events in a way that suggests a strong sense of the direction the plot would take, and of its political import. Its first pages, published by Sheila Watson in white pelican, *(4, 3 [Summer 1974], 36-39) see Miguel Amore watching children play a Kafkaesque game of 'judge,' a more consequential version of which is enacted by nations in the subsequent plot. The game, like Miguel's story from the history book or the novel itself, terminates without resolution when one of its childish players leaves in a huff. The pages published below take up the narrative at this point where the* white pelican *publication leaves off and complete the introductory chapter. That war and poverty each curse the child in the womb is a theme that will be taken up twice more in the manuscript: once when Miguel's fiancée and her brother rush to the hospital a poor woman who has gone into labour while lying in the snow on the street, and again when the fiancée commits suicide in spite of the child she is carrying.*

Henry Kreisel

from The Torch of Hate

And so Miguel could not hear how the game ended. He was sorry. The street was empty now, and he walked up to the house, and leaned on the gate looking at it. He thought about what he had just heard, about the judge and the prosecutor and the accused, and about the stealing of bread. It was very interesting, he thought, only too bad they stopped playing.

The door of the house next to the one Miguel was looking at opened and a woman came out. She was middleaged, and she looked tired and overworked. Her hair was already greying and her face was wrinkled and it looked to Miguel like a railway network or a geographical map. She wore a big white and blue apron that covered her dress so that Miguel could not see it. She had on a pair of slippers and when she came nearer Miguel could see that she was pregnant.

'You're not thinking of renting this house?' she asked.

'No, no,' answered Miguel, 'I am only looking at it.'

'Well, there ain't much to look at,' she said. 'One house is like the other. They're all old and dirty. The best thing to do with them would be to pull 'em down.' She looked at it, and seeing the bench broken, she said, 'So, they've broken that bench, the brats. They can't leave a thing alone until they've broke it.'

The little boy who had been the judge came into the street and when she saw him she called: 'Heh, Bob come on, get into the house, you've been out long enough.'

'I'm coming,' he called back.

'Is that your son?' asked Miguel.

'Yes,' she said, 'he's my oldest. I've got two more, and there'll soon be another.'

'I watched him play with some other boys. He was the judge.'

'O did they play that silly game again?'

'You know the game?' he asked.

'Sure. It's two weeks since they first began to play it. Ever since that fellow was sent to jail for stealing bread.'

'Which fellow?'

The boy came near now, and she called to him: 'Get in, and get yourself washed. Look at you, look at your hands. Get in, quick, get in before I slap you.' He ran into the house quickly and slammed the door behind him.

'Which fellow?' asked Miguel again.

'O, there was [a] fellow from the next street, who stole a loaf of bread, and they sent him to jail for two weeks and called him a thief. For a long time everybody around here was talking about it. It was then the kids picked it up. But I tell you he didn't steal 'cause he's not a thief. He's no thief I tell you. He stole 'cause he has kids crying for bread at home and he has none to give 'em. Look here, my man hasn't worked for years because there's no work for him, and there are three kids crying for bread. And there'll be a fourth soon. O, how I hate it! It would be best if it were born dead.'

'Stop talking like that,' said Miguel, 'it isn't right.'

'Yes, yes, it isn't right. But what will it have, poor child, once it is born? Hunger and misery and pain. No, no, the world's no good. Better not to be born, better not to see it all.'

'There will be better times. You must not despair. There is always hope.'

'Yes,' she said, 'there is always hope. But I've seen people hoping for a lifetime. And then they've died, and gone was the hope, and gone was everything.—But I guess it's no good talking. The children will want food.'

She turned and went back into the house without any further speech.

Miguel walked slowly home. A mother cursing the child in her body! A child that she did not want to be born because there was no room for it in the world.

Did not man and wife beget children in the same way all over the world, whether rich or poor, he thought?

Has therefore not everybody got the same right to love? Could not all children stand up and claim their rights as citizens of the world?

In this so called civilisation?

The woman had the tea ready when he came home.

'Did you spend the afternoon well?' she asked.

'Yes,' he said, 'quite. I had a long walk.'

'That's right, my boy, it'll do you good getting a bit of fresh air.'

'Maybe,' he said, 'maybe.'

He ate silently of the food that she had placed before him. He cut himself a slice of bread and buttered it.

'Is there a lot of bread,' he asked, 'if you can buy it?'

The woman looked surprised at him and then she said, 'Why— Yes, of course there's a lot of bread, of course there is. But why do you ask?'

'Just like that. Nothing particularly.'

He stopped eating and pushed the plate away.

'Why don't you finish your food?' asked the woman.

'I'm not hungry. I've got no appetite.'

'Why—are you not well?'

'I'm well enough,' he said. 'I've watched children play, and I've heard a woman curse the child that is still in her body. That has taken my appetite.'

The woman shook her head. 'What's all this about?' she said, 'you watched children play and you heard a woman curse. . . . I'm sure I don't understand it. No. I don't understand all that.'

'It's better you don't,' he said, and then again: 'it's better you don't.'

He rose and went up to his room, leaving the woman puzzled.

'I'm sure I don't understand it,' she said over and over again, 'I'm sure I don't understand it at all.'

He went to his bookshelf, took out a volume of Ovid who was his favourite poet, turned on the light, made himself comfortable and began to read.

He opened the volume and the first verse he read was:

Aurea prima sata est,
Aetasque vindice nullo.

He translated it:
> *At the beginning there was the golden age,*
> *an age without judges.*

And then suddenly he began to laugh ironically.

Miguel's friend, Robert Cameron, enlisted in the army of the 'North,' is out on patrol with his batman, Thomas, and three others:

They walked in silence. Robert and Thomas in front and the other three behind them. The village was surrounded by a wood and they entered it. It was difficult to walk on the terrain. They saw trails of rabbits in the snow and now and again a crow flew over their heads, and kaa-kaa it sounded through the woods. The wind blew through the trees and shook the snow off the pines and firs and the falling snow hit the men on the[ir] heads and on their backs and made the patrol yet more uncomfortable.

Robert stopped abruptly and pointed with his finger into the snow. 'What is this?' he asked.

They all stopped. 'Tracks of men, sir.'

'Yes,' Robert turned to the sergeant. 'What does it mean?'

'The evening-patrol has come through the wood not long ago.' The sergeant was old and his face was wrinkled. He had been in the army for thirty years.

'I thought so,' said Robert. 'What are we going to do?'

'There is no danger, sir. They have probably left the wood a long time ago.'

They resumed to walk. They could see no further signs of the enemy. Everything was quiet again. They took a cut through the wood until they reached the open plain again. Still covered by the wood Robert focused his binoculars and looked across to the enemy positions. Then he handed them to the sergeant.

'Everything seems all-right,' he said as he did so. 'I can't see the guard. He must be inside.'

The sergeant handed him back the glasses. 'Everything is all-right,' he said.

'I think we shall cross the open here,' said Robert, 'enter the wood on the other side and walk back.'

They walked out of the wood into the open. Robert and Thomas in front, the three others behind them.

There were two sharp reports and the officer and his batman fell down on the snowcovered ground. The three others ran back into the woods and opened fire. After the two shots the enemy did not fire again.

'Let us go back quickly,' said the old sergeant.

'But what about the two?'

'They are dead. It would be an unnecessary risk to go out into the open again. They will probably fire again,' and he turned and led the way back through the wood.

Thomas lay in the snow and his mild brown eyes were open and seemed to be staring at the grey sky, and even in death they had the same devoted expression they had had in life. Right through his head the bullet had gone and killed him instantly. He had not even had time to utter a word. Life had never given him much and yet he had clung to it as does every human being. He had always been satisfied with the little he had and never asked for more. He had adored Lydia though he had never seen her and only knew her from a photograph. He had been satisfied with the little he had had. But even this little was considered too much by the higher forces, and so they had gone and taken from him the last thing he possessed, the very essence of being, life itself. And as if those higher forces had not been able to bring it over themselves to close his eyes, those eyes that could speak so well, they had let them be open in death.

Lieutenant Robert Cameron had been hit in the chest, and there was still a bit of life in him. He gathered himself and stood up slowly, swaying to and fro. He put his hands on his chest to stop the pain there. Then he looked around and saw Thomas lying on the ground.

'Thomas!' he called, 'Thomas!'

There was no answer, for how indeed could there have been. Robert staggered towards his batman and bent down.

'Thomas!' he called again, 'Thomas!'

It was then that a big wave of blood shot out of his mouth, and with his face downwards, the Lieutenant Robert Cameron fell down on the snowcovered earth and lay still.

Big, white flakes of snow fell down from the grey sky on the earth. The earth was covered by them and the trees and also the two men who were lying there, dead.

All through the night it kept on snowing, and, in the very sense of the word, the snow wove a shroud round the two and buried them,

Thomas with his eyes staring at the sky, and Robert with his face buried into the earth.

If the reach of the death scene is still a bit beyond him, if he cannot quite separate the operatic from the realistic style or resist the gloss, the young Henry Kreisel still shows himself capable in this last paragraph of creating a tableau marked by (nearly restrained) pathos. In the companion scene, when Robert Cameron's friend Michael (Miguel), sitting in a bar on the other side of the enemy line, learns of his death, Henry Kreisel opts for a harsh realism, notable for his mastery of an idiom not taught in the schools.

'It's great to be in a town again,' said the same, brutal looking soldier, turning to Michael, 'after having been in God's worst place for a month.'

Out of necessity Michael had to answer him. 'Where've you been?' he asked.

'Been right out on the front. Most boring place yer can imagine. Ain't that so?' he asked, turning to one of his companions.

'Sure is,' said the one, gulping down some brandy, while the other had passed the state of reasonableness and being already completely drunk, he banged on the table with his fists, and a continuous flow of obscenity came from his mouth.

'It can't be as boring as it is here,' said Michael, 'you see some action at least. There's some change.'

'Action,' he growled, 'action, indeed. You hear that ass! Stop banging on the table, dirty bastard. There's no action out there either, friend. No bloody action. And there'll be nothin' doin' until the damned snow's gone. We'll have some real fightin' then, let me tell yer.'

'What did you do out there then?' asked Michael.

'Nothin' brother,' and he took his glass and drank, 'nothin'. Diggin' trenches, and patrol-duty and that's everything, damn it. The only time something happened was last week.'

'Why? What happened then?'

'I shot two damned enemy bastards, I did. They said I couldn't do it. Here, that bastard was one of them.' He spoke with contempt now. 'Said I couldn't shoot 'em. Well, I'll show you, I says. Do you want to bet, I says. Sure, they say. So we put all down our money. They said the bullet wouldn't carry that far. Sure it will, I says. Well, prove it then, they says. Sure I will, I says. On the next day I was on guard. 'Twas an old farm house barricaded with all kind of stuff. Me and this drunken bastard was there. Some time in the afternoon it was, I think it must 'a' been round five when we sees the evening patrol come out o' the wood. I watch one o' them take out his glasses and look across to where we are. Then I sees 'im hand 'em to another fellow and then they come slowly out of the wood. Well, says this bastard here, why don't yer shoot, big mouth. Wait a minute, I says, let 'em get to where my bullet can reach 'em. Ha, ha, he laughs, it'll never reach 'em, big mouth,' he stopped and spat on the floor, 'won't it, I says. Never, says he. Well, watch me then, says I. Then I wait until I think it's the right moment and fire twice, and don't miss once. I got two o' them, all-right, the bastards, ha, ha, ha,' he gave a rollocking laughter, terrible in its austerity, 'and they thought the bullet wouldn't carry that far. Here, ask 'im, the dirty stinker, ha, ha, ha.'

Michael sat, staring at the speaker, who was boasting of a murder, because it had been murder, nothing else.

'When it got to be dark,' the soldier went on, 'I went out and went across to where the two lay. One was an officer and the other some little, obscure fellow, damn him. I took away the disc the officer was wearing, here it is, Robert Cameron the fellow was called.'

A sudden pain came over Michael as he heard the name. 'What was the name?' he yelled.

'Here's the disc,' said he, 'Robert Cameron,' and fumbled in his upper coatpocket and tossed the disc which had once belonged to Lieutenant Robert Cameron across to Michael.

With a voice that was not his own, he asked: 'What did you do with the body?'

'With the body? Ha, ha, ha! The body! We left it lyin', of course, the worms want to get some food sometimes.'

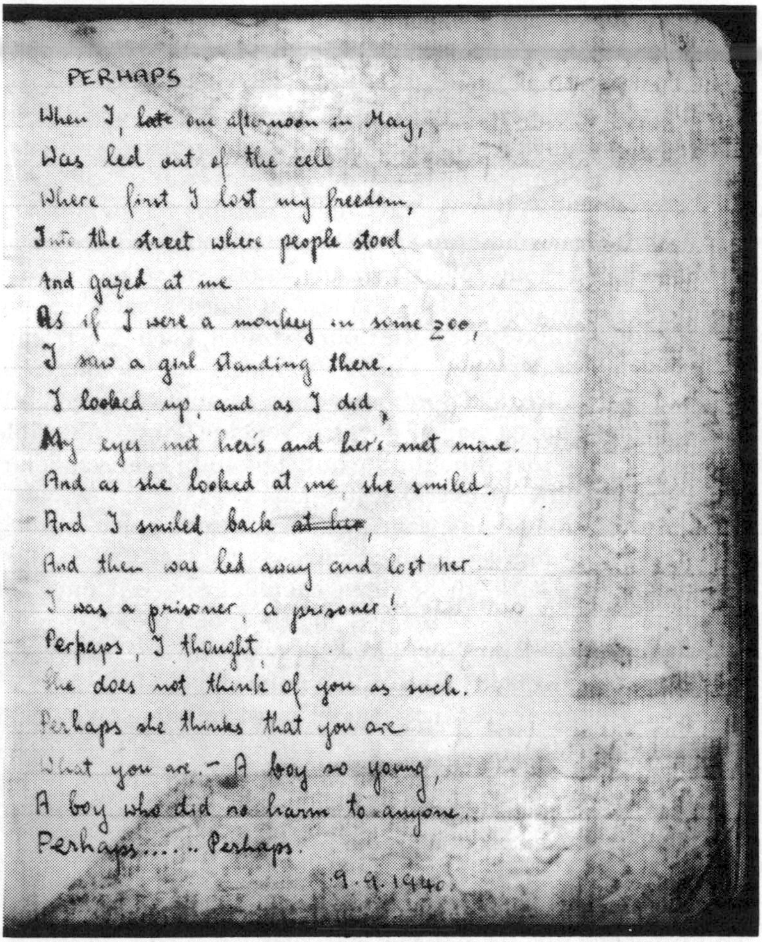

PERHAPS

When I, late one afternoon in May,
Was led out of the cell
Where first I lost my freedom,
Into the street where people stood
And gazed at me
As if I were a monkey in some zoo,
I saw a girl standing there.
I looked up, and as I did,
My eyes met her's and her's met mine.
And as she looked at me, she smiled.
And I smiled back ~~at her~~,
And then was led away and lost her
I was a prisoner, a prisoner!
Perhaps, I thought,
She does not think of you as such.
Perhaps she thinks that you are
What you are, — A boy so young,
A boy who did no harm to anyone..
Perhaps..... Perhaps.

9.9.1940.

First page of ms. notebook kept during internment

The remaining manuscript books contain shorter pieces,
dating from September 9 1940 to March 31 1942. Henry Kreisel
seems to have rather quickly found his voice in prose and most
of these books are filled with short stories. However, he
occasionally turned to poetry, particularly when he wished to
isolate or exalt a moment of beauty or of trauma. Two poems
derived from the early days of internment:

Henry Kreisel

The Violin

We all were laying on our palliasses
Trying to sleep.
The night was dark and hot
And all was quiet.
And I turned and turned
But I could not close my eyes.
Then, one of us got up;
And he took his violin,
His much beloved fiddle
And he put it to his chin
And he began to play.
When the strains of music reached my ears,
I thought that God himself,
Had come and talked to me.
And my heart
That had been restless,
Jumping up and down, was still.
And my cheeks that had been burning,
Cooled.
And it was as if the violin was saying
'Go to sleep, my child, go to sleep.'
And I closed my eyes and I slept.

                                    9.9.1940.

Visit

My mother came to visit me.
She looked pale and her hand trembled
As she took my head and kissed it.
She did not speak much,
Just asked me how I was.
She never took her eyes off me,
And her hands stroke my head,
As she had always done when I was very small.
And then the time was up.
'So soon,' she murmured, 'so soon.'
And then she kissed me,
Kissed me long and deep.
'Be brave, my child,' she said, 'be brave.'

                                                9.9.1940.

*The first stories of Henry Kreisel, not unnaturally, focus on loss
and oppression. In the attempt to find situations sufficiently
distanced from his own, he sometimes turned to romantic
symbols. In 'The Two Poppies,' for example, the happiness of
the young couple is imaged in the two poppies dropped into a
stream, floating first apart as their lives had, then together and
out of sight. Five years later, the wife dead, the husband returns
to the site and repeats her action of dropping the poppies; they
again float first apart and then together, promising this time
togetherness in an afterlife.*

*The characters of other stories are unwilling to wait for
another world to settle the score for injustices, betrayals, losses,
and disillusions that most certainly are not God-sent. In 'The
Sculptor,' the least successful because the most stereotyped of
the stories, the artist searching for Ideal Beauty finds it
personified in a young woman whom he then images in a
'masterpiece' in marble. That she embodies the Ideal does not,
however, stop him from very rapidly making her his mistress, or
her from deceiving him; disillusioned, he takes a destructive
hammer to his statue, his illusions, and his notion of Ideal
Beauty. 'Christopher Bull' places the circumstances of betrayal
and oppression closer to Kreisel's own experience and makes
the response to it less futile. Its antagonist is a bullying office
manager, whose name, which gives the story its title, suggests
both his method of cowing a timid employee, and, perhaps, his
creator's resentment that John Bull had turned against him
after first giving him refuge. In this story, however, the
solidarity of the office workers effects the defeat of the unjust
manager. If there is an element of wishful thinking in this, it
turned out to be prophetic: Henry Kreisel's own release from
John Bull's internment was effected by the solidarity of the
Jewish-Canadian community.*

*Mothers are central to many of the stories about loss, but they
are mothers without the bitterness of the woman Miguel Amore
meets. The poetic treatment of mothers derives very directly
from the adolescent Henry Kreisel's painful separations from
his own mother, first during the year he spent in England while
she was in the Ravensbrook concentration camp, and then
during his internment: the poems include, for example, 'Prayer
[To My Mother]' and 'Letter to Mother.' But it was only towards
the end of his internment that he was able to write directly about*

*his mother in prose. Then he did so in a series of character
sketches of her and his grandparents and their Vienna life. I
suspect that his writing very directly about his mother only at
this relatively late period during his internment was the
consequence of two circumstances. One personal and psychological: that he could stay in Canada was becoming a real
possibility at this point, making the continuing separation
from his mother a matter of choice rather than oppression, and
making nostalgia for the Vienna of his youth attractive without
being overwhelming. The other a question of literary accom-
plishment: by this time he had done enough to realize that one
of his strengths as a writer was the character sketch and his
mother and grandparents were the 'characters' to whom he was
closest.*

*But the first stories show a capability, extraordinary in one so
young, to empathize with the losses and sufferings of figures
representative of motherhood. His own pain at separation is
continually transformed into this imaginative empathy with
the emotions of motherhood, emotions that he reveres as a quiet
but intense power against the violence of contemporary events.
In several pieces, a distanced but strong optimism becomes
evident as the young refugee from the threat of concentration
camps, unwanted in any country, dwells on the glad suffering
and high hopes he sees women bringing to the birth of their
children. Ambitiously, for a boy turned only eighteen, he writes
a 'Letter of a Woman Who Gave Just Birth to a Child, to her
Husband' [sic]. If the 'letter' is rather too liberally sprinkled
with the epithet 'darling,' it does testify powerfully to the desire
for and belief in mothers' love. A later piece, 'Mummie, Who
Are They?' is more directly related to Henry Kreisel's own
experience and is far more accomplished in its narrative. Here
the child's recent illness introduces the sense of insecurity, the
possibility of loss, that had become a permanent part of both
Henry Kreisel's life and fiction. Moreover, the child, who asks
his questions about the two internees he has seen hauling wood,
becomes the vehicle through which Kreisel distances the
personal material which is his subject: while one of the two men
dwells on the physical beauty of the woman, the other dwells on
that of the child as the image of lost freedom; meanwhile, the
child's question forces the mother to think through her
previously unexamined assumption that the internees are 'bad
men.'*

This empathy for a lost maternal world, combined with the felt need to find a way of distancing himself from the personal experiences about which he is writing, is evident in 'Ginger.' A few months later Henry Kreisel would write directly about leaving Vienna in 'Farewell'; here he attempts to distance his autobiographical material by casting the narrator as an adult who becomes acquainted with the refugee child only to find he has disappeared into internment. The story is of considerable biographical and psychological interest. The narrator clearly owes his strong image of the young Ginger's departure from Vienna to Henry Kreisel's own departure. What remains remarkable about the passage is the empathy that allowed the adolescent author to re-imagine that parting in terms of his mother's grief rather than his own. This imaginative recreation of his own remembered departure from Vienna in terms of his mother's suffering, and his projection of himself into both male characters, is perhaps an index of a need to distance his material if he is to deal with it at all; it is certainly an index of his psychological resilience. We see the interned boy avoiding self-pity and narcissism by a literary incarnation of himself as both the unemployed narrator and the befriended 'Ginger,' still remembered in the world outside the camps. Both characterisations have the affectionately intimate knowledge which shows up in most of Henry Kreisel's later writing.

Henry Kreisel

Ginger

You will say that he had red hair, and you will be right. He had red hair. I guess he could not help having red hair for mother nature had blessed him with it and had not asked whether he would have preferred dark hair. It was a fact, he had red hair. But it was different from any red hair that I had ever seen, and if you asked me why I could not say, and if you asked me to describe the shade of the red of which his hair was made I would be unable to do it. I can only say that it was a sympathetic red and that anybody who ever saw the little chap with the red hair was forced to like him and I can state it as a fact that everybody did like him.

I had not eaten anything since dinner-time, and then I had had nothing but some bread and milk and had smoked a cigarette, and now at about seven o'clock I felt cold and hungry. My stomach demanded its rights and would not hear of·my good words. I had a few pennies in my pocket that would just buy some bread and butter, and maybe some coffee and a cigarette.

'Keep quiet,' I said to my stomach, 'you shall have something to eat in a minute.'

I had been looking for a job the whole day, but there was nothing, as usual.

I turned round a corner, and walked down a sidestreet where I knew a little restaurant where you could buy a lot for a comparatively little money.

I do not think there is any need to describe the little restaurant. There was nothing that could be called extraordinary about it; it was a restaurant as you have seen one many a times and that you know therefore.

It was warm inside, and I sat down, took out a paper, began to read, and felt quite comfortable.

There was noone there but myself yet I had to wait for about five minutes until somebody took notice of me. I did not shout for the waiter because I found it undignified to do so.

There is no need for the waiter to know that I am hungry, I thought. At last he came.

'Yes, sir,' he said, 'what can I do for you?'

I did not look at him but pretended to read my paper. 'Bring me some black coffee,' I said, 'and some bread and butter.'

'Yes, sir!' he said.

It felt grand to be called sir, I thought, and I felt like a gentleman.

He returned soon, and put the tray down on my table. I folded my paper slowly and carefully and put it back in my coat pocket, pretending that I was not hungry at all, and doing as if I had just come in to kill some time.

When I looked at the coffee I got a shock.

I had ordered black coffee, and the coffee that was standing before me contained certainly as much milk as coffee.

'He[h],' I said, 'Do you call that service?' I was just going to shout at the waiter but when I looked at him, I said nothing.

He was standing there looking at me with big eyes, a little boy—he could not be more than fifteen years—with red hair, and little freckles all over his face. He put his hand to his mouth in a gesture of fright.

'Pardon me, sir,' he said.

I looked at him. 'What did you say?' I asked.

'O, I meant to say I'm sorry, sir.' He spoke slowly.

'You're a little red-haired devil,' I said. 'You haven't been here for a long time, have you?'

'No, sir,' he said, 'not long.'

'You're not an English chap,' I said.

'No, sir,' he answered, 'I'm a refugee.'

'O, a refugee.—You're alone, then?'

'Yes, sir,' he said, 'all alone.'

'All-right, Ginger,' I said, 'Next time I order black coffee, you bring me black coffee.'

'Yes, sir,' he said ruefully.

I took out two pennies from my pocket. It was the last bit of money I had, and I had intended to buy some cigarettes for it. I gave him it.

'Buy yourself some chocolate,' I said.

'Thank you, sir,' he said.

I went out into the cold again, and thought of refugees. I saw women, hardly able to walk, with tired faces, a bundle of clothes on their back and a little baby in their arms, dragging themselves across the Pyrenees, fighting against the cold, blowing, icy wind, giving the breast to their babies, feeding them, holding their trembling hands over them to save their little bodies from freezing, saw thousands of Jews, men, women and children, having done nothing but being Jews, being thrown out of their houses onto the streets, driven out of Germany, out of Austria, and of Czechoslovakia. I saw mothers with tearstained faces bidding farewell to little children, children of three and of four, and of ten and of fifteen, boys and girls, pressing them close to them, kissing them, sending them out into a dark, black world full of hate, not knowing when they would see them again, sending them into a doubtful future, dark and impenetrable.

I thought of Ginger.

I could picture his mother. Maybe she has red hair, too, I thought. I could see her standing on the railway station, looking at the train that was standing in the hall, looking at the big locomotive as it was puffing big columns of smoke into the air. She hated the train and the locomotive for it would take little Ginger away from her.

She remembered the night he had been born. Fourteen years ago, she thought. How quick the time has passed, she thought. Fourteen years!

She had dreamed of a big career for Ginger, she had dreamed of giving him a good education, of seeing him grow up to be a real man like his father.

She remembered how as a young, pretty girl, she had met Ginger's father, and she smiled.

And she had dreamed how Ginger would marry once, and how he would have children once, and she always liked to think of herself as a grandmother.

And now he was fourteen years, and a train was standing in the hall, and a locomotive was puffing smoke into the air, and Ginger was looking out of the window, and he was going away into a strange and foreign country.

She pressed a handkerchief to her eyes and she tried hard not to show the tears that were in her eyes because she did not want Ginger to see them.

And then the train rolled out of the hall, slowly first, and then faster and faster, and Ginger leaned out of the window and waved, and the wind blew his red hair all over his face, and his mother waved back, and then the train slowly disappeared and she could not see Ginger any more, but she stood for a long time yet, staring into the empty space before her, moving her hand slowly up and down, waving a handkerchief— —

I saw Chinese women being machine gunned from the air, throwing their bodies over their little ones using their bodies as a shield. I saw bullets piercing their bodies, and everything was red, blood, blood, blood!

They were mothers, all mothers!

Whether they were white or black or yellow, they were all mothers. They had all gone through pains to have their children, they had all borne them in the same way. The world is terrible, I thought, it stinks. I spat.

Then I reached my room. There was no fire and it was cold. I took a pen and some paper and began to write a comic story. I managed to write two pages but when I read them I tore them up. I had just put down words but they did not convey any meaning.

Why should I write funny stories, I thought, in a world that is full of tragedy.

'Damn the world,' I said, 'damn it!' I went to bed and slept.

Next day I went again into that little restaurant, and Ginger served me. He was fifteen years, he said, and he liked girls.

He had a special technique of looking at girls. Whenever he used to see a girl coming towards him, and when he thought her worth looking at, he used to run about a hundred yards in front of her, then turned abruptly and walked again towards her. Then he would look into her face first to see if she was pretty and if he thought she was, he would smile at her and there was not a girl who did not smile back at him because nobody could resist his red hair. And when he was behind her he used to look at her legs very critically, and sometimes he would shake his head and say: 'She's no good.'

Ginger was unhappy sometimes because girls saw in him only a boy and he would have so much liked to be a man.

Ginger and I became great friends, and it was about a week after I had got to know him that I found a job. Ginger said he was glad. I took him to the pictures and we both enjoyed the show.

O, yes, Ginger and I were very good friends indeed.

He was not too good a waiter, but I did not mind.

One day I came into the restaurant and they told me Ginger had a cold and was in bed.

I went up to his room and found him sleeping. He had his blankets pulled up right over his face and only his red hair was visible. It looked as if something was burning.

And then, one day in May it was and the war had already been on for some months, I came again into the restaurant and Ginger was not there.

'Where is Ginger?' I asked.

'Two men came and fetched him.'

'Fetched Ginger?' I asked. 'What for?'

'They said he would have to be interned.'

'Ginger interned?' I asked, and began to see black. 'Whatever for?'

'He is a German, they said, he is an enemy alien, they said, he would have to be interned.'

'Ginger an enemy!' I cried out and began to laugh. I do not quite know why but I laughed. The whole affair seemed ridiculous to me.

'He is not an enemy alien,' I protested, 'he is only a little boy and he hates Hitler more than any Englishman.'

The woman who spoke with me, shrugged her shoulders. 'Don't shout at me,' she said. 'I know it, but what can I do about it?'

'I guess nothing,' I said.

I went out. This is unjust I thought. It is a terrible world we live in, frightfully bad and black, full of wars, and of injustice and of misery.

'Damn the world,' I said, 'damn it!'

I went a few times more into the little restaurant, but I missed Ginger. It was not the same any more, and I stopped going there.

I often think of Ginger and I hope to see him again some day.

I hope that his mother's wish will be realised and that she will one day be able to be proud of him and that he will grow up to be a real man as she always wanted him to.

I know that some day Ginger's mother will hold her grandchildren in her arms and play with them, and she will think back of the time he was fourteen, and maybe she will cry a little bit.

O, yes, he was a great friend of mine, that little fellow with the red hair.

12.1.1941

103

papers sometimes but I could see it did not mean much to him, and so I said: "Yes, he will come to me over the wireless."

He looked at me.

"O," he said, "I see!" and bumper made the van, sending me flying to the top and there my head felt a resistance, and as wood is more solid than the skull of my head, I came bouncing down on the seat again, and my head was aching.

"Yes," I said, "Toscanini is in London and he is conducting there, and the concert will be broadcast."

"O," he said, "now I know. It's a symphony concert, yes?"

"Yes," I said, "do you like it?"

He pulled a face. "No," he said, "symphony is not for me. La-la-la it goes all the time, and then you hear some trumpets, tra-ra-ra, and then suddenly the drums bum-bum-bum —— there's nothing in symphony, no, there's nothing."

I smiled but I did not argue. what is the good of it? I knew I would not be able to convince him.

We reached the market by twelve. Some stalls had

from 'The Market and the Symphony No.5 by Beethoven,' ms. notebook kept during internment

115

been music in my ears because it meant fresh. So I
stood at the remnant stall waiting for the fellow to come round.
"Here, are lad, have you something for me?"
I turned. There was an old, old little woman standing
there, looking at the neatly folded pile of remnants, a shawl
wrapped round her head, a little basket in her hand.
"You're late, my lady," I said, "We're packing up in
a minute."
"O, it won't be as bad as all that."
And already she began to look through the remnants,
taking some, unfolding them, throwing them back in the
pile, making a mess. There was no way of stopping her,
so I said, "we haven't got the length you want."
"How d'you know what length I want?" she asked.
"Well what length do you want, and what colour
should it be?"
"I want a black piece about a yard long."
"We haven't got one."
"O, you'll have one," and she kept on looking through

from 'The Market and the Symphony No.5 by Beethoven,' ms.
notebook kept during internment

*An occasional story is directly autobiographical, none more so
than 'Two Streets' which has interest both as a reminiscence of
Henry Kreisel's first impressions on his arrival in England
and as an account of his decision to write in English. The
casting of the call to literature in the form of a 'voice' may seem
romanticized; Henry Kreisel himself, as his memories matured,
would speak of his recognition of a vocation in more circum-
spect language. But while this is the sort of imagery critics often
mock, it is also the sort that very accomplished writers have
often used and it should perhaps be taken here, as elsewhere, at
face value. The absurdity of his conversation with the girl in the
piece remains typical to this day of Henry Kreisel's gentle
amusement with the incongruous aspects of even the most
significant events.*

Henry Kreisel
Two Streets (A Phantasy)

North Street

In the North of England there is a town called Leeds. Not a very
beautiful town, not a town that is famous for its buildings, not a town
famous for musical events, a town whose chimneys and smoke never
in the past have, to my knowledge, inspired a great poet or composer
to write about it.

It is a typical industrial town, populated by half a million souls,
and dominated by factories and chimneys and smoke.

There arrived in this town one day in July at midnight a young
boy of about sixteen, who came from Vienna. He was tired from the
journey and could hardly keep his eyes open. He only dimly recorded
that people had come to fetch him from the station, that these people
were his relatives, that he was put into a motorcar and driven through
the town. He dimly recorded that he came into a very brightly-lit
room, that many people were there and that they all shook hands
with him.

'I can speak English,' he announced proudly. He then started to
speak English and the people in the room smiled, for he spoke with a
queer accent and made many mistakes.

And then he went to bed, forgetting that he was a refugee who had fled Hitler, only knowing that he was tired and wanted to sleep. He fell asleep quickly.

The next morning was hot and beautiful. He woke at ten and at first he did not know where he was and was puzzled by the strange surroundings. He rose and dressed and went downstairs. He had his breakfast and then he went out and explored the neighbourhood. His name was Heinrich, a name hardly pronounceable for English tongues, and people called him Henry.

He was becoming more familiar with the town, and his English was getting better though he had a lot to learn yet.

He didn't believe in sitting down and studying textbooks, and memorizing words, although everybody recommended him to do so. He liked to mingle amongst the people and listen to their talk to make his ears accustomed to the sound of the language, and he enjoyed it. He had always liked languages, for him a language had always been a living thing, breathing and everchanging. Textbooks were dead and made the language look dead too. A feeling of satisfaction overcame him whenever he could follow a conversation to the end and understand it.

And then in the evening he would get hold of a book and look through it, trying to read a page here, trying to read a page there, without the help of a dictionary.

And he thought how wonderful it would be if he were able to write in English. He kept a dictionary, but he wrote in German. He tried once to make his notes in English, but the words didn't come out naturally, and he still made errors, and so again he wrote in German.

'You should study more textbooks,' said his relatives and friends, 'only so will you be able to learn English properly, to learn grammar and orthography.'

'For me,' he said, 'the street is the best teacher. The most fascinating and natural teacher. In the street the language lives, in the textbooks it is dead.'

To which all shook their heads and smiled.

And the days became shorter as summer was slowly gliding into autumn, and day after day, whenever he had time and opportunity, there walked through the smoky streets of Leeds a young boy of sixteen, listening to the talk of the people, absorbing the language, and the more he listened the more did he like it.

And so the streets became the teacher of a young Austrian in his study of a peculiar language, spoken by a very peculiar sort of people called Englishmen, a language that is the most widespread language in the world.

Leeds is divided into districts, and he lived in the seventh district of the town, which is called Chapeltown.

A long, broad street is leading from the center of the town to Chapeltown, and the name of this street is North Street. Although North Street itself is a very nice street, the sidestreets are small and dirty, and a lot of the houses are not worth anything else but to be torn down. Along this street he used to walk often, stopping in front of the shops, looking at the goods. And then he used to walk into one of the many sidestreets and study the contrast. Here the long clean street with broad pavements, there a small, dirty street with a yet smaller pavement, here bright shops, there little houses with broken gates, and from each house there ascended a cloud of white smoke towards the sky.

And the people that hurried along North Street seemed to be different from the people that populated the sidestreets. For it seemed that the people in the main-street wore different clothes. Or was it only his imagination? And indeed it even seemed to him as if they spoke different. And as soon as somebody emerged from one of the sidestreets and walked along North Street his language seemed more refined. Or did he only imagine it? Such was the great contrast. A strange world he thought.

He was a great dreamer, a day-dreamer as people say, and his thoughts were ever wandering, wandering into strange worlds, worlds that were imaginary and only lived in his imagination. And often he would walk and not take any notice of what was going on around him. He had his hands crossed behind him, and his head bent, and so he walked and thought. Somebody once asked him why he clasped his hands behind and he said if he didn't he wouldn't know what to do with them. And the fellow who had asked shook his head and smiled.

In North Street he saw a better world. He saw a world that lived in peace, in North Street he could let his thoughts wander. Sometimes his thoughts ran away and he lost control over them. Then they became confused, and the sidestreets ran together with North Street, and there was only one big North Street and all the people seemed now better, and all the people spoke more refined. And there was no contrast. The small, dirty pavements had disappeared and broad, light pavements had taken their place. And in his imagination the dirty streets melted together with the broad street, and there ceased to be a contrast.

And his thoughts went further than North Street and concentrated on a country. And he saw the fields heavy with wheat and ripe for harvest, and he saw the farmer take in the wheat, and out of the wheat was made bread. And he saw all the people eat of the bread, for there was enough for everybody. And the pictures of starving children were blotted out, for there were no starving children because there was enough bread to feed all.

And the farmer took the money that was given to him for his bread, and he went to the tailor and he said, 'Make me a suit.' And the tailor made a suit for him, and he took the money and went to the cobbler. 'Make shoes for me,' he said. And the cobbler made shoes.

And the country prospered and the people were happy. And the state said: 'We will have clean, broad streets.' And the dirty, little streets were torn down, and broad streets were built in their place.

And as one country did, so did all the others. And the representatives of the countries came together, and they said: 'We are all happy now, and we all have enough. Let there never be a war between us. Let us not say: "This is our country and we will not let anybody enter and close the frontier." For we all have been born alike, we all are citizens of the world and one may live where it pleases him to live.' And they opened the borders and they traded with each other, and everybody had a house to live in, and bread to eat.

And when his thoughts had carried him that far, Henry suddenly encountered something, and he said: 'I am sorry.' And as he looked up, he saw that it was a lamppost, and he rubbed his head with his hand where it hurt him, but his great illusion was gone. For North Street was there just as it had been, and the sidestreets were unchanged.

If I could write down what I just thought, he said, it may be interesting for another to know. But can you write? he asked. Writing was something holy for him, a thing Shakespeare had done and Goethe. There is a park in North Street, and he went into that park, and he sat down on a bench.

An urge overcame him to write down what he had just thought. He tried to resist that urge, but again and again there was a voice within him, saying: 'Write!' 'No,' he said. 'Write,' said the voice.

And the urge became stronger and stronger, and he took out a piece of paper and a pencil. The voice was quiet, and he sat and waited. And again the voice came and said: 'Write.'

'What shall I write?' he demanded. The voice was quiet, and then it said: 'It is for you to know.' He began to write, and this is what he wrote:

'North Street was a country, and the sidestreets around North Street melted together with it, and North Street became the world. And in this world everybody was happy, and it was a world of peace, and the word war was not included in its vocabulary.'

The voice was quiet, and he read what he had written.

'It doesn't make sense,' he said, 'if another reads it he wouldn't understand it.'

And then suddenly the voice spoke again, the one that had told him to write.

'Do not worry,' it said, 'every beginning is difficult.'

'Who are you?' he asked.

'I am the urge,' said the voice.

He smiled, and he released his limbs, feeling utterly at ease. A young woman with a little child entered the park, and she sat down beside him. She took the child on her knee, and began to feed it, but the child would not eat. Children always like to listen to stories, he thought.

And suddenly, against his own will, he said: 'Eat, little one. I will tell you a story.'

The young woman looked up at him surprised, and she said: 'O, will you. That is nice of you.'

What story shall I tell, he thought?

There came the voice again, and it said: 'Tell the story of North Street.'

'No,' he said, 'a child wouldn't understand it.'

'Form the words in such a way,' said the voice, 'that any child will understand it.'

'No,' he answered, 'this is too difficult.'

The child looked at him expectingly and unable to think of any other story, he began to tell the story of North Street. And the words came out naturally, and for the first time he found himself telling a story in a foreign language.

'A young boy was walking on a big street and suddenly that big street disappeared, and a tremendous street came into its place.' And he told the story in easy words, and the child did not take its eyes off him, and it opened its mouth mechanically and let the mother feed it.

'That was nice of you,' said the young woman when he had reached the end of his story. 'And it was a nice story, I enjoyed it myself. I never heard it before.'

'No,' he said, 'you wouldn't.'

He walked happily home, and again he heard the voice: 'You told the story well,' it said, 'now go home and write it down.'

'In what language?' he asked.
'In English.'
'I don't know enough English.'
'Do not argue with me,' said the voice, 'do as I tell you.'
And so there was born on that day in the mind of a young Austrian, while he was walking along North Street, the urge to write.

Chapeltown Road

Sheepscar is a funny name. Henry tried to find out why the square was called Sheepscar, but there was nobody who knew. Four streets were meeting at Sheepscar. One of them, leading to town, is called North Street, and another, leading in the opposite direction, bears the name of Chapeltown Road.

Chapeltown Road might just as well have been called North Street for it is not much different from it, in fact it isn't different at all. The same broad street, and the same sidestreets leading away from it, with one difference: The sidestreets are nicer.

Since that day in North Street the urge had come many more times, but every time he had resisted it. He had neglected it, and it had gone.

He was walking along Chapeltown Road one evening with a girl. They were talking about books, and about music, about films and theatre, things of every-day life and no importance.

Out of one of the sidestreets there came an old man, tall and broad, wearing a long, black coat, and he stopped at the corner. Then he turned round and was facing the two. He was a Jew, and he had a long, white beard.

He stood there, and as the two passed him he smiled and nodded his head. And Henry was so impressed by his majestic appearance that he stopped and watched him.

The old Jew looked up and down the street as if he was searching for something, and he looked like a general after a victorious battle. Once more his eyes met the eyes of the young refugee, and he seemed to say: 'Do not worry, my son, the name of Hitler will be wiped out and forgotten, but Jews will always be.'

The old man turned and walked away slowly.

'What's the matter with you?' said the girl, 'what are you looking at?'

'Nothing,' he said, 'just like that.'

He was quiet after that and let the girl do the talking, for his thoughts were far, far away.

'What do you think about it?' asked the girl.

He had not listened, and now he said: 'Yes, I think it's all-right.'

'What?' asked the girl, 'what is all-right?'

'It is all-right,' he said.

'You don't know what you're talking about,' said the girl.

'No,' he said, 'forgive me, I wasn't paying attention.'

Suddenly there was the voice again. 'Go home,' it said, 'and write about the old Jew.'

'O, go away,' he said, 'and leave me alone.'

'Were you talking to me?' said the girl, 'I'll go if you want me to go.'

'Excuse me,' he said blushingly, 'but I wasn't talking to you.'

'There is nobody else whom you could have talked to,' said the girl, 'take me home.'

'But,' he protested, 'I was only talking to the urge.'

'You are going mad,' said the girl. 'What urge?'

'The urge to write.'

'Please take me home,' said the girl, 'please.'

'As you wish,' he said.

'Now then,' he said to the voice after he had taken the girl home, 'now then, look what you have done.'

He walked along Chapeltown road, and suddenly he again passed the old man with the long beard.

'Go home,' said the voice. 'Go home and write.'

'All-right,' he said, angrily. 'You are a nuisance.'

'Maybe,' said the voice, 'but it is for your best.'

He was glad when he came home, and he sat down, and began to write.

'I saw one Jew in Chapeltown Road today,' he wrote, 'and it was like seeing a million. For such was the power that came from the one.'

He thought what else there was he could write.

'It is well,' said the voice, 'you have told the story well.'

'I have only written two sentences.'

'It is enough,' said the voice. 'You are improving.'

From that day onwards, he never tried to resist the voice. It was no use, for the voice was stronger than he.

And here the story breaks off.

Camp 'B' 4.IV. 16.IV. 17.IV. 1941.

In a story like 'A Typical Day in My Camp Life' Henry Kreisel would humorously complain—for the benefit of his fellows— about the senseless rules, small frictions, and endless waiting they all endured. 'Shall I Buy an Icecream?' is a more serious attempt to evoke the ennui and anxiety beneath the forced and noisy hilarity of a New Year's Eve celebration in the internment camp. By the standards of Henry Kreisel's mature work, the playful opening of this story may seem slight. But remember that its author was eighteen, had begun learning English a little over two years before, and was writing in an internment camp, and then that playfulness about form, and the series of absurd repetitions and reversals surrounding the seriocomic medita- tion about political responsibility all reveal a remarkable self- possession and Henry Kreisel's early and strong sense of his own voice.

Henry Kreisel

Shall I Buy an Icecream?

A funny title you will think and you will expect to find a mysterious and strange plot hiding behind that somewhat odd and remarkable heading. But if you do it is my duty to tell you that you will be disappointed, and that you had better not read the story at all.

There will be no excitement, there will be no hero carrying his heroine through a river in his left arm and fighting crocodiles with his right, there will be no romance, no hero kissing the heroine behind a shady doorway and telling her that he loved her, and there will be no heroine telling him that she just thought like he, and that if only her father would give his consent and so on——

No, dear reader, there will be nothing of the sort, there will, in fact, be no heroine at all.

There will be not much of a plot, I do not quite know if it can be called a plot at all.

Why then, you will ask, are you writing the story? As to that, dear reader, I cannot give you a quite satisfactory explanation, I can only say that somehow I found interest in writing this story and though it has nothing in it that can be called action, I yet found something unusual, something extraordinary, something worth writing in it. But that, of course, is only my humble opinion and that is to say not very important. You may differ from me, and find the idea silly, crazy, mad, or you may find it interesting and worth thinking over, but all that is up to you! And now, having made you familiar with all the facts just as I know them, you may begin to read——

The winter in Canada is cold as it is the privilege of any winter, and on the thirty-first of December of the year I am speaking it was snowing. The year in question is the year 1940.

Millions of people all over the globe are celebrating New-Years Eve and I did not see any earthly reason why I should not. And now slowly I am coming to the point.

The setting of my story is a big room, able to hold two hundred persons or perhaps more.

When we, that is to say a friend and I, were walking into it, it was about half full with men who were sitting on long tables, drinking coffee, playing cards, and shouting.——Notice, I said men!

They were all men, not a single female, not even if you looked under the tables.

On the one end of the room a stage had been improvised by some tables, and a piano was standing in the corner.

On the far end a canteen had opened and people were crowding round it, but—though strangely it may seem—no spirits were to be had.

A little fellow was standing there, selling icecreams. We sat down and did nothing but sit which, after all, is something. More people were coming in, all men.

'Shall we buy some coffee?' I asked.

'No,' said my friend.

'Why?' I asked.

'Because it costs more than it usually does,' said he.

'Oh,' I said, and again we were silent and just sat.

The room was getting very crowded and it was almost unbearably hot. Somebody had sat down at the piano, and began to play some age old, long forgotten hits. Many people passed by me, and a lot were licking icecreams. They were of different colours—the icecreams I mean,—some red, others brown, yet others yellow. I turned to my friend.

'Herbert,' I asked, 'shall I buy an icecream?'

He looked at me, somewhat puzzled and echoed: 'An icecream? Are you mad? People are freezing to death every day, and you want to buy an icecream.'

I said nothing. It must be terrible to freeze to death, I thought, first to see one's nose fall off one's face, then one's arms, one's feet——horrible!

I shivered. There is no danger of freezing here, I thought, it is hot. A violin joined the piano now but a lot of the music was drowned in the shouting. Somebody shouted: 'Three spades,' another: 'Four diamonds,' and a third: 'You silly idiot why do you play three hearts when you could have played four!'

A fat fellow stepped on the stage now, and lifted his hands in an effort to create silence but as nobody paid attention, he had to overshout the crowd: 'Gentlemen,' he cried, 'five cents for any piece of music you want to hear, five cents!'

To make this offer more attractive, a tall fellow who looked like a Japanese, joined the two musicians with an accordion. He did not play very well, and sometimes he would str[ike] some deep, bass chords at the wrong places, and burst my ears.

Somebody ordered the 'Second Hungarian Rhapsody' and the three musicians played the opening bars, and then immediately switched over to some modern Hungarian medley that was as much Liszt's music as it was wine. I felt bored.

'Herbert,' I said, 'shall I buy an icecream?'

'No,' he said short and abrupt, 'I told you before.'

'Why not?' I asked, 'there is no danger of freezing to death here, it is hot.'

'I guess so,' he said, 'but you can get a cold in your stomach.'

'Don't be silly,' I said, 'how can I?'

'I don't know how,' he answered, 'but you can.'

I turned to another fellow and asked him. He said he did not think one could get a cold.

'You see, Herbert,' I said triumphantly, 'you **can't** get a cold in your stomach.'

'Still,' he answered, 'I shouldn't advise you to buy an icecream.'

'All-right,' I said, 'I won't.'

The music had stopped and something seemed to be about to happen. The fat fellow came again, and said the show would start now. People clapped their hands and shouted.

A little chap began to dance to an oriental melody. It was a funny kind of a dance and people laughed. I laughed too, but it was a forced laughing because I did not really feel like it.

And then, suddenly, I seemed to see something else. I was in another theatre. It was a big, a tremendous theatre, it was the world, and the principal character was the year 1940.

It was 11:30, and the curtain had already fallen after the closing scene, and the year 1940 was just making its final bows before the world audience.

It was old and wrinkled, and had a long, red beard, because through the whole time it had been principal character on the theatre so much blood had flow[ed] that it had bathed not in water but in blood. Far away you could already see the infant 1941 coming slowly nearer because it had not learned to walk properly yet. And I could perceive that something was written on its forehead but it was still too far away so that I was not able to read it.

And then the curtain fell for the last time in order to rise again in about half an hour when the year 1941 would make its first appearance.

There was a cemetery outside the theatre, and a big tomb was there too.

The year 1940 was slowly walking down the steps and entered a tremendous marble hall, where all the years that had ever been since the world began were sitting on big, marble thrones. The year 1940 slowly went to its throne and took its seat, and over the throne was written in deep-red color: '1940 YEAR OF BLOOD.'

My friend pushed me, and said laughingly: 'That was funny, wasn't it.'

'What was funny?' I asked.

'The cracks the two comedians made, didn't you hear the jokes?'

'Which jokes, what jokes?'

'You must be mad,' he said.

'I was just watching 1940,' I said.

'1940?' he asked.

'Yes, 1940.'

'You are crazy.'

Somebody was hammering away on the piano like mad. It was hot. People were shouting. There was a war going on in the world.

I turned to my friend. 'Herbert,' I said, 'shall I buy an icecream?'

He looked at me for a while, and said nothing. Then, all at once he almost screamed: 'O, go to the devil and buy yourself an icecream!'

'All-right,' I said, 'there is no need to shout, I'm going already.'

There was quite a big queue in front of the icecounter for a lot of people wanted to buy icecreams. I looked at the fellow who was selling them. He was short and darkhaired; he reminded me of an Italian.

Ha, Italians!

They are at war at present, I thought. I hate Italians because they are fighting against democracy, against personal liberty, against freedom of speech and of writing. I hate Mussolini, their leader, because he is a dictator and I hate all dictators.

Most icecream is made by the Italians, I thought. I remembered a little Italian fellow I knew back in England. He used to push a little cart, and he had a little bell in his hand which he was ringing continually, and he used to shout: 'Ice! Ice!' Little boys and girls would run up to him then, and say: 'A penny-one, please!'

I once asked this Italian what he thought of the world and of its problems, and he said: 'Vat do I care about ze world. Ze big shots are not for my liking, I'm only a worker. Let zem do what zey like as long as zey let me live. Zey can all go to hell!' And he had pushed on his cart, and shouted: 'Ice! Ice!'

I didn't hate him then, nor do I now. He was not an Italian as I really think of an Italian. He had no national feelings. He might just as well have been a Russian, a Greek, a Pole or a Frenchman. He was human, and had no harm against anyone as long as nobody did any harm to him.

Italians make icecreams, I thought.

And maybe, I thought, the Italian that is making the icecream I am going to buy now is a conscious Italian, maybe he is a sympathiser of the Italian cause. I will pay five cents for this icecream, I thought, and maybe this Italian will send a lot of money to the Italian government, and the five cents I pay will be a part, be it only a very small part but still a part, of this money. And I would be aiding a cause that I despise and hate.

The queue was pushing on, and before I knew it I stood in front of the icecounter, and the fellow who looked like an Italian, asked: 'What is yours?'

I thought a bit, and then I said: 'I do not want any icecream.'

He looked surprised and shook his head.

'Why the hell did you queue up then?'

'Never mind that,' I said, and went back to our table.

'Well,' said my friend, 'Where is your icecream?'

'I didn't buy one.'

'Why not?'

'Because of the Italians.'

'Because of what?'

'Of the Italians.'

He thought a bit, and then he said: 'There is no alcohol, so I can't say you're drunk, but you sure are crazy.' Then he turned his attention to the show that was going on. Somebody was singing a song, but I don't quite remember.

Suddenly the light was switched off and everybody cried: 'Happy New-Year!'

And again I seemed to be in that big world-theatre, and the curtain was rising slowly, and 1941 was sitting in the middle of the stage, speaking its first lines.

And now I could read what was written on its forehead in big, black letters. I spelled W-A-R; War, and somebody was hammering away on the piano like mad, and people were playing cards, and somewhere a little, dark Italian fellow was pushing a cart, and shouting 'Ice! Ice!' and somebody was singing, and somebody threw eggs at the chap who sang, and from far away I seemed to be hearing a big orchestra playing a sad tune, and women were screaming in the airraid shelters of London, and children were crying for their mothers, and 1941 had taken up its role as principal character on the world-theatre and three letters were written on its forehead, W-A-R, War, and people were shouting 'Happy New-Year!'

My friend tapped me on the shoulder and I turned. 'Yes,' I said, 'What is it?'

'I think,' he said, 'I shall buy an icecream!'

9.1.1941

another country: personal essays

When Henry Kreisel was asked to contribute to the special 100th anniversary issue of Canadian Literature *(Spring 1984), he chose to write about his own discovery of Canadian literature, a discovery which began with the question 'Has anyone here heard of Marjorie Pickthall?'.*

Henry Kreisel

'Has Anyone Here Heard of Marjorie Pickthall?': Discovering the Canadian Literary Landscape

I caught my first glimpse of Canada in May 1940 from the deck of the *Sobieski*, a Polish ship that was bringing hundreds of civilian internees and prisoners of war from England to Canada. The civilian internees, myself among them, were German and Austrian refugees who'd been interned by Britain after the Nazi conquest of France.

During the journey the *Sobieski* developed some engine trouble, was left behind by the convoy of which she was part, and eventually limped into harbour at St. John's, Newfoundland, for some emergency repairs.

We thronged the deck, glad to see a harbour, and wondering if we were going to disembark there. Newfoundland was not of course part of Confederation in 1940, but it was a British dependency. I was not sure at the time of its precise political status. I knew that it was close to Canada.

About Canada itself I had only the vaguest of notions. It was *terra incognita*, at most a large block of red in the atlas I used when I was a schoolboy in Austria. If I thought about Canada at all, I thought of it vaguely as a huge, but sparsely populated country, rich in natural resources, though I would have been hard-pressed to say what exactly these resources were.

Once, after the Nazi annexation of Austria in 1938, I was talking to a friend who knew everything. We were talking about possible countries we might escape to. He ruled out Canada, because it was virtually impossible to get a visa. Canada's doors were tightly shut. Perhaps that was just as well, he said, because Canada was a cultural backwater. There were no theatres or opera houses there, no serious music was played there, and there was no literature worth talking about. Canada was much worse than the United States, he said. The United States at least was a vigorous country, though quite barbaric. On this point I argued with him, for I had read a few American writers (Upton Sinclair, Whitman, Hemingway, Steinbeck), and thought quite highly of them. But since I knew absolutely nothing about Canada and had at the time no desire to find out, I accepted his superior knowledge.

And now here I was, without a visa, and under rather strange circumstances, looking up the steep, rocky cliffs at the city of St. John's and wondering what it was like to live there.

The *Sobieski* lay at anchor for a day or two, in the mouth of the harbour. We were not taken ashore, but during the day dozens of small boats came out from shore and circled the *Sobieski,* and the people in the boats called out to us as we stood on deck. Suddenly that large, abstract red mass on the school atlas became real for me, a human landscape.

Who were the people that lived there? What songs did they sing, what stories did they have to tell? As soon as I saw the people, it was impossible for me to believe that they had no music and no literature. My all-knowing friend must have been wrong.

We did not disembark in St. John's. Repairs completed, the *Sobieski* sailed on, into the Gulf of St. Lawrence, and then up the great river, a romantic landscape stretching away on both sides. So this, then, was Quebec, the French part of the vast unknown country. People along the shore saw us and occasionally they waved. Again I wondered what songs they sang and what stories they told.

At Quebec City we at last disembarked, boarded trains and began the long internment. For a year and a half (I passed my eighteenth and nineteenth birthdays there) I knew the country only from the confines of internment camps in Quebec and New Brunswick and came in contact only with the officials who administered the camps and with the members of the Veterans' Corps who guarded us.

With some of these guards I struck up something resembling a friendship. One of them, a short, somewhat rotund man asked me to write a letter for him, for writing, he said, did not come easy to him. So we sat down at the long table in the middle of the hut where my bed was, and he began to dictate the first of many letters I wrote for him. 'Dear Wife,' he said and stopped. Then slowly, hesitantly, he formulated some questions, about his wife's health, about what she was doing, whether she had heard from their daughter, from their sons. He had not much to report from where he was, he said. The food was good, the work not too hard, sometimes he was bored.

The word got around that I was good at writing letters and three or four other guards used my services. I found out where they came from, places and provinces I had never heard of, from Kenora in Ontario, from Gimli in Manitoba, from a small village on the Nova Scotia coast. The great red expanse on the map became humanized, though the letters I wrote revealed little of the Canadian psyche.

Once I asked one of the guards if he knew of any Canadian writers, but he looked perplexed.

So for eighteen months I lived in Canada and yet was not really in the country. We did get copies of the Fredericton newspaper, but one could not discover the presence of a literary life in the city or in the country from reading it.

After several months we managed to get some books sent into the camp. We could even request some titles. I asked for some Canadian books of fiction or of poetry. None was ever sent. When I inquired why, I was told that unless I could give the title of a particular book or the name of a specific author, it was impossible to fill my request. A classical Catch-22 situation! I didn't know any titles of Canadian books or the names of any Canadian writers, and so I couldn't get any books to find out. I asked one of the officers if he could help me. Officers, I thought, were supposed to be educated and might be expected to know something about their national literature. But I drew a blank. So I went back to reading European writers. In the camps, therefore, my quest to discover what Canadian writers might have to tell me about the people of the country I wanted to know ran into the sand.

When I was at last released from internment in November of 1941, I went to Toronto and enrolled in Harbord Collegiate to prepare myself for the Ontario grade XIII examinations. English was of course one of the major matriculation subjects. Now at last, I thought, I would learn something about Canadian literature, for surely in the last year of high school some of the major figures of the national literature would be studied.

That was certainly the case in the Austrian schools I knew. We studied some of the great German writers, but the important Austrian writers were studied as a matter of course. No one ever thought to question the fact that students should study the national literature.

To my surprise that was not the case in Ontario in 1941. When I looked at the reading list, I found an anthology of poetry, mainly British, Shakespeare's *Henry V,* and *Lorna Doone,* an interminable mid-nineteenth-century novel by R.D. Blackmore. I still sometimes wonder who decided to inflict this novel on the long-suffering students of Ontario and why.

Harbord Collegiate was known as a school with high academic standards, its students among the best in the province. But when I asked some of my new friends if they could recommend some Canadian books I might read, no one seemed able to tell me, and I was too busy trying to make up for four lost years of study and prepare myself for the final examinations to pursue the matter with any kind of urgency.

When we had finished at last with *Lorna Doone,* we began to read a few of the poems in the anthology. There were some narrative poems by Alfred Noyes and John Masefield, a few lyric poems by Keats and Tennyson, sonnets by Shakespeare and Wordsworth, and a poem by Marjorie Pickthall.

I remember reading the poem before class and being quite taken by it. Its sad tone, its *weltschmerz,* its vague religiosity appealed to my youthful, romantic sensibility.

When we began to study the poem in class, the teacher asked, 'Has anyone here heard of Marjorie Pickthall?'

Silence. No one raised a hand. No one spoke.

'Well,' he said, 'she's a Canadian poetess. A very fine Canadian poetess. She has a great command of language. Listen to these cadences.' And he read the poem, and read it very effectively.

For me it was an important moment. At last a figure had appeared in the literary landscape that had seemed quite empty and barren. The teacher told us a little about Marjorie Pickthall. She had been a rather fragile woman, and had died young in 1922. (That was the year I was born, and so felt at once a connection between us!) He told us about the devastating blow her mother's death had been for her. It was all very touching. I could relate to her suffering. I believed that one could not be a poet without suffering. A teacher in Vienna had once told us that. Poets suffered more than other people, he had said, and that's why they were poets.

Marjorie Pickthall was thus the first Canadian literary voice I heard. I asked the teacher once after class why we didn't read any other Canadian writers. He seemed somewhat taken aback. No other student had evidently ever raised this point. He said something about Canada being a very young country that had not yet produced a significant literature. This was the first, but by no means the last time that I heard this curious line of reasoning.

But were there not at least some writers worth reading, I asked. He mentioned four names: Leacock, Haliburton, Carman, and Roberts.

I thanked him and wrote the names down.

I began to frequent Toronto bookstores, and there at last the literary landscape began to open up. Whenever I asked for some Canadian books I was directed to a little ghetto called 'Canadiana.' It seemed to me then, and still seems to me now, a curious practice of segregating our writers. But at least they were there. I began by reading Leacock and Haliburton because my teacher had recommended them, and read them with great enjoyment.

In the fall of 1942 I enrolled in the honours course in English Language and Literature at the University of Toronto. Now at last, I thought, I would be able to get a systematic overview of the national literature, for one of the first-year courses was 'American and Canadian Literature.' It was, alas, a misleading description. The Canadian part of the course consisted of three or four lectures at the end of the academic year. These lectures were given by Claude Bissell. They were very good lectures, but there was not very much that he could do in three or four hours. R.J. McGillivray taught the American material. When I saw the reading list for the course, I expressed my disappointment because there was so little Canadian material on the list. McGillivray said that if I was interested, I could write a major term paper on a Canadian writer. He suggested A.M. Klein, who had recently published *Hath Not A Jew*, and whose background was similar to mine. So the very first term paper I wrote at the University of Toronto was on a Canadian poet. It was a great experience for me. For the first time I heard a modern Canadian voice and began to wean myself away from the poetic vocabulary of the Romantics and Victorians. Klein's was also the first urban-Jewish voice I heard, and this was very important for my own development as a writer. Through Klein I came to A.J.M. Smith and F.R. Scott and the other poets whose work appeared in *New Provinces.*

Most of my fellow students were not much interested in Canadian literature, or were at best defensive about it. Canadian writers were never 'as good as' any number of British or American writers. This always seemed to me a ludicrous way of arguing, because the proposition was based on totally wrong premises.

When I went to school in Austria nobody ever said that Grillparzer, say, or Stifter was not as good as Goethe and Schiller and therefore we needn't study them. We studied Austrian writers because they had important things to say about the country. Then why shouldn't Canadian students study Canadian writers who might have important and interesting things to say about Canada? The image I got after listening to some of my friends was that of a literary foot race, where Shakespeare always came in first, followed by Milton and Chaucer, and one or two thoroughbred British classic writers; after them came two or three American writers, and, then, bringing up the rear (always the rear), came two or three Canadian writers, destined to be forever last.

At the same time there were writers at the University of Toronto who were much admired by students and professors alike. E.J. Pratt was at Victoria College and Philip Child was at Trinity. Northrop Frye at Victoria was beginning to exercise his extraordinary influence, and Marshall McLuhan was beginning his explorations at St. Michael's College. Many people were telling me about Earle Birney, who had recently published *David and Other Poems,* but who had left to join the army just before I arrived on the scene. The stories I heard made him seem a dashing and exciting figure, and when I finally got to know him, in Vancouver in 1950, he lived up to his legend. There were also professors like Norman Endicott, not himself a creative writer, who were tremendously interested in the creative work of their students and offered constant encouragement and help.

So I found a paradoxical situation: a defensive, hesitant attitude towards Canadian literature as manifested in its relegation to the bottom of the official curriculum on the one hand, and encouragement and a desire to foster that literature on the other hand. As an outsider I found all this strange, because the little that I found time to read of Canadian literature seemed to me very interesting indeed, and nothing to apologize about. The literary landscape was in fact much richer than I would ever have expected it to be.

In 1943 I met Robert Weaver and James Reaney. Up to now Canada had been for me the confines of internment camps, and then the two big cities—Toronto and Montreal. The rest of the country barely existed in my consciousness. Reaney, both in his inimitable conversation and in the evocative things he wrote, introduced me to the world of small-town Ontario, and Weaver, who was more interested in prose than in poetry, introduced me to modern Canadian fiction. It was Weaver who told me about Morley Callaghan and Philip Grove and got me to read some of their novels, and it was Weaver who told me about a new writer, Hugh MacLennan, who'd published his first novel a couple of years earlier, and lent me a copy of *Barometer Rising.* Weaver didn't have much money, but he always managed to buy books, or else he got review copies.

Henry Kreisel on graduation from the University of Toronto

Weaver also knew a lot of literary gossip, and I found it absorbing to listen to his stories, as I still do whenever I see him. He made the literary landscape come alive. He also knew some of the writers who were writing for the CBC, people like Lister Sinclair and Len Peterson, and he introduced me to them.

Once he told me that Philip Grove usually came to the public library on College Street on Wednesdays and always sat in the same seat, in the rear of the reading room. So I went down to the library one Wednesday, and behold, there indeed was Grove, dressed in a very old-fashioned suit, and wearing a high, starched shirt collar, sitting very erect, reading and occasionally making a note. I watched him for a while, trying to make up my mind whether I should go up and talk to him. I'd just read *Fruits of the Earth* and I tried to think of something I might say to him about it. In the end, I didn't do it and just walked away without speaking to him.

In 1944 Weaver, Reaney, the late Robert Sawyer, and I thought that we should get together once or twice a month to discuss modern literature and perhaps read from our own writings. So we launched what we called The Modern Letters Club. Weaver arranged for places where we could hold our meetings, usually in the common room of one of the residences. It was all very informal. We never had a constitution, or by-laws, or anything resembling an organization. Word got around and we usually had twenty or thirty people at our gatherings. These were always lively. People could read anything they liked—poetry, fiction, dramatic sketches, or critical articles. Some professors showed up, too; Norman Endicott quite frequently, Northrop Frye and Barker Fairley occasionally, but they never imposed their presence on us.

I used to look forward to our meetings because we all had the feeling that we belonged to a community and that literature was the most important activity in the world. The debates went on until we were told to leave, and the talk continued out in the street and in coffee shops near the campus. We never published a journal ourselves, but quite a few of the pieces first read at our meetings found their way into print.

For two or three years the club was going very strong. Then the meetings became less frequent, the atmosphere was less electric, and so we just stopped. In 1947 and 1948 most of the original members graduated and drifted apart.

In the fall of 1947 I got a job at the University of Alberta, and at last the immense part of the country that was still *terra incognita* for me became real.

I discovered to my surprise that even though Edmonton was a much smaller city than Toronto and the University of Alberta much smaller than the University of Toronto, there was a lively regard for literature. W.G. Hardy, who had written some very successful historical novels, was in the Department of Classics, and F.M. Salter, my colleague in the English department, had for some years been giving a course in creative writing that had become famous. In the spring of 1947, W.O. Mitchell, one of Salter's prize students, had published *Who Has Seen The Wind*. Many other writers, among them Christine van der Mark and later Rudy Wiebe, were his students. I myself showed him a draft of *The Rich Man*, and he was very helpful and very encouraging.

Salter was a Maritimer and he talked enthusiastically about the writers of Atlantic Canada, and so illuminated for me another part of the literary landscape. It was also Salter who introduced me to the work of the writers of the West, to people like Robert Stead and Martha Ostenso, and Sinclair Ross.

And yet, when after two years or so I asked my senior colleagues why we didn't offer a course in Canadian literature, the paradoxical attitude I had first encountered in Toronto surfaced again. Canada was a young country, there was not sufficient material for a full-year course, our literature wasn't yet quite good enough.

To my image of the literary foot race I now added the image of a town crier, or a CBC announcer, calling out one day, 'Hurrah! The great day has at last dawned! Canadian literature is now good enough to be taught in our schools and universities!'

One man at least was already doing it in 1947. Desmond Pacey, a New Zealander, was offering a full course in Canadian literature at the University of New Brunswick, but Pacey was at that time regarded as something of an academic maverick. Yet increasingly, graduate students were writing theses on Canadian literature, but it was not until the 1960s that formal courses in our own literature became standard offerings in our universities.

My own discovery of the terrain was at last completed in 1950 when I went to British Columbia for the first time and met Earle Birney and Roy Daniells, and through them Alice and William McConnell, who in turn introduced me to Ethel Wilson and to Dorothy Livesay and to Marya Fiamengo.

The great landscape was full of life, full of interesting writers. There was one great gap. Quebecois writers remained shadowy for me, and it was not until the mid-1960s that I began to read them.

In the 1950s Wilfred and Sheila Watson came to Edmonton and became the inspiration for many aspiring writers. They were marvellous friends. Eli Mandel, Robin Mathews, and Henry Beissel became my colleagues and my friends. Robert Kroetsch and Rudy Wiebe were students here and became my friends.

The 1960s brought a wonderful outburst of literary activity. It was no longer possible to keep abreast of everything that was going on. The old attitudes lingered on. In 1961, the late Douglas Grant, then editor of *The University of Toronto Quarterly*, asked me how long I thought *Canadian Literature* could keep going. He thought the material for articles would soon run out. And from time to time some of the older cultural pundits bemoan the fact that few Canadian writers have truly international reputations. I am always tempted to ask how many Dutch or Yugoslav or Brazilian writers they can name.

The young writers I know are fortunately not much bothered by this kind of soul-searching. They know who they are, they know where they are, and many of them are puzzled by Frye's famous question, 'Where is here?'

As for me, I could hardly have imagined when I caught my first glimpse of Canada in May of 1940 how marvellous the voyage of discovery would be.

Henry Kreisel has several times spoken and written about his decision to write in English. In this essay he talks specifically about the importance to him of Joseph Conrad and A.M. Klein. A first truncated version of the talk, one with the final section and its discussion of multiculturalism removed, had earlier been published in Tradition-Integration-Rezeption: Annalen Zweites Symposium Deutschkanadische Studien, *Karin R. Gürttler and Herfried Scheer, eds. (Montréal: Université de Montréal, 1979), pp. 105-14. A second version, 'The "Ethnic" Writer in Canada,' was given at a 1979 University of Alberta conference on 'Ethnicity and the Writer in Canada' and included considerable discussion addressed to the issue of multiculturalism. It was published in* NeWest Review, *5, 3 (November 1979), 7, 16 and 5, 4 (December 1979), 7, 14 and again in* Identifications: Ethnicity and the Writer in Canada, *Jars Balan, ed. (Edmonton: University of Alberta Press, 1982), pp. 1-13. Most of the material of the expanded version has been retained in this printing of the essay.*

Henry Kreisel

Language and Identity: A Personal Essay

I

It was in a large, overcrowded army barracks in the little town of Pontefract, in Yorkshire, that I made the deliberate decision to abandon German and embrace English as the language in which, as a writer, I wanted to express myself. The barracks, part of an army camp, had been hastily converted into an internment camp for German and Austrian nationals who had been rounded up in the large northern cities, chiefly Leeds and Sheffield. It was the middle of May 1940. The British government, at least partly in response to the fateful events that were then unfolding in France, had decided to intern all so-called 'enemy aliens,' though most of the internees were in fact refugees who had left Germany in the years since Hitler came to power in 1933, and Austria after the *Anschluss* of 1938. Most of the internees, myself among them, were Jewish, but there was also a significant number of political refugees among us, Socialists and Communists, and some devout Christians, both Protestants and Catholics, who had fled from Germany and Austria for reasons of conscience.

This was the first stage in a journey that was to take many of us to Canada, where we spent nearly two years in internment camps, mostly in Quebec and New Brunswick.

Strange though it might seem, the internment experience as I see it in retrospect, and as to some extent I apprehended it also at the time, had important liberating effects. First of all, it freed me from a dreary and soul-destroying factory job and gave me some time and opportunity to set into motion a deeply-felt ambition to try my hand at writing fiction. In the attempt to try my wings I had to make a decision that was, for me at least, momentous. I had to commit myself to a language that was not my own, that I had spoken for barely two years, and in which I had done hardly any writing at all. But I knew that I would never return to Austria to live, that henceforth my life would be lived in English-speaking countries, and that I wanted therefore to embrace, totally, the language, and with it the attitudes, the cast of mind, the way of thinking and feeling, of English civilization. I was only dimly aware that this would mean, on a very deep level, an entirely different approach to feeling, and therefore an alteration of basic parts of one's identity, but it would not be until very much later that the full dimensions of that decision were to manifest themselves and to produce a crisis that caused me much anguish and that was, in one form or another, to persist for some years, and that would re-occur from time to time throughout the whole of my adult life. Basically, it had to do with the nature of the material of my writing, both creative and critical, with the approach to that material, and with the linguistic means of expressing that material. With hindsight, and the experience of nearly forty years, I have come to the conclusion that I have never fully resolved all the difficulties inherent in a situation that arose when I tried to render European experience in an adopted language. And it was to take many years before I dared to tackle essentially Canadian material. I can say now also that without the help, the presence in my imagination, of Joseph Conrad, the Pole, and A.M. Klein, the Canadian Jewish poet, I could not have resolved the crisis at all, and the adventure I so boldly undertook in that overcrowded army barracks in Pontefract would have inevitably ended in total failure.

But at seventeen I was very romantic. Endless possibilities opened out before me, even in an internment camp, even in dark days, even in moments of depression. Perhaps especially in moments of depression, when some vision, however distant, seems to shed a kind of radiance, a glow, that illuminates the darkness and helps to mark, dimly perhaps, with the light constantly overwhelmed by shadows, the outlines of some path that would lead me out of the darkness into the light.

And really, it is a good thing that young people can dream of boundless possibilities, that they are quite unaware, or only very dimly aware, that in the waters in which they propose to swim there are submerged rocks. Ignorance really can be bliss, because, blissfully ignorant of danger, they do not suffer from fright. The daring young man on the flying trapeze really can accomplish things that an older, wiser man would not even dream of attempting.

So, seventeen years old, sitting on a straw mattress (the only space readily available in that crowded barracks hall in Pontefract), I boldly projected, not a simple short story, but a novel. That novel was to deal with the attempt of a young man, an orphan (I even invented his name, suitably international and romantic: Miguel Amore), to discover his moral identity in an immoral universe, symbolized by a Kafkaesque city, unnamed and menacing. The novel was to be called *Miguel Amore*, but I also thought of calling it *The Torch of Hate*. During the next year and a half, it was in fact written—285 pages in four large notebooks. I thought that these had long since been lost until, to my surprise, they turned up in an old suitcase that I had faithfully dragged along with me without ever really looking to see what it contained. (I found there also a diary I kept during the period of my internment, and that I allowed to be published in the journal *white pelican* in 1974.)

So I set out to become an English writer. (Canada was of course not in my consciousness at all. I barely knew that the country existed.)

Some doubts about the whole enterprise nevertheless soon crept in. Because as soon as the dreams had to be turned into reality, some real linguistic mountains had to be climbed. And I became aware that I did not have much equipment for the climb. I did not even have an English dictionary.

Suddenly I found myself asking some fundamental questions. Could one really change one's language as if it were a shirt? And could one simply throw the discarded shirt away? I came to know people who had been emotionally and psychically so bruised by the Hitler experience that they wanted to shed the language which he spoke, and which they felt he had corrupted. Halting and awkward though their English was, and though they could speak the language only with a thick and heavy accent, they nevertheless refused to speak German and insisted on speaking English. They would thus forcibly suppress part of their innermost selves, and cast it off with the language of their mothers, the language of their childhood memories. It was the expression of a rage so furious, of a despair so profound that they were willing to tear out the very roots of their psychic being, to obliterate the very core of consciousness of which language is the prime instrument. As if one could create a new identity for oneself by denying and destroying the old. Here I learned at once, and in a very practical way, how closely linked identity is to language, how intertwined are the emotional and psychological centres of the personality with the language in which that personality expresses itself.

The road of forcible suppression of my native language I did not want to take. Such violence I did not want to do to myself. Though my country had been taken from me, the language of Grillparzer, of Goethe, and above all of Schiller (the poet I most admired) could not be taken from me. It belonged to me by right, and I exercised that right in the long and passionately written letters I sent regularly to my mother. (Some of these have survived, and so I don't have to rely on the memory alone when I recall them.) Yet I did want to change languages; I knew that, and knew also, intuitively, that this would mean, if not a total change, then at least a major modification of identity, since I was prepared to make a total commitment to the new language, and everything that is connected with language, even though I was not yet sure, and would only learn slowly and painfully, what that commitment meant. At the time I only felt it as a necessity, as one way, not of obliterating, but of reducing my psychological dependence on my native language.

There was among the internees at Pontefract a small, owlish-looking man of about thirty-five, though he seemed older. He had only a few wisps of hair, his shoulders were stooped, he walked with a curious slouch. Most of the time he sat on his straw mattress, deeply immersed in books he had brought with him. They were, as I found out, Latin texts. For he was, someone told me, a distinguished classicist. He had been a Docent, and had published. His whole manner did not, however, invite one to approach him. Nevertheless, I did. I told him what I had determined to do. I wanted to write in English. Did he think it could be done?

He peered at me over the rims of his glasses, looking like a curious bird whose feathers I had ruffled, whose peace I had disturbed. He sat on his straw mattress, with his legs tucked under, in the lotus position.

Then suddenly, in a high-pitched voice, he screeched, 'Haben Sie Latein studiert?'

A strange question. I did not know what relevance it had. Yes, I said, I had studied Latin. For six years in the Gymnasium. 'Das ist nicht genug,' he said. 'Nur weiter. Nur weiter. Weiter Latein studieren. Dann können Sie's machen.'

Like an oracle having delivered its cryptic message, he indicated by his manner that he had said all that was necessary. He returned his attention to his book. Identity for him was clearly tied up with the ancient and once international language. I was puzzled, but have since often pondered if perhaps he meant to tell me something about discipline, about the necessity of immersing oneself with single-minded devotion to the study of language as language. I remained standing, waiting to see if the oracle would perhaps deign to say something more comforting. Sensing that I was still standing there, he raised his eyes and peered up at me again. 'Chamisso hat's gemacht,' he said. 'Der war Franzose und ist dann ein deutscher Dichter geworden. Josef Conrad war ein Pole und ist ein englischer Schriftsteller geworden.'

That was more comforting than his bleak instruction to study Latin. It gave me hope and I plunged at once into deep water, only to find that I was drowning. A diary entry of May 30, 1940 records that two chapters of *Miguel Amore* had been written, but that I was dissatisfied and angry, and decided not to write any more.

A few months later, in an internment camp in New Brunswick, I had the good fortune to meet Carl Weiselberger. He was much older than I, but we became friends. He had been a distinguished journalist in Vienna, and was to have a distinguished career with the *Ottawa Citizen* later on. Weiselberger, a warm and gentle man, was wonderfully understanding. I showed him some of the things I had written and opened myself up to him, expressed both my ambitions and my fears. He understood the problems. He was critical, but never destructive. He constantly encouraged me to do more and more. And he also told me about Joseph Conrad. For a long time Conrad remained an image, an important psychological presence. But I could not read him because I could not get any of his books. Not until many years later did I occupy myself intensively with Conrad, both with the man and the writer. I then found out that the circumstances that compelled him to leave his country and adopt another civilization and another language were very different from the circumstances I faced. But this merely demonstrates the extremely complex psychological forces that are at work when a writer sets out to appropriate a language that is not originally his own, and attempts to use it as an instrument of creation.

The matter becomes even more complicated (if I may be allowed to digress for a moment) when a writer feels that his native language is, in some profound way, not his own. There is some evidence, for instance, that James Joyce, one of the great magicians of language, felt that way about English. In a significant passage in *A Portrait of the Artist as a Young Man*, Stephen Dedalus, speaking to the dean of his college, who is an Englishman, thinks: '—The language in which we are speaking is his before it is mine. How different are the words *home, Christ, ale, master,* on his lips and on mine! I cannot speak or write these words without unrest of spirit. His language, so familiar and so foreign, will always be for me an acquired speech. I have not made or accepted its words. My voice holds them at bay. My soul frets in the shadow of his language.'[1]

It would take a separate paper to explore Joyce's bewildering relationship with language, but I have long believed that he saw himself as the conqueror of a language that had in the first instance been imposed upon a conquered people. And by the use of an alien instrument whose absolute master he had become he would create, not only his own identity, but that of his people, and he would forge, as Stephen Dedalus puts it, 'in the smithy of [his] soul the uncreated conscience of [his] race.'[2]

II

In Conrad's case there were extraordinarily intuitive processes at work, though their causes can be fairly reliably reconstructed. They have their roots in the completely unsuccessful Polish uprising against Russian domination in 1863, in which his father, Apollo Korzeniowski, played a leading role. The collapse of the uprising was followed by the forced exile of the father, which Conrad shared together with his mother, by the mother's death at the age of thirty-four in 1865, and then by the death of the father four years later, after he had been allowed to return to Cracow, a sick and broken man no longer considered dangerous by the Tsarist authorities. All this, as Conrad later noted, under 'the oppressive shadow of the great Russian Empire—the shadow lowering with the darkness of a new-born national hatred fostered by the Moscow school of journalists against the Poles after the ill-omened rising of 1863.'[3]

Conrad's past included not only the exile of the father, in which the son was of course involved without conscious choice, but also, an

altogether more momentous matter, the self-chosen exile of the son.
When Conrad left Poland, he was in a sense exchanging one kind of
exile for another. For to be a Pole and not to be allowed, at least
officially, to use one's own language, to see national customs and
institutions defiled and outlawed, the country itself arbitrarily
divided between three great imperialist powers and Poles excluded
from its governing, was to be exiled in one's own country. But this at
any rate was a condition which millions shared and fought against.
By choosing to uproot himself and go to sea, he was escaping from
the stifling atmosphere of an oppressed country, but he was at the
same time also removing himself from the patriotic struggle in which
his whole family had been deeply involved, and for which his father
had sacrificed his life.

Since Conrad first made his choice (if one can even use the word
'choice' here) when he was a boy in his early teens, he could not have
been consciously aware of all the issues, but the tremendous
opposition which his mere intention aroused, and the extraordinary
steps taken by his guardian to try and dissuade him from actually
carrying it out, must have made the seriousness of his planned step
quite clear to him. That he persisted and finally broke from the land
of his origin, 'under a storm of blame from every quarter which had
the merest shadow of right to voice an opinion,'[4] shows, not mere
stubbornness, but a deep emotional need, a need so strong that it
enabled him to defy the 'astonished indignations, the mockeries and
the reproaches of a sort hard to bear for a boy of fifteen.'[5] Years
afterwards he still feels the need to justify his action, for the echoes of
the reproaches linger on, the commotion aroused in the society in
which he moved still agitates him, and the voices of the past still
demand to be answered:

> I catch myself in hours of solitude and retrospect meeting
> arguments and charges made thirty-five years ago; . . . finding
> things to say that an assailed boy could not have found, simply
> because of the mysteriousness of his impulses to himself. I
> understood no more than the people who called upon me to
> explain myself. There was no precedent. I verily believe mine
> was the only case of a boy of my nationality and antecedents
> taking a, so to speak, standing jump out of his racial surround-
> ings and associations.[6]

If Conrad's need to leave Poland was intuitive, his first transformation—from the Polish youth to the British seaman—was

calculated. 'I had thought to myself that if I was to be a seaman then I would be a British seaman and no other. It was a matter of deliberate choice.'[7] The second transformation—from the British seaman to the English writer—was not. At least according to his own testimony. In his 'Author's Note' to *A Personal Record*, he notes that the fact of his not writing in his native language had been much commented on, but goes on to disclaim any deliberate choice in the matter:

> The truth of the matter is that my faculty to write in English is as natural as any other aptitude with which I might have been born. I have a strange and overpowering feeling that it had always been an inherent part of myself. English was for me neither a matter of choice nor adoption. The merest idea of choice had never entered my head. And as to adoption—well, yes, there was adoption; but it was I who was adopted by the genius of the language, which directly I came out of the stammering stage made me its own so completely that its very idioms I truly believe had a direct action on my temperament and fashioned my still plastic character.
>
> It was a very intimate action and for that very reason it is too mysterious to explain.[8]

The beginning of his writing life, he says later on in *A Personal Record*, was not determined by 'the famous need of self-expression which artists find in their search for motives. The necessity which impelled me was a hidden, obscure necessity, a completely masked and unaccountable phenomenon.'[9] One might have thought that the early, searing experiences of Jozef Teodor Konrad Korzeniowski had something to do with that masked and unaccountable phenomenon.

The English writer Conrad, however, had some difficulties in dealing with the Polish experiences of Korzeniowski. With the ghost of the past he could not openly grapple in his fiction. Overwhelming as the experience of his childhood and early youth was, it does not enter his imaginative work directly. With the exception of one or two rather insignificant tales, Poland does not appear in his fiction. The Polish experience had to be transmuted by the alchemy of his creative imagination, and appeared in his fiction with its identity transformed. One can see, in *Nostromo* for example, behind the South-American sombreros, the faces of men whose ancestors were feudal landowners or silent, sad-eyed peasants in a less tropical land; one hears that experience echoed in the memories of oppressed people and their aspirations for liberty; one finds that experience in the many tales of political outrages and massacres that can be found in Conrad's fiction from the very beginning to the very end. In his letters, in interviews, in autobiographical writings, he freely acknowledges his Polish identity, but in his fiction he must deal with it obliquely. There the consciously fashioned identity of the British seaman (who can often be seen in the *persona* of Captain Marlow) and the English writer takes precedence.

III

Conrad gave me courage, but also caused me despair. He taught me to have respect for my adopted language, especially because it was an acquired instrument, and one had to earn the right to use it. He caused me despair because he made me realize that I was not a magician of language, and that my gifts were extremely modest when compared to his. But to know one's limitations is never a bad thing.

Conrad's solution of how to deal with the raw materials of his experience could not be mine. It was A.M. Klein who showed me how one could use, without self-consciousness, the material that came from a specifically European and Jewish experience. I began to understand that identity was not something forever fixed and static. It was rather like a tree. New branches, new leaves could grow. New roots could be put down, too, but the original roots need not be discarded. In the end, I thought that I could perhaps use a double perspective that allowed me to see European experience through Canadian eyes, and Canadian experience through European eyes, and so to say something that, however modest, might have some value. Thus language and identity could be brought into focus, each modifying the other, but without the one destroying the other. And the new language could be made to express the old as well as the new. It was a constant struggle. That one had to accept. There were many aborted efforts, many failures, a few modest successes. One was grateful when something succeeded, and learned to accept failure. What mattered ultimately was the attempt, now and again, to break the silence.

For a writer, of course, the question of language is crucial, and the 'ethnic' writer, particularly of the first generation, must come to terms with the question of what language he will use. That, as I suggested, is a very complex decision, and I am inclined to believe that it is fundamentally a decision taken on the deepest subconscious or even unconscious level, almost compulsively, a response to a deeply felt need, though neat rational explanations may later be furnished, either by the writer himself or by others.

For some writers of the first generation a change of language is not possible, usually because they are too old when they immigrate and their linguistic pattern is too solidly ingrained for them ever to feel truly able to play the instrument of another language. I am thinking of poets like Walter Bauer, or George Faludy, or Waclaw Iwaniuk.

For the writers of the second generation, or for those writers of the first generation who are able to adopt the language of the country in which they now live, the central problem has to do with the raw material of their art. For they must first of all muster the courage to confront that material honestly. There are ever-present doubts whether the material will interest the majority of the people living in the country, whether indeed the material is inherently valuable. I certainly confronted such doubts when I first set out on my way nearly forty years ago. One must climb curious psychological mountains. But linguistic mountains also.

How, if you are going to write in English about people who do not in fact speak that language, do you render their speech? Do you make them speak a kind of broken, pidgin English, so that what emerges is the worst kind of stereotype? When you do that, you at once rob your people of their dignity, make them into caricatures, less than human. How, if you are a second-generation 'ethnic' writer who is dealing with people of the first generation, do you render their lives, their struggles in a strange, cold land, their sense of alienation and their slow setting down of new roots in often stony soil?

One of the central patterns in the writings of the second generation, and one of the most painful to confront, has to do with the cultural pressures that operate in an immigrant society and that become particularly acute for young children as they grow up and are torn by conflicting loyalties and ambiguous emotions about their own identity. That theme is at the core of such novels as Adele Wiseman's *The Sacrifice,* of Mordecai Richler's *Son of a Smaller Hero* and *The Apprenticeship of Duddy Kravitz,* and of John Marlyn's *Under the Ribs of Death.*

It is the writers of the third generation, Myrna Kostash in *All of Baba's Children,* say, or Monty Reid in a book of poems called *Karst Means Stone,* who can now look back at the past in order to reinterpret it and re-evaluate it from a new and more secure emotional base. They operate, it seems to me, in a new and improved climate of perception, a climate at least in part created by the policy of multiculturalism. For this policy at its best asserts the value of the contributions of many different people to the culture of this country. And one of the central functions of the writer in a society is to help raise the consciousness and thus the understanding of his or her readers.

All writers face the dangers of falsifying experience. But the 'ethnic' writer is perhaps particularly prone to pander to the perceived appetites of the audience, and to play up the exotic and picturesque aspects of his material and thus to diminish and ultimately to corrupt its value.

This was a temptation whose power I have often felt and it took all the discipline I could muster to resist it. A.M. Klein taught me to seek in the memory the strength and vividness of my deepest roots. He taught me that without the sustenance that flows from these roots no creative activity of any significance is possible.

But he taught me something equally important and, ultimately, perhaps of greater significance. For without abandoning the roots of his consciousness, which were ultimately grounded in Old Testament and rabbinical literature, he added legal lore (for he was a lawyer) and the whole range of English literature from Chaucer through Shakespeare to T.S. Eliot, as well as the influences of French and French Canadian civilization. Out of these influences he created his own linguistic and emotional instruments with which to render his earliest and strongest memories of the slums of Montreal, 'the ghetto streets where a Jewboy/Dreamed pavement into pleasant Bible-land.'[10] Out of the memories of his childhood and youth Klein recreates the world of the immigrant Jews, a world now largely vanished. These men and women he recalls with a certain amount of nostalgia, even with sentimentality, but also with a good deal of satirical wit. The same warm humanity is there when Klein moves out of the narrow and special environment he knew as a child to observe and comment on the life of French Canada.

Just as he amalgamated Hebrew and legal lore, and Shakespeare and T.S. Eliot, so also he intermingled Jewish, English and French culture and experience. Not to create an undifferentiated stew, but to give each element its proper and unique weight, to observe and render people other than his own with sensitivity and seriousness.

I took heart from studying him. He emboldened me to move out of my own original cultural group without ever abandoning it, to embrace the wider Canadian reality; to dare, for example, in such a story as 'The Broken Globe,' to render the experience of an old Ukrainian farmer of the first generation and his conflict with his son.

---

[1] James Joyce, *A Portrait of the Artist as a Young Man* (Harmondsworth: Penguin, 1960), p. 189.

[2] Joyce, p. 253.

[3] Joseph Conrad, *A Personal Record*, in *The Mirror of the Sea: A Personal Record*, Dent's Collected Edition (London: J.M. Dent & Sons, 1946), p. 24.

[4] *Ibid.*, p. xiv.

[5] *Ibid.*, p. 110.

[6] *Ibid.*, p. 121.

[7] *Ibid.*, p. 119.

[8] *Ibid.*, pp. v-vi.

[9] *Ibid.*, p. 68.

[10] A.M. Klein, 'Autobiographical,' in *The Collected Poems of A.M. Klein*, compiled by Miriam Waddington (Toronto: McGraw-Hill Ryerson, 1974), p. 271.

'Problems of Writing in Canada' is an earlier and more intimate look at Henry Kreisel working in a new language and a new country. It was prepared for a CBC talk in the mid-fifties, after he had published The Rich Man *and before* The Betrayal.

Henry Kreisel

Problems of Writing in Canada

There has been a great deal of talk in recent months about the problems of so-called 'new' Canadians. In the last few years hundreds of thousands of people have come to this country from all parts of Europe in order to settle and begin a new life here, and we have heard and read, in radio talks and in articles in the press, something of the problems which they have had to face, and which they continue to face, in their attempts to integrate themselves into the life of our country. Their problems are economic, but also psychological and cultural, because the transition from one way of life to another is not always easy.

Suppose now that among these new arrivals there is the odd person who wishes to devote himself to literature. A quixotic notion? Perhaps. Assume it, anyway. Suppose further that this man has come to Canada from some Central European country, so that his native language is a language other than English; and yet he decides that, having cut his ties with the old world and the old country, he must adopt this new land, and, above all, its language, and that if he is to express himself at all it must be in English.

That was the decision I made when I came to this country in 1940. I had left Austria, where I was born and partly educated, after Hitler annexed that country in 1938. I was then fifteen years old. The next two years I spent in England. There I worked in a tailoring factory, but also managed to learn enough English to begin a fairly systematic reading of classic English literature in the evenings and on my days off. I even began to have some notions that I might myself perhaps write something some day. When I reached this country, I made two decisions. I decided that I would stay and work in this country if this country would have me, for such charms and allures as Europe once held for me were gone, and I decided further that I would devote myself to the study of English literature, and that if I were to write anything myself it would be in English. I remember making these decisions very consciously and very deliberately, but without the full realization that in the waters in which I proposed to swim there were submerged rocks. At seventeen one tends to be romantic, and to have exaggerated notions of what is possible. Still, in this case ignorance perhaps was bliss because, blissfully unaware of danger, I did not suffer fright. Not that I was completely blind to the difficulties that faced me. I knew, even at seventeen, that a language is more than a collection of words and grammatical rules, and that to master it one had to understand also the traditions, the attitudes, the frame of mind of the people who speak the language. Could a foreigner do that? Could he change his language as if it were a shirt? And could he simply throw the discarded shirt away? I was troubled and perplexed. And I remember talking the whole matter over at great length with a friend, an older man who had been a very successful journalist in Vienna.

'Perhaps,' he said, 'perhaps it can be done if one is young enough when one starts.'

'How young,' I asked, 'is young?'

But he wouldn't commit himself. 'It has been done before,' he said to me with an amused smile. 'Joseph Conrad did it. Go and see what he did.'

So I went and read Conrad. The result was despair. For how could one hope to emulate that master? But there was also hope. Hope derived from Conrad's despair. 'I had to work like a coal miner in his pit,' I found Conrad writing to a friend, 'quarrying all my English sentences out of a black night.'[1] It was comforting to know that the great Conrad had not come by his triumphs easily. And Conrad also taught one to have respect for one's adopted language, especially because it was an acquired instrument, and one had to **earn** the right to use it, even if one could never hope to use it in so masterly a way as he had done.

I have often heard it said that the writer who changes countries, as it were, has an advantage over the writer who stays put. He observes his new country with fresh eyes, the argument goes, he sees things more sharply because he can view both the old and the new country with a certain amount of detachment, and place people and events in their proper perspective. The argument sounds convincing at first, but it contains at best a half truth. Certainly, the newcomer sees some things more sharply than people who have lived all their lives in one place and have come to take a great many things for granted, and some of his insights may well be perceptive and original and even valuable. But—and this is especially true of first impressions—his observations are often a compound of what he has heard and read about the new country, of preconceived notions, that is, modified by what he now sees and hears at first hand. That is the way most travel books are written, and very often they tell us more about the feelings and prejudices of the writer than they do about the country which he describes. It is only very rarely that the newcomer can give us a really profound picture of a country and its people in a work of art. There are too many things he doesn't know or doesn't understand, and there is often a tendency to make people and things look quaint and picturesque merely because they are different. There are some countries—Mexico, for instance, or Italy—where life seems very highly coloured and exciting, and where people often seem to act out their private lives in public. The exotic surface of life, the rich historical associations, the very climate, thus become sources of drama and therefore act as powerful stimuli to the creative imagination.

Canada is not such a country. The surface of life here seems almost too placid, the tempo of life too even. Canada is not therefore a country that offers a writer—and especially one who comes here from abroad—ready-made dramatic situations. This drawback (if it is a drawback) he shares with the native Canadian writer, of course. In recent years, indeed, the search for the **Canadian** character, for a **Canadian** identity, has been the number one intellectual parlor game of serious-minded Canadians. Hugh Kenner wrote, in a rather snide way, that 'the Diogenes who would shine his torch on the Canadian face is rather in the position of the spinster continually looking beneath the bed and finding nobody,'[2] and Chester Duncan said, 'We haven't discovered what we are or where we're going and therefore we haven't much to say.'[3] Similar views are widely held, I think, and I have often heard them voiced. I am beginning to suspect that to hold them is to take the easy way out, but they do reflect some of the difficulties which writers in Canada have felt they had to cope with. Certainly it has been my experience that it is only after a long time that one begins to sense, and partly to understand, the strong undercurrents of passion and emotion which exist here as elsewhere in the world, but which are often hidden beneath a rather thick crust of reticent Puritanism. To the man who comes here from abroad, Canada is not an easy country to come to know and to write about.

At any rate, I found that when, after many trials and many errors, I felt confident enough to undertake the writing of a novel, I turned, almost instinctively, to a European experience, although I had very naively thought when I first came here that I had done with Europe altogether. *The Rich Man*, which is, so far, the only long piece of fiction that I have published, begins in Toronto, but the central scenes of the book play themselves out in the Vienna of the 1930s, on the eve of great and catastrophic events—the annexation of Austria, the war, the horror of the Nazi concentration camps.

Soon after I had finished writing *The Rich Man*, I set to work on another novel. Stirred and moved by the experience of those who had survived the torment and the torture of the concentration camps, I wanted to write about a man who returns to the wreck and ruin of his former home. For so, I thought, might I have returned had I been less fortunate. Of this novel I wrote about a hundred pages before I felt forced to abandon it. For I found that a tremendous gulf of experience now separated me from the material I wanted to deal with, and sympathy and imagination alone were not enough to make up for the lack of precise and intimate knowledge.

As a writer I was now standing between two worlds. I no longer really knew Europe, and I did not yet feel that I really knew Canada. And only intimate knowledge can confer authority upon the imagination. It is only now that I am beginning to feel that this country is in me as well as that I am in this country. It takes a long time, much longer than I had thought when I set out upon my journey, to circumnavigate the submerged rocks.

---

[1]Letter to Edward Garnett, August 28 1908; in G. Jean-Aubry, *Joseph Conrad: Life and Letters* (New York: Doubleday, Page & Co., 1927), II, 82.

[2]The opening sentence of Hugh Kenner's essay, 'The Case of the Missing Face,' in *Our Sense of Identity: A Book of Canadian Essays*, edited by Malcolm Ross (Toronto: Ryerson Press, 1954), p. 203. (First published in *Here and Now*, 2 [May 1948]).

[3]I have not been able to trace this quotation. Henry Kreisel believes he took it from a CBC broadcast.

the writer's letters

(and some notes on a convention)

In 1946, Henry Kreisel submitted The Angels Weep *to McClelland and Stewart Limited. During 1946 and 1947 the firm attempted to negotiate American publication. High hopes were placed in Little, Brown—to whom the manuscript was taken personally by John McClelland—until Angus Cameron, their editor-in-chief, rejected the novel 'with regrets.' His report commended the author's 'warmness of approach and . . . feeling for family life.' 'However,' it went on, 'it seemed to us that this quality would not redeem the novel from its essential lack of form and pointlessness. It also seemed rather difficult to conceive that in 1936 the old man could have returned to the Europe of anti-Semitism and found it apparently such a vacuum of political feeling and activity.' Henry Kreisel's very encouraging editor at McClelland and Stewart, Sybil Hutchinson, did not agree that the novel lacked form and wisely suggested that Kreisel himself knew best about Vienna in 1936. In the letter printed below from the author's carbon copy, Kreisel points out the extent of Cameron's misjudgement.*

The novel was next sent to Reynal and Hitchcock. Their reader responded to the first forty-five pages with high serious-ness: 'Excellent! Atmosphere, pathos, poignancy and admirable English. A Chekhovian suggestion at times with a smack of Andreyev. Something in it too that reminded me of the first chapter of Pan Tadeusz. And there is, of course Wladyslaw—St. Reymont's A Polish Scene. *Read that story again. Then parallels between this excerpt and that tale of St. Reymont's are striking.' Presumably the reader followed his own advice and directed his attentions elsewhere, for Reynal and Hitchcock did not pick up the book either. And, if Henry Kreisel could derive some satisfaction from the 'admirable English' of his evidently middle-European novel, he was unimpressed at being found so derivative; his annotation to 'St. Reymont' reads, 'I never heard of the man.'*

A last attempt was made to place the novel through a New York literary agent. This reader, a less pompous peacock than the previous one, wrote, 'I think it has not solidified for him yet in characterization or in plot.' He also suggested that the novel should end on 'a note of hope,' a suggestion that led Sybil Hutchinson to threaten that, if Henry Kreisel complied by the then-fashionable device of sending his characters off to the

United States at the end of the novel, she wouldn't remind Mr.
McClelland of the advance on royalties for his next book.

When no American firm took The Angels Weep, *McClelland*
and Stewart did not publish it either. Henry Kreisel put the
novel away. The next time its publication was mooted,
McClelland and Stewart approached him: Sybil Hutchinson
wrote on April 8, 1948 to say that the company was 'desperate'
for a novel that fall and to ask whether he could rewrite The
Angels Weep *in two months. She suggested strengthening the*
Toronto background and heightening the European scenes to
make the threat of Nazism more explicit. She also reported
McClelland's objection that the title's connotations of misery
(at least for those who did not read Shakespeare) might spoil
sales. Henry Kreisel did rewrite; the novel appeared that fall as
The Rich Man.

to Sybil Hutchinson, July 6 1948

. . . I am of course very disappointed by Little, Brown's reply,
though by no means downhearted. I was prepared to get a long series
of rejection slips before I ever started to write the book, and the really
quite unexpected sponsorship which you have so kindly given to my
novel has been most heartening to me.

I must say, however, that the reasons Mr. Cameron gave for
rejecting the novel strike me as rather odd. He complains of an
'essential lack of form and pointlessness.' Your reassurance that you
disagree with him has made me very happy.

The structure of the novel is so simple as to perhaps make it seem
formless. It is true that the novel is episodic, but surely I am right in
claiming that the episodes taken together form an organic unit. The
personality of Jacob Grossman is intended to give unity to the work
and knit the episodes together.

The action of the novel is plotted along the simple classical curve
of rise and fall.

(1)   Jacob Grossman's position shown as it really is.
(2)   Meeting with Tassigny; purchase of the painting; con-
        sequent growth of his ego.
(3)   His sense of importance further enhanced by the recep-
        tion given him by his family.

(4)   He reaches the pinnacle of his brief authority when he shows off the picture. His triumph carries with it symptoms of decline because Albert and Shaendl are not taken in.

(5)   In the steambath the whistle of a passing launch reminds him of the factory siren.

(6)   In Albert's shop he recognizes Albert's superiority. Further signs of his coming exposure given by Albert's silent deliberations about asking for a loan.

(7)   Albert's death. Jacob approached by Reuben for money.

(8)   Confession of his poverty. Departure. He flings away the painting which by now has become a symbol of his rise and fall.

Use is made throughout the novel of 'leit-motifs,' contrasts and repetitions, designed to emphasize certain important points.

My answer to the comment pointlessness would involve me in a literary argument which would take too long. I should start off by asking Mr. Cameron what he considers to be the 'point' of *The Playboy of the Western World*.

I come now to the third point, the treatment of anti-Semitism and of politics in the novel. . . .

In 1936 the Schuschnigg government seemed firmly established. There was only one political party in Austria, both the Social Democrats and the Nazis having been outlawed in 1934. The Socialists had been completely broken then, and recovery for them was hopeless. The Nazis, with help from Germany, were slowly rallying, but they did so very inconspicuously. The Vaterlaendische Front, Schuschnigg's organization, grew tremendously because all Nazis joined in order to tarnish [sic] their underground activities. My father's best friend, a man who came to have dinner at our place every Sunday for years, was an illegal Nazi, yet we did not find [out] about this until after the annexation!

To a man like Jacob Grossman Austria would most certainly have seemed like a very peaceful country. He is not an intellectual. He came to visit his family. Political under-currents do not interest him, because they are not tangible, but rather something abstract which he cannot comprehend.

Neither was the Europe of 1936 the Europe of anti-Semitism in the sense in which Mr. Cameron thinks it was. Mr. Cameron is under a distinct misapprehension, confusing the Europe of 1936 with the Europe of 1938, 1940, and 1946. It must not be forgotten that the poison spread by Hitler had not yet taken effect. The attack was still in a stage of preparation. German Jews, strange though this may seem, were still in possession of their businesses, and were living relatively unattacked in Germany. It was not until 1938, sure of his power, that Hitler struck. The annexation of Austria was the signal, and six months later, on November 10, 1938, he staged the bloodiest pogrom in history. All Jews were disenfranchised and their property confiscated. This whole dismal chapter is clearly traced by Heiden in his book *Der Führer*.

Austria has always been anti-Semitic. But in 1936 the anti-Semitism in Austria was not militant. It became so in 1938. Many Austrian refugees claim that anti-Semitism in Austria **before** Hitler was not nearly so bad as it is in Canada and the U.S. today. I do not think so, but judging the situation by outward symptoms it would seem to be true. Signs like 'Restricted Clientele' were inconceivable before Hitler. Neither was it customary to ask a person to state his religion when he applied for a job. The social life between Gentile and Jew was not nearly as divided as it is here, and there were hundreds of mixed marriages. Two Jews were ministers in Schuschnigg's cabinet.

To the little man Jacob Grossman, spending only four weeks in Vienna, spending most of his time in a Jewish district with his immediate family, things would not seem strange at all.

Would an American of the same social class as Jacob Grossman, spending four weeks in Toronto, go back to the States politically informed? Could he diagnose the complex under-current of Canadian political life? Would he know anything at all about the French Canadian problem? If you asked the average Canadian, would he be able to tell you about the significance of the recent meetings of the Provincial Premiers?

Jacob Grossman takes it for granted, as most Jews of his class do, that anti-Semitism is a necessary, almost inevitable evil. He prays for one thing only—that no bodily attack be made upon him. This may sound cynical, but it is a fact. In 1936 no one killed Jews. Not even the worst pessimists dared to predict the horrible events of 1938 and the years that followed. If truth be told, not even the Nazis themselves knew then that they were destined to reach the murkiest, lowest depths of human civilization.

But Mr. Cameron is right, of course, in thinking that the foundations of everything that has happened since were already firmly laid in 1936. It is very easy to see the causes by the light of subsequent events. In 1936 it was not so very easy. The press of the world was very busy throwing a heavy smokescreen around European Fascist and semi-Fascist activities. The handful of people who attacked Fascism were themselves attacked as warmongers and Communists. Could we have had Munich if people had listened to them? Did they not laugh at Churchill and Eden, surely no Communists?

I tried, as honestly as I could, to portray the under-currents of anti-Semitism and of political life in the Austria of 1936.

The question of anti-Semitism is raised on the very evening Jacob arrives in Vienna. In the taxi the little boy Hermann says to him that his father believes things are getting bad for the Jews in Austria, and that they would have to leave. 'Papa says the people hate us. Why do the people hate us, Uncle Jacob?'

Twice more the issue is raised in prominent places. Albert speaks about it in his store, and Jacob finally encounters it personally when he goes to eat out after he has confessed his poverty and listens to the proprietor of a little café, who tells him that the Jews have all the money, and that Hitler is doing great things for the Germans.

The greatest political tragedy that befell Austria came in 1934 when Dollfuss crushed the Socialists. I have tried to symbolize that tragedy in the figure of Robert Koch, poet and writer, reduced to playing the fool in a side-show. You will also remember that he gives a fairly full picture of Austria's political mess when he talks to Jacob in Albert's shop, and that Albert rounds out the picture after Koch leaves.

On the very first evening the family gets in a fight because Albert tells them that there's going to be a war, and that they don't know what is going on in Europe. Reuben laughs and says: 'We know nothing. Only Albert knows.'

They didn't know anything. They were blind to what was happening around them. 'They' were the common people all over the world. In 1938, after Chamberlain came back from Munich there were tremendous demonstrations of joy in England. He was called the saviour of the world, and people were dancing in the streets and shouting: 'Peace in our time!' and they believed it, because they wanted to believe it.

The Austrians, having been so terribly defeated in World War I, were trembling at the mere thought of war. So afraid were they of war that I have seen women bursting into tears at the mere mention of the word.

The people of Vienna, their democracy crushed in 1934, and the Social Democratic party which had ruled Vienna for over twenty years utterly wiped out, were in 1936 politically completely apathetic, thus opening the way for the Nazis who conquered Austria without any opposition, ideological or otherwise. I think I have succeeded in the novel in painting this picture of general apathy. Mr. Cameron's comments about the political vacuum which Grossman found are, albeit unwittingly, an acknowledgement of success. Albert Reich and Robert Koch are the products of this decadent society— capable men both, but defeated and crushed by their environment.

The overhanging cloud of doom is symbolized by the street-urchins who surprise Jacob and the children in the cave, and their vicious shout 'Wait till we get you alone!' lingers on after they have disappeared from sight. . . . I do not insist on that interpretation, but the meaning is there if one cares to look for it.

Economically Austria was a bankrupt country, deep in the throes of depression. One chapter is given over to the painting of this picture, and Reuben is chosen to be the focus of it. Depression is a thing he would obviously know about, because he is hit by it. You will remember the walk to the steambath and later on in the same chapter the conversation in the steambath itself. . . .

[*In script on the back of a page:*] History is written by educated men after the events when the smoke has cleared. It is made by millions of little men, working, loving, suffering, and dying, blind persons in the grasp of an implacable destiny and ignorant of its working. And the few who see and warn the rest are never heard and their voices die in the wilderness.

Professor Malcolm W. Wallace of the University of Toronto English Department wrote to Henry Kreisel on November 30 1950, praising The Rich Man *and especially the characterization of Jacob and of Shaendl and her children. Henry Kreisel has found among his papers a draft of his response. The draft shows a good many cancelled passages; I have silently omitted them when printing the letter.*

to Professor Malcolm W. Wallace [December 1950]

. . . What touched me most in your letter was the statement that though I have not made Shaendl strikingly beautiful, you would always think of her as such. This is a great compliment not to me, but to her, for in the course of writing the book I myself fell completely under her spell, and was carried away by her strength and the nobility of her character. And through Shaendl I have also paid a tribute to my mother who stood model for her.

There is one other thing I feel I must say to you. (I have often spoken about it to my friends.) I discovered early that such creative powers as I have lay in characterization, but it was not until I heard your lectures on Shakespeare that I realized how character can be moulded and revealed. Though I had read a good deal of Shakespeare by myself, you opened a great and boundless world to me and showed me things I had never seen before. I have never forgotten your exposition of *Anthony and Cleopatra*. I can still see you standing there in front of the class, reading: 'Unarm, Eros. The long day's task is done, and we must sleep,' and then Cleopatra's great lines: 'Peace, peace!/Dost thou not see my baby at my breast,/That sucks the nurse asleep.' This was a marvellous experience for me, and it was listening to your reading and to your comments that brought home to me with full force how a writer can lay bare the soul of a man in a flash. . . .

This letter to Robert Weaver of the CBC gives news about the Kreisels' visit to Vancouver, where Henry Kreisel had been teaching summer school at the University of British Columbia. The letter reveals some personal restlessness; its writer is also trying to decide whether to stay in the university and, if he does, whether to face 'another two years of semistarvation' in order to get the 'union card' for academic employment, a Ph.D. (He did, in the event, take leave from the University of Alberta to gain a Ph.D. from the University of London.) Most of the letter, however, is taken up with Weaver's criticism of an early draft of the radio play 'He Who Sells His Shadow.' Henry Kreisel returned to this play in 1956, when he rewrote it for production by the CBC the same year. It is published for the first time in this volume. He now readily admits the limitations of the play but retains an affection for it as saying something that cannot be said too often. I have excerpted his original defense of its method.

to Robert Weaver, October 3 1950

. . . I have thought a great deal about your criticism of the Shadow. . . . I wonder in this case . . . whether you have not judged the play too narrowly. When you say that the modern D.P. has no real alternative to his present situation, you are not wholly right. A certain section—the Jews in Nazi Germany for instance—undoubtedly had no real alternative. But a good many others did in fact have an alternative. A great many writers, for instance, did in fact sell their shadows to Hitler. A man like Thomas Mann did not. But Otto Hahn, a great chemist (and a Jew) accepted the status of an 'honorary Aryan' and kept on working for the regime. The artist in a Stalinist country also finds himself in the position where he must either conform—that is sell his shadow—or simply stop being an artist. And in the present hysteria in the States that condition also exists, though it is perhaps not so acute. But even when you remove the symbol from the realm of politics, there is applicability. What of the genuinely serious writer, for instance, who sells himself to Hollywood or becomes a highly paid ad man? In other words there are many degrees of displacement and alienation, and the process is by no means restricted to the arts. You tie me down to **one** state of displacement. But I never say that Peter is a 'displaced person.' At most I commit myself to saying (through the Man) that he 'has joined the legions of displaced men,' but he has done so voluntarily since he has come to the conclusion that [he has] lost too much by making the deal in the first place, and that the gain was not worth the loss.

I feel on the defensive, because I shouldn't have to explain. Perhaps the fault lies with me, perhaps with you. I cannot be sure. But I want to bring up a rather important matter—the nature of symbols in dramatic writing. The . . . symbol, as I conceive it, must primarily make an emotional impact. I believe that a symbol may exist on different levels, and that there may even be a certain amount of contradiction between the levels. . . .

Henry Kreisel, on the Kahlenberg,
Vienna Woods, 1954

*Robert Weaver continued for many years to support Henry
Kreisel's work and to broadcast it on CBC. When they differed,
as in the previous letter, the matter could be discussed. But not
all the criticism Henry Kreisel received was so well-informed.
Weaver reported in one letter that the CBC had received
complaints about both the language and the incidents of
'Annerl' when they broadcast it, and that one of his colleagues
had suggested the usefulness of censorship. But it was 'The
Travelling Nude,' read far too literally, that drew the greatest
criticism. After its publication in* Prism *(Fall 1959), a former
student from a creative writing class taught by Henry Kreisel
and Wilfred Watson wrote to him in a vein that indicated that,
whatever she hadn't learned, she had mastered the jargon of
short story critiques: 'To begin with, I cannot accept the
premise that anyone in this country would be permitted to
travel in the nude——but even if such were the case, the story
does not seem "solid" to me. Not you, in fact. Perhaps I am
biased, but after Homecoming, the Rich Man and The Broken
Globe, it puzzled me. I do not feel that it quite comes off, as it
were.' A prominent critic was bothered less by the premise than
by its embodiment; he decided against including the story in an
anthology on the grounds that it was 'a little too strong meat for
my book.'*

*Bill McConnell considered 'The Travelling Nude' and
'Homecoming' for a volume he was editing,* Klanak Islands: A
Collection of Short Stories *(Vancouver: Klanak Press, 1959). He
perceived an 'indecision in tone' in 'The Travelling Nude' and
decided on the second story, querying only the ending. In
response, Henry Kreisel wrote about the genesis of both stories.*

to Bill McConnell, January 10 1959

['Homecoming'] is a chapter in a novel which I began, but was
emotionally unable to finish, because the subject proved unbearable.
That was four or five years ago. Last year Paul Wright [of CBC] asked
me to show it to him after I talked about it. He liked it, and asked if he
could broadcast a part of it. HOMECOMING was clearly self-
contained, and they sort of cut it off after twenty minutes, if you know
what I mean. CBC after all is time-bound. What I propose to do is
type out for you the section that follows, and perhaps you can then
find a better place for the ending. . . .

I am also pleased that you liked the Travelling Nude, although with reservations. I wrote the story last summer. I tell you how I conceived it, and that will perhaps explain the indecision in the tone which you found in it. What I aimed at was a study of a non-conforming personality who is an artist, but not really a very good or original artist. I thought of Mahler as a man who, though really aware of this fact, does not want to admit it, even to himself, except when he turns the irony on himself, which he does when he describes the stages of his artistic development, and the activities at the Ontario College of Art. His temperament, however, brings him into conflict with conventional middle-class society. This society thinks that he is mad. First his father thinks so, then the adults whom he is teaching, and finally his boss, who is really his father again. But since Mahler isn't really sure of his talent, he has no defence against that society except an ironic awareness of both his own and his society's limitations. He half-believes his father and his boss when they tell him that he is mad, although I think he also believes that he is in the end saner than they, for they are hopelessly confined by their complete lack of imagination and by the humdrum world of solid things which is all they know. Mahler's problem (and here I see him almost as a tragic figure, though he always remains in a comic framework) is how he can save himself from being drawn into the world of his father and his boss and so eventually lose the limited imagination which he does possess. Hence he asserts at the very end the reality of the travelling nude. She has a name. Valerie. (Which means the truth.) But she has no surname. In the end, then, Mahler is left without a job, and still wondering how he can come to terms with the world.

I would certainly appreciate any comments you may have, for apart from Esther, only Wilfred Watson, Eli Mandel, and you have had any idea of what I was doing or at any rate trying to do . . . .

Henry Kreisel wrote the 'Postscript' to The Betrayal *in a great rush of energy shortly after submitting the rest of the manuscript to McClelland and Stewart. But the postscript was in fact two postscripts, a circumstance which his editors, Jim Totten and Joyce Marshall, found troublesome. The letter below is Henry Kreisel's response to Joyce Marshall's suggestion that the two be made one.*

to Joyce Marshall, March 25 1964

. . . I have been considering and reconsidering your suggestions, because I value anything that comes from you. I also talked to Jim Totten, whom I saw briefly just after I got your letter. I can see that you might find two postscripts 'just a little awkward.' I was aware of this 'awkwardness' myself, but decided to risk it. . . .

You see, what I decided to do was to have two distinct emotional movements in the postscript. The first movement, dealing with Stappler's return only, was to begin on a quiet note, almost idyllic. (I begin with a Wordsworth quote, which in the context, and to me, is ironic, though I don't particularly want to draw very strong attention to it. Tintern Abbey begins, 'Five years have passed . . .' etc.) Then Lerner goes on to talk about the 'paradisal' summer, recounts the love affair from which he has recovered, and is now again leading a quiet life. This stillness Stappler once more interrupts, as he did earlier, but this time with much less powerful effect. Then he leaves again, but stays in correspondence with Lerner, and the second emotional movement deals with his death.

If we were to telescope the two movements, Lerner would of necessity have to write after Stappler's death, but that would mean that the death of Stappler would dominate everything, and the tone of postscript 1 could not be what it now is. Then, too, I don't want to focus on Stappler's death, but rather on his life. 'Du lebst noch,' says his old professor. 'You are still alive.' I feel very strongly, therefore, that by telescoping I would lose more than I would gain.

But I have a suggestion which might go some way towards eliminating page-breaks. Instead of having two distinct chapters, could we have one chapter only, with two dates. . . .

One of Henry Kreisel's most careful readers was Hugo McPherson, who reviewed The Betrayal, along with Douglas LePan's The Deserter and Fred Bodsworth's The Atonement of Ashley Morden ('Betrayal, Desertion, Atonement,' The Tamarack Review, 34 [Winter 1965], 106-11). He was the first of Kreisel's critics to invoke Conrad and to suggest an unengaging coolness in the character of Lerner: 'Both his [Kreisel's] narrative technique and his choice of situation recall the intensity of Joseph Conrad. But if Theodore Stappler is a plausible brother to Lord Jim, Dr Lerner is no substitute for Conrad's narrator Marlow. When Marlow tells one of his "inconclusive tales", we feel that we have pierced through morality to the darkest impulses of experience. Professor Lerner, by contrast, is somehow too calm, too comfortably ensconced in his world to communicate powerfully the passions he has glimpsed. His aloofness is perhaps characteristic of the winter-bound Canadian consciousness—an irony of which Mr Kreisel is undoubtedly aware.' Henry Kreisel's response clarifies his use of Conrad.

to Hugo McPherson, March 25 1965

Dear Hugo,

I read your review in Tamarack yesterday and since you talked to me briefly about it when we saw each other in Toronto, I thought I'd tell you that I was really pleased with what you had to say. From the point of view from which you looked at the three novels you reviewed you had to see them in the way you did. More specifically, you had to see The Betrayal in the way you did. I should not wish to quarrel with your interpretation, although I want to make a comment. I make the comment to you as a friend, not as a reviewer.

What you had to say about Stappler bears out my own conception of him and your comments were illuminating. I accept your play on the name ('the stalker') as a kind of unexpected bonus. You might be interested to know that I actually derived his name from the German word 'Hochstappler,' which is untranslatable. It describes a person who pretends to be more than he is.

The particular comment I want to make is about Lerner. He was not conceived as a Marlow figure, but on the contrary as an anti-Marlow figure. Critics in general, while noting the Conrad influence, haven't noted the way in which the Conradian pattern has been inverted. I felt that we had had quite enough novels in the post-war period in which writers tried to 'pierce through morality to the darkest impulses of experience.' Now, I wanted to deal with dark impulses and with dark experience, but I didn't want Marlow to tell it, I wanted a guy like Lerner to tell it, a sensitive 'Director of Companies,' if you like, or indeed, a liberal member of the liberal Canadian university establishment. (At last, you see, the liberal establishment has allowed Jews to come in, and there is Lerner. Kreisel, too, if you like.) I believe that once you see Lerner, not as a Marlow, but as someone quite different, he becomes, I believe, a much more complex figure (because conceived as an ambiguous, ironic figure) than any reviewer except Weiselberger in the *Ottawa Citizen,* and Eli Mandel (in conversation) has yet seen him as. . . .

Sharon Drache, an Ottawa writer who was publishing in Dialog *and* Quarry, *had written to Henry Kreisel to ask whether he had ever met A.M. Klein. In answering her, he described the mysterious circumstances of almost meeting the poet in the fall of 1956. Sharon Drache responded that 'Your letter sent shivers through my system, the mysticism of the man lives in many of us I'm certain. . . .' Henry Kreisel's attempt to describe the event that wasn't one and Sharon Drache's response to that description were the genesis of the short story 'The Almost Meeting.'*

Three Letters to Sharon Drache

May 14 1980

. . . You ask about A.M. Klein. I have had a long, silent, almost mystical bond with him ever since 1942 when I first read him. I had just entered the University of Toronto, and had made friends with a young professor, Claude Bissell, who was to become president of the U. of T. later. Bissell thought I would like Klein and gave me his copy of *Hath Not A Jew.* I was moved and impressed, and since I was taking a course in American and Canadian literature (the Canadian part of the course was a joke, since only two weeks at the end were given over to it!) I asked Dr. McGillivray, who was giving the course, if I could write a paper on Klein. In the fifties and sixties I did a number of broadcasts on him for CBC. Last year I gave a paper to a conference here and there I set out my relationship with him. . . .[1]

Your question of whether I knew Klein personally is more complex. I met him—almost—twice! I used to go to Montreal fairly often, and in fact I still do. On one of these occasions (in the middle fifties) I was at Irving Layton's apartment for dinner. The talk came round to Klein. Klein had already become something of a recluse, but he still saw friends from time to time. I expressed a desire to meet him. I knew that he knew of me, because both Frank Scott and Art Smith had told me on separate occasions that Klein had read *The Rich Man* and had been very moved by it. Irving said he would phone Klein, tell him that I was at his apartment, and invite him to come over. I was delighted when he came back into the dining room and said that Klein had agreed to come because he wanted to see me. About half or three quarters of an hour later the phone rang. Irving went to answer it, and when he came back he said that Klein had phoned. He was at a drugstore, about a block from Irving's apartment, and he wanted us to come down there and pick him up. It seemed strange to me, but Irving said that he might have got confused about the address. So we walked to the drugstore. When we came there, there was no sign of Klein. In fact, nobody was in the store. We asked the pharmacist if someone had made a phone call a few minutes earlier. He said yes, and described a man who was clearly Klein. But after the phone call, the pharmacist said, the man thanked him and walked out. We looked around outside, but there was no sign of him. Irving phoned his house a few times after we came back to the apartment, but there was no answer.

The second occasion on which I almost met him occurred a few months afterwards, late January or February. It was cold and snowy. I was in Montreal for three days, and on the last evening, on the spur of the moment, I phoned Klein's house. A woman answered, probably his wife. I told her who I was and asked if I could perhaps see Klein that evening, because I was leaving early the next morning. She said she would see. A few minutes later, she came back to the phone and said yes, Klein would be pleased to see me. She gave me the address, which I actually had, and also told me what bus to take. It was a long ride. I walked a block or so from the bus stop to his house, but when I came there, the house was dark. I rang the bell. No one answered. I checked to see if I had the right house. There was no doubt. I rang the bell again. I waited. Nobody came to the door. No light went on. I stood there for a few more minutes, and then I walked away. . . .

October 7 1980

. . . I thought you might be interested to know that just after I had written to you about my almost meeting with Klein, the CBC approached me and asked me to write a story for the new season of Anthology. I had for many years been toying with the idea of using that near encounter for a story, but could never find the right form or setting. But with my letter to you still very fresh in my mind (it was the first time that I had actually set down the experience) I sat down and began to sketch out a number of possibilities, until at last, in August, I found the key, and wrote the story, perhaps for me the most difficult I have ever done. I recorded it about two weeks ago. It was broadcast over the Western network last Saturday, and I have had a very good response. The national network will carry it in November. . . . You stood in a way as godmother to the story, because your sentence ('Your letter sent shivers through my system . . .') was very important for me.

October 30 1980

. . . It occurred to me that I might unwittingly have given you the impression that the story is 'about' Klein, but that wouldn't be correct. I deliberately made the character David Lasker different from Klein, though there are some affinities. And the other figure is certainly not me. I had to find ways to distance myself from the characters so that I could handle the intricacies of the theme. Nevertheless, if you hadn't asked me a certain question, I wouldn't have written the story. Things move in mysterious ways.

---

[1]Published as 'Language and Identity: A Personal Essay,' *Another Country*, pp. 119-30.

*Henry Kreisel is not only a gracious and generous correspond-
ent of those interested in his work, he is a marvellous writer of
personal letters: keenly observant and gently humourous. His is
an eye for the telling detail, an ear for the exact phrase, and a
spirit whose generosity embraces the people he meets. The two
letters and the note published here demonstrate him at his best
as a correspondent and a travel writer. The first was written to
his wife, Esther Kreisel, in the summer of 1948, when he had
been invited along for the ride by a CBC agricultural broadcast-
ing team who were visiting the Experimental Station set up
near Lethbridge by the Federal Department of Agriculture. The
letter is of special interest as a record of one of his first
impressions of prairie landscape and prairie people (who
seemed more than willing to put on a show for the visiting
broadcasters).*

to Esther Kreisel [early summer 1948]

'They order these things better in France,' says Sterne, and I repeat
his words because they always pop into my head, and I should add
that they order things well where we are now—see letter heading.
This is a marvellous place—about a thousand acres of beautifully
kept and cultivated land, magnificently well equipped (at least so it
seems to the uninitiated layman's eye of mine), presided over by an
eccentric character named Dick Painter, of whom more anon.

We had a smooth ride all the way to Lethbridge; time passed
quickly, and there was some good talk. They stopped at Crossfield, a
small place just outside of Red River, to interview the wife of a well-
to-do farmer. She, having been informed, was all prepared, spruced
up, hair neatly curled, white blouse and grey silk stockings—a rather
pretty woman of thirty-seven married to a man very much older than
herself. She had prepared a sumptuous lunch of roast beef and
trimmings, very beautifully served and altogether satisfying. Then
they interviewed her, and she in rather breathless tones informed the
world that the girls' club of Crossfield is learning all about vegetables
and fruits and how to make jellies and jam. And yes, there is a boys'
club too, called the Pathfinders I believe, and they, o yes, they do some
sort of handicrafts—and she produced samples for us—a bull's head
hammered out of a copper plate, traced after a pattern (no original
designs at all, which seemed a pity), some plaster things, you know

the sort. 'We will take these to Calgary,' she said (and it's all recorded), 'to the exhibit on there, so that people will see that boys **can** do something with their hands.' This last sentence our lewd minds construed into a meaning which I am sure the gentle woman did not intend to convey. And while the recording was being made Jack Craine and I paid court to a marvellous orange Persian, about nine months old, whose loud and satisfied purrs filled the room, producing something akin to static noise, so that Alec had to stop it. She then lounged in an easy chair, looking suspiciously at the equipment and the microphone, but being rather too regal to bother about inspecting it. And when all was done, and Alec started to wind up his coils, she suddenly jumped down and dived for them, but finding nothing there, and as if by such rough and undignified behaviour she had somewhat compromised herself, she stalked from the room, haughtily, her tail up in the air. 'I must have a long tail with which to express my emotions.'

So on, past Calgary, and there the country changes, and becomes really quite beautiful, with the foothills gently curving and rolling, and the still snowcovered mountains lifting themselves in the background. This is probably the finest time of the year to travel through this country, because everything is green and fresh and pleasant to the eye. Later, I am told, the sun scorches and burns the grass, and the country begins to look brown and somewhat desolate. To the west the mountains stay with you almost as far as Lethbridge, but to the east the country flattens and becomes smooth, like a polished table. A curious contrast to the eye, the mountains on your right and absolute flatness on your left. A very prosperous area this. For the past ten years the farmers in this area have made an average of $8000 a year, some much more than that. Prosperity is in the air. Modern buildings and equipment everywhere, and fine cars on the road. What, one wonders, would the Italian peasant think were he to come here, and see these vast stretches of land, not all under cultivation even, while he squats miserably on a couple of acres of dry and rocky land? It makes one feel uncomfortable to see these vast stretches inhabited by so few people.

Lethbridge, bulging with wealth, almost visibly so, to judge by a hasty look, is prettier than any other city in this province, at least as far as my experience goes. Tree lined streets, broad and clean, perhaps make this impression.

The experimental station is about five miles outside the city, and there in front of his house, Dick Painter was waiting for us and greeted us in friendly manner with a gentle oath. A real character. A big man, very potbellied, he calls himself one of the biggest bull-shooters in the country. And he can indeed tell marvellous stories. He is a biologist, who graduated from the U. of T. exactly four days after I was born, June 9, 1922. He claims he learned his profane expressions, of which he has as extensive a collection as you are likely to find anywhere, there too. He took over (about three years ago) a couple of delapidated buildings, which he turned into veritable palaces. There is his own house, beautifully laid out by the judicious tearing down of walls, and furnished with excellent taste, and then a sort of guest house, where we are now staying, adjacent to the main building. This guest house is a well-nigh perfect reconstruction of a bunk house, with added comfort and a curious kind of beauty. The walls are made of honey-coloured cedar wood, and so are the two double bunks, though the cowboys very likely slept on less comfortable mattresses than we, and did not have a shower bath and flush toilet either. On the walls a series of silhouettes, of horses and bulls, and cowboys and cowboys being thrown from horses and cowboys roping cattle. A cowhide on the wall near the door, covered with the signatures of people who have stayed here. Seeming coal oil lamps hanging down from the roof, though more conveniently serviced by electricity. Guns on the walls and bookshelves filled with Westerns. Here we sat last night and listened to Painter's stories about the opening up of this country, while all the while his dogs lay stretched on the floor, or curled themselves up on our bunks (no house kitties here). There is a whitish grey, wiryhaired Sealyham dog (I think that's the way it's spelled) looking somewhat like a Yorkshire terrier, though rather more lowbellied, and not so straightlegged, and a blackhaired bastard who is her son, product of a rather unfortunate affair between herself and a black cocker. 'That goddamned bitch had to have a couple of illicit fucks,' is the way Painter phrases it. The product, a very lovable dog indeed, is called Mr. McGuffy, his mother's name Mae West. Perfect names these. He breeds fighting cocks too, rather fearsome looking animals, and naturally there are horses here, too, one of which I will ride after I finish this letter.

   With us last night, too, was Dick's supervisor, a man with a grooved and weatherbeaten reddish fiftyish face, and a body as youthful as that of a twenty-year old. He is one of the few people actually born here (he's over fifty), taciturn of speech, more at home with the long bullwhip, in the skill of which he gave us a marvellous demonstration at midnight. After that to bed. . . .

Shortly after their arrival in Edmonton in 1947, Henry and Esther Kreisel met Rita Rowan, the energetic and tenacious secretary of an organization called 'Friends of the Indians.' As Henry Kreisel describes it, she 'dragooned' them into joining, though perhaps such military persuasion was not necessary since they thought the group worthwhile. The 'Friends' sought mainly to help Indians who came to the city from the reserves, but they also aimed to help the Indian people organize themselves. To this end, they ran workshops to teach them how to thread the maze of government bureaucracy, to fill out forms, to lobby. They also lobbied themselves for the interests of the Indians. Much had been accomplished by 1950: the Indian organizations, run now by Indians, had become much stronger negotiators on their own behalf. However, the 'Friends' lingered on, although without the Kreisels from 1952 to 1954 when they were in England (where Henry Kreisel studied for a Ph.D. at the University of London). On their return to Edmonton, they were—again to use Henry Kreisel's word— ' "reactivated" ' by Rita Rowan, in time for the first major convention organized by the various Indian associations. The 'Friends' were invited, as a mark of appreciation, to send a non-voting delegation of six members. On June 21-22, Henry and Esther Kreisel were among the delegates at the Indian Convention at Driftpile. (Driftpile is located a few miles south of Lesser Slave Lake, about half way between the Alberta towns of High Prairie and Slave Lake.)

Henry Kreisel's keen observation and imaginative interest in the new landscape and new people among whom he found himself are again evident in the notes he took about the drive to Driftpile and the convention. The social concern—the outrage at injustice, the longing for a better world—so evident in the writings done during his internment, now, fifteen years later, shows itself as a matured and mellowed empathy, much informed by practical wisdom.

Notes on Indian Convention at Driftpile, June 21-22 [1955]

. . . On the drive North again the vastness of the country is what impresses. The bush now is green, so the landscape is softened. Parts of it were burned out by forest fires, and the trunks of trees stood there bare, and stark, leaves and bark burned away. In the twilight they looked eerie, like gibbets. So, one imagines, the via Appia must have looked when the bodies of Spartacus' followers were hanging there after the grisly revenge of the victors.

A magnificent sunset. Sun going down behind a large cloud bank which it coloured purple and red.

Driftpile. For us merely a stop along the highway. Eight miles from Faust where we stay. (A magnificent old cat, Jo-Jo, there to greet us in the lobby of the little hotel.) On one side of the dusty road, the wooden hut in which the convention is to be held, on the other side a wooden shed which is used as kitchen-cum-dining hall during the convention. Beside it some Indian families have pitched their little tents. Children torn between curiosity and shyness. With demurely bowed heads they accept candy.

Albert Lightning is the first Indian who greets me. He is standing on the steps of the hall, John Lansoc beside him. Albert wears a ten-gallon hat, a dark-grey striped suit and a red bow, tied in the old-fashioned way. Albert has a great sense of occasion.

The convention gets under way slowly. Mimeographed copies of the resolutions are handed out. There are 67 resolutions to be debated. By the time the afternoon session starts, they are well into them. The hall is now crowded. There they sit, men and women, erect on the hard wood benches. They do not move, do not wriggle, do not shift position the way I have to. A few of the women have babes in arms and when the infants get restless, give them the breast. Then they go to sleep again.

Here then one gets insight into the problem of a people still to a certain extent primitive, but moving out of the tribal pattern, being forced out of the tribal pattern whether they want to or not. One gets a glimpse at any rate into what the situation all over Asia must be like, for the great revolution in our times boils down to questions of health and education and the well-being of the people everywhere. People want to live better and they want these things **now,** not in the future, not when it pleases some others who are now sitting on fat asses. One can imagine meetings in countless Chinese villages in which just such issues as I heard discussed were probably thrashed out—from Cold Lake came delegates who wanted the support of the association in their demand for new wells. From up North (White Fish Lake) came a delegate who wanted nothing in particular but strongly voiced the woes of his people. Sentence by sentence (Albert translating) he stammered out his tale. 'We are isolated. We are poor. The government does not allow us to hunt all the year round. How shall we eat?' He had a hooked nose and wore a plastic patch over his left eye, the pale pink of the patch a curious contrast to his brown leathery skin. He had grey walrus mustaches, and (I sat opposite him at dinner) seemed to slurp his soup through them.

When to hunt and when not to hunt became one of the great issues of the first afternoon. Forsland, the government representative, tried to explain that certain birds (migratory birds like ducks) could not be shot out of season because an international convention governs these regulations. Jim Croweagle got up and argued that birds were trespassers, and trespassers on private property could be shot! Then, amid laughter, he said that his principle could be extended to include the white man, who was after all a trespasser on Indian soil!

The most poignant moment came during the discussion of matters concerning treatment of disease, when a young man got up and talked of the death of his child. He spoke in Cree, sentence by sentence, Albert Lightning translating. This made the whole thing more dramatic, and the hall was hushed, listening to him. It was late afternoon, hot and dusty. Beside me a woman looking more Eskimo than Indian suckled an infant now and then upon her ample, blue-veined bosom.

'Last year,' said the young Indian, 'my baby became sick. It was tuberculosis. The doctor said she should go to the Charles Camsell hospital. We took her there. After two days she died. My wife and I went to the hospital. They asked me if they could do an autopsy. I asked my wife. She refused. Then I refused also. They told us to come next day to fetch the body home. We did so. They gave us the coffin. When we came home and opened the coffin, we saw that the body had been cut open.' He sat down, and for a moment there was a poignant silence which seemed to brood over the hall.

The two doctors there, Faulkner and Oxford, appeared uncomfortable. Autopsies must be authorized, yet there are times when the law requires autopsies to be performed. Perhaps, said Faulkner, there was a misunderstanding. A failure of communication between the hospital authorities and the man. (It is, I think, possible.)

All the issues dealing with health, and many others, boiled down, so it seemed to me, in the final analysis, to a question of human dignity. (One resolution asked that hospital personnel [white] treat older and more backward patients with greater courtesy.) They are aware that their status is not what it should be. I fully understand that position, and sympathize with it. To be treated, not as second class, but as human beings. That after all is what provides the social dynamic in a great part of the world. It is perhaps the central issue of our time. And the people who have superman pretensions must be firmly put in their place.

On Wednesday morning the convention still did business, because not all the resolutions could be dealt with in the two days allotted. We left before it was all over. On behalf of our group, I made a short speech of farewell. Their organization, I said, is essential and indispensable in the fight for a better life.

*In 1968 Henry Kreisel attended a conference at Brisbane where Professor Roy Daniells of the University of British Columbia gave a paper in which he used the term 'marginal.' Henry Kreisel evidently queried him about it at the conference for in a letter of August 16 1968 Daniells returns to his use of the term, connecting it to marginalia by recalling Tennyson's allusion to a book in which the text was but a fly-speck on the page surrounded as if by a cloud by numerous marginalia in an immense margin. He also explained that what **he** meant by 'marginalia' was the things a writer did not say but which were nonetheless a necessary part of the reader's knowledge if he were to understand the writer's theme or develop it. He further suggested that Henry Kreisel's own novels could, by this definition, be called 'marginal.' Henry Kreisel's response carries on this discussion and is of considerable interest in this country plagued until recently by the notion that its entire literature was marginal.*

But not all the conversation between these two friends was of such academic propriety. Professor Daniells had wanted to stop at Fiji on his return to Vancouver and had given up after two weeks of unsuccessfully trying to book a hotel. Henry Kreisel did have what seemed to be a hotel booking and did stop in Fiji on his way home. In October, having had no response to his earlier letter, Roy Daniells wrote, in the light fantastic manner, for a description of the Fijian visit. The description, when it came, outdid fiction. Indeed, the events of that visit have remained in Henry Kreisel's memory as material he plans to turn into a short story.

to Roy Daniells, October 21 1968

Dear Roy,
    Your charming note of Oct. 18 just arrived. There was on my desk also the note you wrote me on August 16, and which I have been meaning to answer for ages and ages, but things kept intervening, and I meant to make my answer properly baroque—an occasion which almost necessitates one's putting on glorious robes (if only in imagination) and getting oneself in the proper frame of mind, impossible to do in the hurly-burly of registration and all the other myriad activities in which I seem to become embroiled. But I must

write to you, and obviously if I wait until the proper baroque mood strikes, you may never hear from me at all.

I did stop off in Fiji, and had a most remarkable time there, although the visit began most inauspiciously. I arrived around midnight—hot, humid airport, slow-moving line through customs and health inspection—only to find that when I got to the Air-France counter, where I was to pick up my hotel reservation, there was no one there. 'Oh,' I was told by the Quantas people, who occupy the space next to Air-France, 'he has gone home hours ago,' he being the Air-France plenipotentiary. I protested that I had a hotel reservation, and that perhaps someone could phone the Air-France man. 'Oh, but he has gone to bed now.' 'Well, couldn't we wake him?' 'Oh, but he has no phone.' Pause. Touché. Irrefutable logic. 'But even if we could phone him, what good would that be?' Clearly by now I was involved in a metaphysical argument with a patient Indian. The fans whirred in the airport. Nearly everybody who was on my flight had cleared out, and the airport was nearly empty. 'Well,' I said, entering into the speculation, 'he might be able to tell me where my hotel is.' 'Oh, but he wouldn't remember. You see, he doesn't know your name.' 'No, but you could tell him. There can't be that many people with reservations that they have to pick up at the Air-France counter.' Pause. 'True, but if he had a reservation for you, he would have left it with us at Quantas. That's what he usually does.' 'Perhaps he just forgot, and it's in his drawer.' 'Oh, but his drawer is locked.' 'Well, then, perhaps you could phone a hotel and see if I can get a bed.' 'I could phone, but it would be no use. All the hotels are booked.' 'What should I do, then?' I had already resigned myself to spending a night curled up on one of the benches at the airport. He said, 'I could perhaps get a bed for you in a guest house.' 'What's a guest house?' 'It is not so posh as a hotel, but it is clean.' 'All right. Try.' He made a phone call, and said to me, 'There is a bed at the Kabaka guest house.'

I got into a taxi and was whisked off into the black night by a bearded Indian taxi driver. 'How far is the guest house?' I asked him. 'Oh,' he said, 'a little distance.' The darkness made the drive seem endless. 'How far is it from the guest house to the centre of town?' I asked him. 'A little distance,' he said. So I abandoned that line of questioning.

Finally he splashed through what seemed a ditch (it had been raining) and stopped in front of an unlikely-looking place—a rectangular building, white concrete it seemed—with a single weak electric bulb illuminating a sign reading 'Kabaka Guest House.' In front there were about half a dozen young teenagers, lounging about, and slowly coming towards the car and peering at me. I must admit I felt a bit apprehensive, stranded somewhere in the middle of nowhere. Then the proprietor of the guest house emerged—a youngish man, who greeted me very ceremoniously and assured me that the hotel was very clean, although I had made no comment to the contrary. I asked the taxi driver how much I owed him, and he said five shillings. I only had a pound, and he said he had no change, whereupon my host took the pound note from me, and said he would settle with the taxi driver, and the rest of the money would pay for part of my room and breakfast. Then he showed me to my room, up a flight of concrete stairs. A small little room, but clean. I asked if the door could be locked and he said he could get a key, though no key could have protected me had anyone wanted to get into the room. After a while my host (Mr. Lal) returned and asked me if I would like to come down and have a drink. I said yes, and he took me into a dingy little backroom, where two men sat drinking. I sat down on a ramshackle wooden chair and Lal got me a glass and poured me a drink. There was a silence as they looked me over. I finally told them that I was from Canada and had just come from Australia. 'Canada,' said one of the men, a heavy, swarthy man, sweat gleaming on his forehead, 'Canada.' Then he said something in Hindi and they talked for a while, and then one of them disappeared, and about five minutes later came back with a small old man, and said, 'He has two sons in Canada.' The old man stepped forward and embraced me, as if through me he could embrace his son(s). It was quite touching. He could only speak a little English and the others translated for him. His sons were in Vancouver, he said, and he wanted to know what Vancouver was like. I told them, and then they wanted to know if I lived there, and I said no, and tried to tell them where Edmonton is. I drew an imaginary map on the table, but this meant nothing obviously. So I began to speak about the climate in Canada, and told them about the cold prairie winters. This made an enormous impression, and they sat like little children, their eyes fairly glued on me. 'Twenty below zero,' said one of them, and then they tried somehow to grasp this fact, but it was clearly almost impossible for them. They had no points of experience to which this concept could be related. One of them said after some deep thought, 'It is one hundred times colder than it is right now here' (the temperature was about 80 degrees).

When I went to my room, I was again a bit apprehensive because the young teenagers kept loitering about, and I could hear whispered conversations drifting up through my window, but finally managed to fall asleep. In the morning I went down to have breakfast, and then rented a car and drove to Lautoka, about fifty miles from Nandi. There I watched a soccer match and got to know a young Indian who worked for the sugar mill. He invited me for lunch and [I] heard a good many things about the island that I wouldn't have known otherwise. Then he took me through the sugar mill, and late in the afternoon I drove back to Nandi. Just before I reached the town, a heavy tropical rain came down and I decided to go back to the Kabaka guest house. I was most royally welcomed, and Lal prepared a truly sumptuous supper for me, and absolutely refused to let me pay for it. Most embarrassing. So I went out and bought a bottle of whisky, and invited him to join me. After a little while his father-in-law came by with two other men and they joined in, too. At one stage Lal said, 'Tell again about the cold.' And once again I thrilled an audience! At about ten o'clock the father-in-law said I must come and spend some time in his house and then he would take me to the airport. Before I left, Lal asked me to come to the back of his house and meet his wife and daughter. I did so, and was later told by an Indian on the staff here that this was a most unusual honor. Normally the Indians of Fiji don't show their women to strangers and certainly the women don't join in the conversation of men when the men are drinking together. So I drove to Lal's father-in-law's house (or hut really) and he brought out a bottle of whisky and a group of men came in (I don't know how they knew about the party) and we sat and talked for about two hours or more. Then one of the men, who was a taxi driver, asked us to get into his taxi and they all took me to the airport and, all aglow with whisky, they gave me a most spectacular send-off.

I had been meaning also to make some comments on your 'marginal' image. I've thought a good deal about it, especially after you explained it in your earlier note. I have no real quarrel with it, because I see what you are after, but I'm not altogether happy with it as an image, first because it has to be explained, and secondly because I can think of so many exceptions or qualifications that make it difficult for me to keep the image in focus. The first problem the image poses is a problem of reference. If something is 'marginal,' then it must be marginal to something. So that if the point of reference is a specific **Canadian historical experience,** then clearly my own novels, for instance, are marginal to it. And so is Klein's *Second Scroll.* But what about his *Rocking Chair?* I have even more problems with the image if I remove it from the Canadian context, applying a test I learned from you, but applying it in reverse. You used European concepts of art and applied them to the Canadian context. Let's take the examples of Kafka and Beckett. If you set Kafka beside Hasek (*The Good Soldier Schweik*), then Hasek is clearly more central to Czech experience, and Kafka is marginal. But what a margin! But at the same time Kafka is much more central to modern world literature than Hasek. In the wider context Hasek becomes marginal. Beckett is an Irish writer, but also a French writer, and in some sense he is marginal to both literatures and at the same time central to an international literature. I realize that your conception of the margin makes some provision for accommodating writers like Kafka, but at the same time the image of the 'margin' doesn't stand by itself. It has to be explained, and that weakens its impact. On the other hand, I grant you that it has the qualities of 'teasing' us 'out of thought.'

interviews

Felix Cherniavsky interviewed Henry Kreisel in 1974, when he was still Vice President (Academic) of the University of Alberta, but after he had declined to stand for the presidency and had announced that he would not continue in university administration after his term ended in 1975. This particular juncture in his career accounts for the turn the conversation takes and for his expressed wish to return to writing fiction should the Muse not have deserted him.

A longer version of Felix Cherniavsky's interview was first published in Sphinx *(II, 3 [Winter 1977]), 10-20. The excerpts which follow are reprinted by permission of* Sphinx.

Mervin Butovsky's November 6 1980 interview was part of a larger project involving a number of Canadian Jewish writers. In this interview Henry Kreisel is more explicit than anywhere else about the Jewish context of his writing. The interview is published for the first time here.

Felix Cherniavsky

Certain Worldly Experiences:
An Interview with Henry Kreisel

Cherniavsky Since you published your two novels, Canadian literature has come into its own. As you return to a life of writing and teaching, how do you see yourself as part of the Canadian literary scene?

Kreisel I see myself primarily as probably one of the first people to bring to modern Canadian literature the experience of the immigrant. A.M. Klein showed me that it was possible to use within a Canadian context one's total experience, that I didn't have to write in some artificial way about a Canadian topic. On the other hand, I didn't have to set my stories in the United States. I used, then, my double experience because, although my novels are not autobiographical in any full sense, still they make use of the European experience and they make use of the Canadian experience. In *The Rich Man*, I tried to relate the Canadian experience to the European experience by taking an immigrant back to Europe and thus gaining a double view. In *The Betrayal*, I brought a European to this country and particularly to Edmonton. In *The Betrayal* I also saw the European experience of the war through Canadian eyes. Looking at my own work, I think writing about this relationship of Canada and Europe has been my contribution. In a number of my stories the same kind of interplay has formed the focus. 'The Broken Globe' is essentially Western Canadian, and it's interesting that this story has now been translated into many languages and has been dramatized. What becomes clear is that when you write about the places you know, even though the setting is very localized, it can have universal significance. What I will be writing in the future, I really don't know. I have to explore the new consciousness that I've arrived at. I would think that in some way the Canadian and European mixture will still be part of this consciousness because it's part of my consciousness. A writer is always using his basic experiences in a number of variations.

Cherniavsky Do you have any intention of writing a Canadian version of C.P. Snow's *The Corridors of Power?*

Kreisel   That is also possible, of course. I've been involved very, very intensively in university affairs, university and government relationships, but it's been such a treadmill, such a hectic, constant response to immediate crises and to conflict, and attempts to resolve conflict, that I have not had the time to sit back and think what it has meant. I do desultorily keep a journal, and I have noted some things down as they were happening. I hope, since all experience ultimately is grist to a writer, that that experience will also in some way manifest itself in what I do later on. As I said, I don't know exactly how because I have to reflect on what the experience has really meant and what is significant in it.

Cherniavsky   This is going back more than thirty years, but I understand that you wrote on 'Exile and Alienation in Modern Literature' in your Ph.D. thesis. Who were the writers you focused upon in that study? Did they influence your works in any particular detail?

Kreisel   Well, I've always been deeply interested in literature, but I've never been a dispassionate scholar. I've made my way in a different sort of manner. I did do all the academic work and I did it, I think, very well, but in both my Master's thesis and my Doctoral thesis, I focused on subjects that would be of some interest to me as a person and as a writer rather than simply focusing on something as an academic exercise. In my Ph.D., I looked at writers who had experienced either exile or alienation. That was at a time—1952—when the word 'alienation' was not yet very widely used. Later on, of course, it became an 'in' word, but at that time it wasn't really yet much in the general usage of the language. I wanted to look at exile and alienation because, in a sense, that would tell me something about myself. I mean I was, in one way, an exile. I had lived in Austria, was born in Austria, and then became an exile, a refugee, during the Hitler time. Because I was an outsider, certain of the alienating features of modern society were clear to me. I could see the political forces that were making for alienation.

   I did a number of things in that thesis. I focused essentially on four writers. Conrad was clearly an exile figure, and I'd read Conrad quite a lot. D.H. Lawrence was a figure of both exile and alienation. Joyce was in one way the classic exile, and finally Virginia Woolf. She might seem a strange choice to you because she clearly was a member of the establishment and in no way an exile, yet there is in her work, I discovered, a kind of inner psychological alienation. I used her really for this inner kind of alienation. I looked also at the whole history of alienation as we see it in literature, at writers of the nineteenth century, particularly at the various developments that have since begun to separate writers from a mass public in a way that had not happened before. So I also looked at the whole relationship of writer and bourgeois, at Balzac for example. I remember doing a major analysis of *Lost Illusions*. Thomas Mann again is predominant in his analysis of the writer-bourgeois relationship. I mean from *Buddenbrooks* on, certainly in works like *Tonio Kröger* and *Death in Venice*. My thesis looked at the way in which alienation was reflected in the fiction of, shall we say, the late nineteenth and early twentieth centuries. It came out of my perceived need to understand some of the movements, some of the developments, that go far beyond the writers, far beyond artists.

Of course, alienation then became a very fashionable word because it does express a widespread feeling. This way again, as so very often, writers were prophets, sensitive instruments, that could pick up and render situations that became very common afterwards. At first sight, one might say Joyce was a unique figure, as was Conrad, but in point of fact they had sensitive antennae that picked up things that became very, very widespread.

Cherniavsky   In your dissertation did you have occasion to examine any Canadian writer as a figure of alienation?

Kreisel   No, I didn't. I had to limit it because otherwise it would have been unmanageable. But I would say that my involvement in university affairs is, in a way, a personal response to my early feelings of alienation and exile. I always felt the need to make a contribution to the wider society. I wasn't content simply to be a teacher or an isolated writer. I also felt the need to involve myself in the affairs of the country which had received me and to which I'm grateful. Curiously, when I was asked to undertake various tasks, university administration was a way in which I could satisfy that feeling of being part of a larger society, of not being exiled, not being alienated. I never thought that it would take me to the posts I had. I wasn't really ambitious to occupy the posts that I've occupied, but opportunities came, and when they came I didn't turn them down. I finally came to the conclusion two years ago that I didn't want to go on; I'd done what I felt I could do, I needed to do other things, to assert other facets of my personality. That's when I decided to conclude my term and not to seek another term or another post.

Cherniavsky   Perhaps this is too early for you to answer, but in what way do you think your highly responsible administrative duties have affected or might affect your artistic and creative capabilities?

Kreisel   Well, it's very hard to say whether they will affect them positively or negatively. I am taking a step into the unknown, when I want to do again some creative work. I hope some of my creative capacities are still there. I haven't really exercised them in the form of fiction in the last six or seven years. I have written some things but nothing of really any major significance because I have been so deeply involved in the practical affairs of the University at a time when universities went through major changes and relationships with government became paramount. It's been an interesting experience to see how governments work from the inside. I talked about this to W.O. Mitchell a few weeks ago. We talked about writing and about experience, and I said that one of the major things that I've learned is what it means to be involved at the top level in a corporate structure. Because, of course, a large university is run as a corporation, and as a senior official of the corporation you are willy-nilly involved in the corporate life, in the realities of that corporate life. Not many writers really know what it's like from the inside to have to run a corporation, the pressures that are generated on the people who have responsible positions, the dealings that one has to have with the large bureaucracy inside the university and with the outside bureaucracy of the government, both federal and provincial. It seems to me that that may well be a fruitful form of exploration now that I've had that experience from the inside. I think it has been very valuable and very interesting because the corporation really has an extraordinary life of its own. Senior university officials, from the president down, face so many barriers and restraints that they have little room to manoeuver. To see the power modern government exercises has been really an eye-opening experience, but whether it will be useful to me as a writer I don't know yet.

Cherniavsky   With reference to *The Betrayal,* you refer to the influence of Conrad, but you don't mention Eliot.

Kreisel   Though I differed from Eliot ideologically, his vision of the modern world as a waste land was very influential on me. In *The Betrayal* I saw Vienna during the period of 1938-40 as a waste land city. I also used, as a kind of overall concept, some of the Dantesque visions of *The Inferno,* in which hell becomes a metaphor for certain worldly experiences.

Cherniavsky   This is a personal reading, but in *The Betrayal* the immediate setting is Edmonton—a city which, to the protagonist Stappler at least, seems to be a spiritual and cultural desert. Do you think Stappler would regard the Edmonton of 1975 in this light?

Kreisel   I don't think that such a reading, even for the time, is necessarily accurate. The true desert is in Stappler's heart; so naturally he sees the mid-winter landscape as a reflection of his own inner state. I think it would be truer to look at Lerner, whose response is much more positive to the city and to the development of the University. I repeat that Stappler's desolation is within himself, and the outside world never moves his inner self. I never did regard Edmonton as a waste land at all; it was very welcoming to me certainly, and I've always been grateful for this. It's always had an interesting and rather rich life of music and drama, and from the beginning I was involved in the Studio Theatre and its early productions. Naturally, there's been a tremendous development in the last fifteen years as the city grew and affluence made it possible to do things that couldn't be done before; so I think it would be wrong to read what Stappler sees as an absolutely accurate reflection of an objective reality.

Cherniavsky   What would you now say are the main strengths and weaknesses of *The Betrayal?*

Kreisel   That's a difficult question because I haven't re-read the work, except for certain extracts at public readings. I don't normally re-read my work; I like to think about other things. But I would say its main theme of course is that of betrayal, not only of a specific betrayal but of broken promises in the modern world. The book's main strength, I think, is the relationship of a single event on a personal level to the larger inhumanities that have taken place, particularly in the European world. It's very hard for me to say what its successes or failures are. I suppose I could, if I re-read it quite objectively, now reach some more conclusions but I really think that's better left for others.

Cherniavsky   You made a number of references, oblique and sometimes direct, to other writers. Were you aware of this at the time?

Kreisel   Oh yes, I think in many instances I was and in others I suppose I used things unconsciously. Perhaps it's a weakness of the book. People have also said that the figures in *The Betrayal* are not as fully rounded as in *The Rich Man*, and I think that's probably true because they are figures in a morality tale so that they are less three-dimensional, if that is the right word to use, than they would have been in other situations. It's an austere book.

Cherniavsky   Have readers raised any ambiguities or points of interpretation in *The Betrayal* with you?

Kreisel   I think the role of Lerner has not been fully understood although Sidney Warhaft in his introduction to the New Canadian Library edition does a perceptive analysis of that. At the ending of the book, Stappler plays the hero and, finally, stands as a positive hero. I myself had ambiguous feelings about that ending. I saw his whole action as an exotic romantic escape that one finds quite often in the nineteenth century novel. I myself was convinced that's what he would have done. I wrote that conclusion in a great burst of passion over only two or three days, hardly sleeping at all. I don't know whether it comes off.

Mervin Butovsky
Interview with Henry Kreisel

Butovsky You were born in Vienna which means that of all the Canadian-Jewish writers, you're probably the only one who is not of Eastern European background.

Kreisel Well, that is partly true. Vienna, strictly speaking, is not in the East, but my family was an Eastern European family. My mother was born in Poland and my father was born in Rumania. I think my mother came to Vienna in 1916 during the War. Her father had three young daughters still living at home; he had sons as well, but they were older and they were in the army. Rosa, the oldest surviving daughter, told me, a few months ago, how her father was really concerned about what might happen to the daughters at that time, with soldiers moving back and forth. So he bundled them all off to Vienna, the Austrian capital of the region they lived in, Galicia. They were Eastern immigrants, as it were. They stayed in Vienna, in Leopoldstadt, which was very much the Yiddish centre, the ghetto, if you like, and I grew up there.

Butovsky So your parents and family were Yiddish-speaking?

Kreisel Yes, the entire family spoke Yiddish. My mother and my father used to speak German to each other and we spoke German to my grandmother, but she spoke Yiddish to us. I knew Yiddish from the very beginning. But I didn't really speak Yiddish until I came to Canada, curiously enough. It was really in Toronto that I sometimes spoke Yiddish to people who couldn't speak English. In Austria I spoke German essentially, but there were a lot of Yiddish-speakers around me and I remember going to the Yiddish theatre with my mother. I went, of course, to the great German theatres as well, but we went to the Yiddish theatre too. So, I was surrounded by Eastern-European Yiddish culture, although it is true I am not, myself, Eastern born. I would really be like a second generation Canadian writer—like, say, A.M. Klein, who came to Canada as an infant. So, to that extent, I am really not such an exception. I don't come from an assimilated Austrian or German family but from a very strong Yiddish family and my roots emotionally go back to Eastern Europe, in the shtetl.

Butovsky Were your parents still traditional in their religious beliefs?

Kreisel My mother was very traditional; my father less so. But, my grandparents had a very strong influence on me, particularly my grandmother. My grandfather died when I was about ten, I think, but I have very strong memories of him as well as of the time when I used to go to shul* with him. My grandmother was a very, very strict Orthodox Jew who wore a sheitl.** So I have a very strong Orthodox background, although I have long since moved away from Orthodoxy. My mother was fairly strongly Orthodox. My father saw himself as a modern man and he went to shul on Yom Kippur and Rosh Hashanah and maybe on some other holy days.

Butovsky Did you draw upon your grandparents for *The Rich Man* family?

Kreisel Yes. I drew on my grandmother particularly, and I drew on the family up to a point—for the sisters particularly; the older sister is modelled on my oldest aunt. There were four sisters who lived in Vienna and they were very close and they used to come to my grandmother all the time. So, I drew on that and drew on a visit of my Uncle Adolph, who went to the States, early on, around 1918 or 1919, right after the War. He went to the States and came back to Vienna—it must have been in 1930 or so, after they had not seen him for more than ten years. It may have been later, maybe 1933. So, I drew on that, on his return. But, the story itself, the germ of the story itself came from Toronto, because I worked during the first year of my stay in Toronto in a hotel in Muskoka and I got to know a lot of people. It was a hotel that catered to lower middle-class and working-class people. A lot of people who worked at Tip Top Tailors came there. And I know the germ of a story was someone saying to me—'see these guys; well, before the War they saved up money and then they would be able to get back to Europe and they would be the rich men.' And, that was the germ,

---

shul: small synagogue
**sheitl:* Orthodox Jewish women cut their hair and wear a wig (*sheitl*)

actually, of the story. When I began to work with that I used certain aspects of the political setting as well: Vienna just before the disaster and after the events of 1934, when the Dollfuss regime finished the Socialists, as it were, and established a kind of dictatorship. Well, it was a dictatorship, I guess, of the 'blacks' (the Christian Democrats were called 'blacks'; the Socialists were 'reds').

Butovsky Your early education in Vienna, was it a Jewish traditional education?

Kreisel Yes, in part. I didn't go to a Jewish school; I went to the normal public schools, to the Volksschule first and then to a Gymnasium. But I had the traditional Cheder education for many years, two hours a day every afternoon, so that I learned the traditional things, which were almost Yeshiva-like. I mean, I learned the Gemorrah, Rashi, and so on; so, it was a fairly strong traditional Jewish education, just short of a Yeshiva.

Butovsky Were you, as a child of East-European immigrants in Vienna, aware of a conflict between your culture and Viennese culture? Did you feel an outsider in those days?

Kreisel Yes. I think one felt that up to a point, partly because anti-Semitism was quite strong in Vienna. It was traditionally strong and had become stronger after the wave of immigration from the East. These were people who were quite distinct, in a way, a lot of Hassidim, who wore the long caftan and the shtreimels. Our neighbourhood had a very strong Eastern European shtetl atmosphere, so I was always aware of differences. But, we had a very strong sense of our identity, and I never felt alienated. We felt we also belonged to Viennese culture, because we went to the public schools. The school that I went to was very mixed, both the elementary and the middle school, so that we always had contact with the total population and, at the same time, we had a very strong sense of our own roots. And, as I said, we would go to the Yiddish theatres (and there would be Yiddish writers coming through and giving readings) and we would also go to the great state theatres. So, I had both the great German and the international repertoire in the opera and in the theatres—it was very rich. You knew at the time, and it became more apparent later, that it was a rich cultural tradition.

Butovsky   How did the events in the late thirties, at the time of the Nazi invasion of Vienna affect you personally and what transpired?

Kreisel   Well, of course, that ended any thought that one could stay. It was different to some extent from the experiences in Germany, because in Germany the transition from the Weimar Republic to the Nazis, though swift, was not then quite so radical. It took the Nazis a few years, to about 1936 or 1937, to begin the real Draconian process. The Nuremburg Laws, for example, came into effect in 1935 or 1936; and, in fact, after the first fear in 1933, when some German Jews left, a fair number— I don't think this is widely known—actually returned because they thought it wasn't so bad; one could survive. The full murderousness of the regime had not yet really manifested itself. That came only after the full consolidation of power by Hitler, after the 1934 events when he killed off Roehm and established his absolute power over the Party and only then began to move very quickly. By 1938, of course, he had begun to put his program into full force. When he took over Austria, there was no period of grace. The full fury of the anti-Semitic attacks began, literally, the day after the German armies came in. It was a very traumatic experience because the Austrian population moved very strongly over to Hitler. The endemic anti-Semitism burst into flames. We were physically attacked in school and this was a terrible shock, because here were people we thought were our friends, boys who had been with us for ten years, often, through Volksschule, through the Gymnasium, who suddenly turned around and became—not all, but most— virulent. So, it was clear to the Austrian Jews, from the beginning, that there was no hope. Though the Austrian Jews were, to some extent, fortunate; the Polish Jews had no chance of escape since they were, of course, caught in the War, but the Austrian Jews had some chance, if they could get visas. And here we were lucky because my mother had relatives in England. She had a niece there (who was not much younger than she), the oldest daughter of her sister, and her family immediately began to work to get us out. They decided that they would first take out the two oldest children: myself and a cousin. So I was lucky. I got out in July of 1938, four or five months after the Anschluss. My brother came out in January of 1939 with my aunt. My parents had a number of harrowing experiences. They had attempted to get out illegally. For a while the Belgian and Dutch governments tacitly allowed people to come in; if you had a passport, they would let you in and then there were relief agencies and so on. It seemed that it was not going to be possible for my cousin to bring everybody out, because the British Home Office was beginning to make certain noises—'O.K., you have already brought a younger Aunt. . . . You have already brought out four or five . . . that is enough!' We could not go to the United States where my father had relatives and my mother had a brother because my father was born in Rumania and, as you know, immigration into the United States was determined by place of birth and the Rumanian quota was locked up for one hundred years or so. There was absolutely no chance of my father getting a visa to the United States. They decided to go to Belgium and to do this illegal bit;—as a matter of fact I use this in *The Betrayal*—they paid but something happened. I don't know exactly what happened, maybe this particular person was really corrupt—I have invented a fable for it—but they certainly were not able to cross. When they came to the border they were taken off the train and my mother was sent to a women's concentration camp and my father was sent to Dachau. For my mother, it was a terrible, terrible experience. She had been such a *frumme Frau*,* such an orthodox woman and a very, very proper person. For her, suddenly to find herself—as she told me—with prostitutes and criminals, was something that she never ever got over. It was something unspeakable, a Kafka situation. She had somehow been judged and taken to concentration camp. And then my relatives in England really began to work. They put everything they had into trying to get them out. It was still possible during those first few months for people to be released from concentration camps, if they had a valid visa. So I'm really very grateful to them. They really pulled out all the stops; they mobilized members of Parliament, everybody they knew or could get access to, to get a visa for these two people and they were successful in July of 1939, a few weeks before the War. They sent

---

frumme Frau: pious lady

the visa and my parents were both released and got on a train and came to England. I think they arrived in England at the beginning of July, 1939, and, of course, the War began in August. After that, it would have been finished. I used the general atmosphere of those days for *The Betrayal.*

Butovsky   Did you continue your schooling in England?

Kreisel   No, I went to work in a factory. I didn't know English well enough, and in any case, times were very difficult and I needed to earn some money. I didn't want to be completely a burden on my relatives, because they had other obligations and I wanted them to help other people. So, I went to work, and I didn't actually start my schooling again until I came to Toronto in 1941. So from 1938 to 1940 I was working; and, in retrospect, I think it was a good thing.

Butovsky   You came over to Canada as part of a group of wartime internees?

Kreisel   Yes. I was part of the internees group. As a matter of fact, I found the diary that I kept then a few years ago. Sheila Watson who was one of the editors of the *white pelican* asked to publish it and it was fairly extensively quoted in Eric Koch's recent book, *Deemed Suspect*. The diary became an historical document; once it was out, archives all over the place wrote me.

Butovsky   What were your circumstances when you arrived in Canada?

Kreisel   At first, we were simply internees, and then for about one year we were actually designated as 'Prisoners of War'! It is all laid out in the diary.

Butovsky   Did that experience condition your feelings for Canada or England?

Kreisel   Well, I was very Anglophile and, in a sense, have remained an Anglophile, because I saw England as a saviour. I thought the English were, on the whole, generous; not, in retrospect, when I read the documents, as generous as they might have been, but more generous, curiously enough, than Canada.

Canada was tightly shut. Nobody thought of coming to Canada, because the doors were really closed; they were not accepting any refugees at all. So, when we were interned in England, the first feeling was of a kind of betrayal, because here we were, refugees, anti-Hitler certainly, and suddenly we found ourselves interned by the other side as enemy aliens. Eric Koch quotes one of the officers in Canada as saying that when he first saw the refugees or so-called 'Prisoners of War'—he didn't know who they were, but he could see that these were Jews, because a lot of Orthodox Jews were with us—he is supposed to have said: 'I didn't know so many Jews were Nazis!' But, I never—nor the internees as a whole—blamed Canada, because while we might have blamed Canada for not letting people in, we realized that, as far as the internment itself was concerned, the responsibility was England's. Canada simply agreed to accept a certain number of prisoners of war but England didn't have enough prisoners of war at the time. They were trying to get out of France and wherever else they were, and they were not taking any prisoners in. So they just made up the number Canada had agreed to with civilian internees. But as far as Canadians were concerned, it wasn't part of the deal. When they got these people they really didn't know what to do with them. So, insofar as any responsibility has to be assigned, it is really England's, because Canada was merely the agent acting for England. This situation lasted about one year, until it became known to the Jewish Congress, the Quakers, and other groups, who pressed the government to release these people. They asked in effect, what are you doing to these people? First, they were going to send us all back, but then shipping space was scarce. My father was allowed to go back for compassionate reasons, because my mother and brother were there, but I stayed. In retrospect, it was a very lucky break, though I didn't know that at the time.

Butovsky   So, you were incarcerated for over one year?

Kreisel   Yes. From May, 1940, until November, 1941; a year and one-half.

Butovsky   Would you say the treatment was relatively humane?

Kreisel   Yes. The treatment was relatively humane where I was in the camps. But, there were a few camps . . . again, the treatment was humane but . . . Eric Koch, in his book, says that one camp, Camp 'R', had a mixed Nazi and Jewish population and there it was pretty dicey for a few months until they divided the people. But, basically, I would say the treatment was humane. Certainly, my father, who had been in Dachau, thought he was, as he called it, in a sanatorium, compared to the treatment he had experienced in Dachau and even that was before the death camps were instituted. He really thought it was like a holiday camp compared to that. There were some people who became bitter because they had been torn away from careers, people who had been professionals and had had positions in England. I had been pulled out of a factory and so I didn't think I had given up a terribly great position.

Butovsky   Was it, in fact, a labour camp?

Kreisel   No. It wasn't a labour camp though they did have work, of course. In New Brunswick, we cut trees and worked in the forests; in Quebec, we made nets and performed other duties. We were paid twenty cents a day. There were also facilities for studying, curiously enough, and some people prepared themselves for matriculation. I didn't. I wanted to do my own thing. I began to write there and I read a tremendous amount.

Butovsky   Was your first writing personal accounts of your experience?

Kreisel   Some of it, but most of it wasn't. I obviously make use of autobiographical experiences, but I am not an autobiographical writer in the sense in which Thomas Wolfe was or D.H. Lawrence was.

In fact, I remember once giving a reading at Simon Fraser and the person who introduced me, who had met me in 1950 or 1951 when I taught at the University of British Columbia, said that he had been astonished when he met me because he had always imagined an older person had written *The Rich Man*. He was astonished because it wasn't the kind of book that a twenty-three-year-old usually writes. It didn't deal with awakening sexuality, or the kind of autobiographical themes that you would expect a very young man to be concerned with. Recently I was looking over some of the stuff that I had written in the internment camp, and the stories were not, in general, autobiographical. I did write some poems that were directly concerned with the internment experience, but only a few.

Butovsky   Where did you resume your education, and what did you study?

Kreisel   Well, when I resumed my education, I first had to finish off matriculation because I didn't have that, so I went to Harbord Collegiate in Toronto, a school that had a very large Jewish student body. There were a lot of first generation and second generation students. It was a marvellous academic school, whose students throughout the 1930s and 1940s had carried off a lion's share of scholarships. They were highly motivated and I immediately found myself like a fish in water because these were people who came out of the same tradition as I did. So I entered Harbord in November, 1941, and wrote my senior matriculation in 1942. I quickly caught up in the languages— Latin, Greek, English—and History. I won a four-year scholarship to the University of Toronto. I finished the year and then went off to the University of Toronto for I had made up my mind during the internment period that I wanted to study English. I really had switched over into English and made it my first language. I had decided that I would write in English, and I really wanted to learn the English literary tradition, so I entered the department of English language and literature. And, I remember Malcolm Wallace—he became a good friend of mine later on—wondering whether that was the right field for me to enter, because I hadn't studied English for long. I had attended a classics Gymnasium, where the languages were Latin and Greek, so I only began learning English in England. This was only four years before, and so he wondered whether I was really in the right field. Shouldn't I be in modern languages or in classics? But I said, 'No, no, that is not what I want,' and it worked out. As a matter of fact, I headed the class at university.

Butovsky   Was part of your determination to study English based on your desire to be a writer?

Kreisel   Yes. I think I wanted to be a writer and I wanted to write in English because I knew I would not go back to Austria under any circumstances. I cut that off. I knew that I wanted to live my life here and for psychological, emotional reasons also, I wanted to shed that other life. I didn't, as some people did in the camps, turn against the German language. I felt: why should they take Goethe and Schiller away from me? I was a great admirer of Schiller's, particularly of the *Sturm und Drang* period. I was a great admirer of his idealistic philosophy. Why should I give away what belonged to me as well? Thomas Mann belonged to me too, so I didn't want to say that I would have nothing to do with our language. Kafka belonged to me, so why give that away? They had taken enough away without taking away some of our consciousness. On the other hand, I wanted to integrate myself into a living culture and not get lost in nostalgia. I was too young and all the nostalgia was bad. Actually, I always see Vienna in ironically ambiguous terms— it is the city of light, but it is also the city of darkness. I think it is also the waste land city for me.

When I made this conscious decision for English, I wanted to know the English tradition thoroughly, not just what you could pick up in the street, but from the inside out. I had no intention, by the way, of ever becoming an English professor, that wasn't my reason. As a matter of fact, most people thought I was rather mad to do it; whoever heard of someone studying English around College and Spadina, where I lived? What kind of a 'mishagas' is that, studying English? What are you going to do with that? Because, as you know, universities had not hired anybody for twenty years at that time. They certainly never hired a Jew.

So mine was seen as a quixotic move, particularly by my parents. I kept getting letters saying why don't you study law or medicine or accounting, and I would have to defend myself and say this is what I want to do and I don't know what I am going to do with it. I was doing my Master's Degree in 1947—I had a fellowship then at the U. of T.—so I thought that I would finish that and try to get a job at the CBC or something. Then suddenly, universities opened up in 1946, in 1947, 1948, because the veterans were coming back. I wanted to get married—had met Esther—and I heard there were jobs available, so I went to Professor Woodhouse—I had been his fair-haired boy—and

said that I had heard there were jobs available and perhaps he
could recommend me for such a job because I would like to
teach for a while and earn some money, and then decide
whether I wanted to go on and do some further work. And he
looked at me and said, 'I will send you to Alberta!' He was a
kind of czar of English studies because Toronto was the only
graduate school and everybody was running to him and
suddenly they had these masses of students, and they needed
instructors. And, he said, 'I will give them only your name,' and
the reason for that as he told me later, was that if he gave them
two names there was a possibility they would not take the Jew.
But he wanted me to have this job and, indeed, they wrote to me
and I wrote back and gave them the straight goods. I gave them
my background, they offered me a post, and that is how I came to
be here. It was a two-year job, a temporary job. As you can see,
after thirty-four years, I am still here. But, when Esther and I
first came out, the reception here was very warm and we were
immediately accepted into the small university community, and
treated as if we belonged. So, we have had a very warm spot in
our hearts for this place and whenever opportunities came to go
back east or go to Vancouver, we always decided against it—I
think, because of that reception. What a contrast to Austria, and
quite a contrast even to Toronto, although I have very warm
feelings for Toronto for much the same reason: in Austria—
when I was a boy—Jews were specifically excluded from
scholarships, but here I was a foreigner, a Jew, and I won the
scholarships that I was capable of winning. So I have always
had a very warm feeling for Canada, because this country gave
me, and others too, opportunities that Europe did not give.

Butovsky   Does your literary career begin with the early writing in
the internment camp?

Kreisel   It really begins in Austria, because I remember writing
when I was twelve or thirteen. I wanted to write and I used to
write quite a lot of stories in German. In a way, I always was
drawn to writing, to the drama. I was obsessed with the theatre.
In some ways, I have always wished I had written for the theatre.
I have written occasionally for CBC drama, and one play, *He
Who Sells His Shadow*, CBC did twice on the old Wednesday
night 'Stage Series.' But, when I first came to Toronto, then

here to Alberta, drama in Canada was pretty moribund. There were really no opportunities, so I moved into other forms of writing, but drama has always been a great attraction for me.

Butovsky Who would your literary mentors have been in those early days? Who would you have considered to be models for your work?

Kreisel In the early days, I think, the people I read in the camps were people like Thomas Mann. I think he was a model, particularly his novellas. And Kafka was a model. In this diary I mentioned, Sheila Watson has also published an excerpt from a novel I did in camp—although I have never been able to read it through again. But, she looked at it and took this particular excerpt, which is very Kafka-like in feeling. I think he was a strong influence on me as well as the Russian writers, Tolstoy and Dostoevsky. I used to read them a lot and some of the modern Americans like Hemingway and Steinbeck and there was a period also when I liked—because Bob Weaver liked him a lot and got me to read him—James T. Farrell. I used to read quite a lot of Farrell and not so much of Faulkner, but Faulkner was part of my M.A. thesis, and Fitzgerald. Then, later on, Conrad became a major influence, but he was, from the beginning, a great presence.

When I was in camp and was beginning to consider writing in English, I had a very clear consciousness that this was a major undertaking. In actual fact, it wasn't all that rare. Lots of people have switched languages. But it's sufficiently unusual because most people stay with the language which is theirs from birth. So, Conrad became a presence. I held on to his image even though I didn't have any Conrad novels: nobody had brought any to camp. They brought Tolstoy, there was a lot of Thomas Mann around and Shakespeare and Dickens, and so on. But I could never get a Conrad novel. Even so, he became a guiding light. He was somebody who had done it and had become a great master.

Butovsky Had you any acquaintance with any Hebrew or Yiddish writers?

Kreisel I was acquainted with the major Yiddish writers. I knew
Sholom Aleichem. In fact I had a very, very close acquaintance
with him, because in my aunt's house, in my grandmother's
house and in their neighbours' houses, people used to get
together on a Saturday night after Shabbos and there were two
or three people who could read Sholom Aleichem. And they
used to read his stories and I used to go and I loved to hear them.
I have often read Sholom Aleichem to groups myself, but in
English, because I cannot read Yiddish well enough and there
wouldn't be enough people to understand it anyway, but I used
to hear the stories in Yiddish. Then we used to read Sholom
Asch a lot; I even remember Sholom Asch coming to Vienna.
People came from all over to hear him. The hall was packed,
and he read in Yiddish from his short stories. I also heard David
Opatoshu when he came. And then there were the stories of
Peretz and Mendele Mokher Sforim. So, I knew pretty well all of
the great Yiddish writers, because my mother read and talked
about them. People also got together at each other's houses to
read other 'Meinsalich,' 'little stories,' as they were called. And, I
still remember that when I was in Toronto—my wife's family
came from Eastern Europe as well—they got together in people's
houses and they used to read the stories from *Forward,* the New
York Yiddish newspaper. I remember one evening, I was
listening to one lady who was reading a story while the others
really listened; it was a soap-opera story about how a man got a
girl into trouble and then left her with a child and I remember
one woman crying out: 'Man darf ihm stechen mit ein messer'
('He should be stabbed with a knife'); she really got upset. I
think I stand in that Yiddish tradition of reading aloud.

Butovsky This would have been parallel to your own education in
German and in German literature?

Kreisel Yes, that is right.

Butovsky Were you aware of Canadian writers in your early stage
of development?

Kreisel When I was in camp, I wanted to read some Canadian
writers because consciousness comes to me through writers
rather than through reading of history, although I like to read
history as well; but there weren't any of their books in the camp.

When I came to Toronto and went to Harbord, there were one or two little items by Canadian writers in the readers that we had. At the university, I asked some of my friends who were studying English literature to tell me who were some of the Canadian writers I should read, and they knew virtually nothing. Somebody mentioned Morley Callaghan who was at that time trying to disguise the fact that he was a Canadian writer by setting his stories in a general city-scape which could be taken for American. And I took a course in the first year which was misnamed 'American and Canadian Literature.' I say misnamed because Canadian literature got one week at the end—Claude Bissell came in to give it. The other part on American literature was given by McGillivray, but he allowed me to write an essay on A.M. Klein who had just published *Hath Not A Jew.* The very first essay I wrote in Toronto was on Klein. Klein became one of my great culture heroes, because he showed me that you could use your culture, you could use your tradition and you didn't have to be afraid; you didn't have to try and invent something for the audience, but could work out of your own tradition—he had a very important psychological impact.

And I began to read further; then Robert Weaver and I and a few others started the 'Modern Letters Club' in Toronto. Essentially, it was to be a club where we could read our own stuff, but we also discussed literature, mostly American literature, mind you. But we also began to ask: where are the Canadian writers? It was at that time that I really began to read Canadian writers. Of course, I knew Pratt at the University and then got to know Frye, and at that time one really got to know them. I used to go and have a beer with Frye and we've remained friends. And, you know, you could really talk to these people, the way I see and talk to you now. I used to go out with the boys at University College and we used to go over to Victoria College and talk to Pratt. Philip Child was my mentor—he supervised my Master's thesis—and he wrote a number of novels which I knew, too. I began to be **involved** in Canadian literature, with the actual practitioners; then, I met Frank Scott, P.K. Page, Earle Birney, and so on.

Butovsky   On the question of being able to address your own background: did you ever sense that there was some sort of contradiction or, at least, difficulty, in addressing a Jewish life in terms of English literature, a literature which in itself had incorporated certain stereotypical images of Jews? Was there something one had to overcome before being able to draw upon one's personal life in writing?

Kreisel   Yes, up to a point there was. The question arose: when they speak, how should they speak? I am not sure that I solved that problem in *The Rich Man*, but I knew I didn't want my characters to speak as sort of caricatures and so when they speak there are rhythms. The German or Yiddish is translated into speech rhythms rather than into some kind of pidgin English. Yes, I think I felt there was some kind of a problem there of how to render people without making them ridiculous or making them into clowns.

Butovsky   Because the use of an accent would usually be the signal for comedy?

Kreisel   Yes. The accent could be a signal for comedy and I felt that to be a problem. Later on, the Jewish writers became almost dominant in American literature and that was no longer a problem, but in the forties it still was. Still, I felt that that was the thing I knew and, ultimately, it was the thing that I had to express.

Butovsky   As you said before, your writing *The Rich Man* was an uncommon situation because it is a young man's novel where the protagonist is a middle-aged man, which means, I suppose, you felt compelled to address yourself to that subject despite the fact that there might have been personal experiences that were more immediate.

Kreisel   I didn't want the family simply to be a replica of my family, but a family such as I had known. It was a very typical Jewish family in Austria at the time and not anything unique. A number of sisters living close to their mother—that was how families lived, essentially a shtetl family. So I didn't think that there was a problem of addressing the subject itself. I felt that the subject that had emerged as I was working with it had a vitality of its own, and that the experience was important enough within its own frame that I didn't have to apologize for it.

Butovsky   I am just wondering where the self-confidence came from at twenty-three years of age.

Kreisel   I've thought of that too. I began the first sketches of *The Rich Man*—I know exactly when—in the summer of 1944. So I was twenty-two. I was actually going to get a summer job in a factory or wherever, and I was going to start to write a short story. I was looking for a job and I was sketching events and suddenly I thought maybe there was something more there than a short story. So, I went to my sponsor at that time, Mrs. Mendel—I dedicated the book to her—a very aristocratic German-Jewish lady. They had come out in 1933. Her son-in-law was a Professor of Biochemistry at Toronto. She belonged to that very assimilated upper middle-class German-Jewish group. They were not religious Jews, but they felt they were Jews, the same circle from which Thomas Mann's wife, Katia, came, very aristocratic. Here I was, a little Eastern Jewish boy and they were wonderful to me. They got me out of the camp. They sponsored me and helped me. So, I went to her and I told her that I had something I would like to write; would she be willing to give me my allowance over the summer—she gave me $40.00 a month. It was wonderful because one could live on it, and I earned some extra money and I had my scholarships and so I didn't need all that much, but I needed three or four months of support—in other words, about $200.00. And she immediately said yes, was more than pleased to do it and she was very excited. So, I got great support from her. I used to go out—she lived in Oakville—every two or three weeks and I would read to her what I had written; so I was reading *The Rich Man* to her as it was being written. She was terrific. She had a marvellous Picasso which is now in the Toronto Art Gallery, a wonderful Picasso of the Blue Period, a woman kneeling with her head down. So there was this Picasso behind me, while I was reading *The Rich Man*. She would sit with her shawl about her shoulders. It was nice to have a Picasso there, simply just there. That was the first version and then I did a second version around 1948, I guess, when I was here. Then reworked it; but the first drafts were done in 1944, when I was twenty-two. How did we get on to this?

Butovsky   I was asking about the self-confidence you had at the age of twenty-two.

Kreisel   I myself am sort of amazed, but I think that there was such a strong psychological drive, not only to achieve something, but also to prove that I could do it. Otherwise how could I have entered the course in English language and literature at the University of Toronto if I didn't have some kind of absolute self-confidence? I've thought about it and I think that the very strong belief in my capabilities was inculcated by my mother. I think that gave me strength.

Butovsky   Do you think it was her influence also that set you in the direction of cultural vocation rather than success per se?

Kreisel   Yes. I think so, because success, per se, was not of great interest to her—mind you, she wrote me letters saying, why don't you go into law and so on—but she never minded that I did something else, and neither did my father. She was very strongly interested in cultural affairs and also had a strong sense of a Jewish literary tradition. This has remained strong in me even though I'm not a practicing Jew who goes to the synagogue every Friday and Saturday. But I've retained a very strong Jewish consciousness which also gives me this feeling that I come out of a great tradition; that was always there. The Yiddish tradition. And the Biblical tradition which was strong. So I think there was this confidence that even though I didn't naturally belong, say, to the English tradition, I belonged to a strong literary tradition, that I was doing something which was part of the people from whom I came.

Butovsky   To what extent is your literary impulse, rooted in its attachment to this rich cultural and historical tradition, a response to the conditions that sought to destroy it? In effect, both *The Rich Man* and *The Betrayal* are retrospective novels; they seem to reclaim a past which has been lost.

Kreisel   In retrospect, I would say that that was true. I wouldn't say that I was conscious of it when I was doing it, but I think it was true. I have not been as prolific a writer as sometimes I would like to have been and that was in part because I can only write when I feel something of real importance has to be said. I would never have been able, I think, to have been a professional writer who is out there writing. That may be good, that may be bad, but I was also driven to do a lot of other things.

I also wanted to be within a community and have the status that this community can confer, so I wasn't only a writer, but a scholar, teacher, administrator. There have been long periods when I didn't write much. In part that was because I really was busy; as you know, if you have a job like that of a Dean or Vice-President, in the university, you really are busy. On the other hand, I have to be honest and say that maybe I wanted to be busy, for whatever reason, because nobody forced me. I could have said no, I don't want to do it any more; I am doing something else. I don't know. I cannot analyze myself that well because sometimes I don't want to, particularly. The fact is I did other things and my time was so fully occupied that I didn't write. But then the impulses came back. I knew I had to get out of administration and back to literature.

Butovsky In your early reading, was there a place for American-Jewish writers? Were you familiar with Michael Gold or Ludwig Lewisohn or Meyer Levin?

Kreisel I really got to know those writers in Toronto. I remember reading *Jews Without Money*, and I remember reading Lewisohn's *Up Stream*.

Butovsky Did you read *The Island Within?*

Kreisel Yes. I read *The Island Within* as well, and Levin's *The Old Bunch*.

Butovsky Do you think these books had an influence on you?

Kreisel Less, I think, than the Yiddish writers, actually. I used to read Zangwill, too—he has been nearly forgotten now—I read *Children of the Ghetto*. When I began to be conscious of what I wanted to do, naturally, I read people who had written about similar things. I know I read Michael Gold in the forties, but I don't remember that being a real sort of influence.

Butovsky As a student of English literature, were you inclined toward particular authors that might have served as models for you?

Kreisel Yes. I was inclined toward the moderns and for this reason:

I was never a conventional scholar, although I have written a fair amount of stuff on Canadian and English literature. I decided I was going to use my scholarly work to help in my creative work, that is, I was going to choose topics that would have some importance for me as a creative writer. When I prepared my M.A. topic at Toronto, I wanted to explore the realistic tradition because I saw myself writing in that tradition and even, to some extent, in the naturalistic tradition. But I wasn't a naturalist and I knew that—I wanted to explore the realistic mode and to look at various writers and how they had used the realistic method. So I proposed a topic to Child and he agreed on the topic 'Aspects of Realism in the Modern American Novel.' I chose Dreiser and Norris, and some of the early realists. I looked at the way they approached their subject and the way they dealt with reality. And then I did a chapter on Faulkner, particularly on *As I Lay Dying*, the early novel which was a kind of interiorization, a realism of stream-of-consciousness. And, then I did Steinbeck because of his biological attitude to realism, the biological terms which he used to describe society, and also because I liked him at the time. I liked reading *The Grapes of Wrath* and *Tortilla Flat* and others. So, I used these novels to make clear to me where I stood because, by that time, the first drafts of *The Rich Man* were being written and I wanted to know what I was doing. I wanted to explore the ways in which writers use the realistic method, so the thesis, in a sense, was not simply a scholarly exercise, but also an attempt to clarify ideas for myself. Later, I knew that if I was going to stay in the university I would have to get a Ph.D., so I went to England. I wanted to work with Jacob Isaacs. I had read some of his works and I felt we would be *sympatico,* and it turned out that we were, although many people often didn't like him.

Butovsky   Was he at the University of London at that time?

Kreisel   Yes. He had been in Jerusalem and then London. He was a very difficult man for some people. When I told Woodhouse and the others that I was going to work with him, they almost had a fit. He was known as a very erratic person and at London if you don't hit it off with a supervisor, that is curtains! Luckily we hit it off. For my Ph.D. I wanted to explore the condition of exile and alienation because, again, it was something I felt I was working through—and so, in fact, my Ph.D. thesis was on the theme of exile and alienation in modern literature, and dealt with Conrad, Joyce, D.H. Lawrence, and Virginia Woolf. Joyce and Conrad were the two writers that I particularly liked. And when I turned to poetry, I liked Yeats and Eliot very much. I also liked the realistic writers. I would find it a bit difficult to read them now, but at that time Bennett and Wells and others were powerful. So, these were also influences.

Butovsky   Did you have any difficulty with what would be considered strong anti-Semitic elements among some of these modern classic writers like Lawrence and Eliot?

Kreisel   Yes, I do. Just as I have some difficulty with Wagner—and I happen to like Wagner's music—, but one has to say also that one cannot lump all of anti-Semitism into Hitlerian anti-Semitism. One cannot accept it, but one has to come to terms with it. I have never been able to come to terms with Pound's anti-Semitism for different reasons.

Butovsky   Because he was a confirmed fascist?

Kreisel   Yes. But, the others, certainly Lawrence, had Jewish friends and so it wasn't the same kind of animosity.

Butovsky   I was struck by the fact that in *The Betrayal* you used literary quotations from T.S. Eliot. Would this reflect your own leaning at that time?

Kreisel   Well, in part and also, since I consciously saw *The Betrayal* as a Waste Land theme and an exploration of Waste Land attitudes, I used them. I still think 'The Waste Land' is a very great poem and again, I think, there are Conradian echoes as well, particularly, in *The Betrayal*, echoes from *Lord Jim* and *Under Western Eyes* and *Heart of Darkness*, the conscience-stricken human being, who cannot forgive himself for having failed at the moment of crisis. . . .

Butovsky   In *The Betrayal* you comment on the relationship between the Canadian sensibility and the European, the Canadian being innocent without experience of evil while the European is endowed with a knowledge of human tragedy. As a writer of Jewish experience, do you feel that Jewish consciousness, too, speaks out of a kind of experience which Canadians were untouched by when you first met them?

Kreisel   Why, sure. I may have simplified almost too much, but to some extent when I came West there was a kind of innocence here, particularly at that time; we hadn't been tested in the same way.

Butovsky   Because the war was so remote?

Kreisel   The war was remote and, to some extent there was a positive element to it, because it brought prosperity in one sense. I did feel a lot of the war problems were very, very remote to people. I think things have somewhat changed now, we have come into the mainstream. Once again, we didn't have the kind of experience that the United States had with Vietnam, so we have been able to keep certain illusions of innocence. Canadians tend to think of themselves as not racially biased and so on, which is an illusion, actually. They just have not been tested in the same way as, say, the Americans were or the British now are. We are beginning now, as we become more of a multi-racial society, to face certain tests also. Then we were, to some extent, out of the mainstream, we were onlookers . . . Jewish-Canadians had, in fact, only vicariously been through the wringer.

I know from my wife's situation that no Jew could escape the Hitler, the Nazi presence, because we all knew that we were not exempt really, that our personal exemption was just an accident. I once said to a friend of mine here—and he was really shocked—that nothing after the Hitler experience was ever able to get to me, because I would always say to myself that it was a miracle, just an accident of fate that I escaped what so many millions had to endure. It was not my doing, it was just luck. But, in a sense, one was really burned.

I remember Elie Wiesel was here a few years ago and I introduced him at a lecture he gave, and we hit it off. He was in the fire, but when he asked me to send him something of my writing, I sent him the two novels and he wrote back to say, 'You know the fire also, even though you weren't directly in it, you know the fire also.' And, that is true, I think, of all of us. Even people like yourself who were born here; nevertheless that was an experience that seared us all.

Butovsky   Did you see your role as a Canadian writer, as the act of being a witness? Did you feel that somehow or other Canadians had to know this too?

Kreisel   I don't know that I ever consciously thought that. I mean, I didn't see myself as a missionary, or a person who had to bring the message. I didn't feel that, but subconsciously or unconsciously, I don't know. Certainly not consciously. I didn't think I had to tell these people, partly because I knew that others—like Wiesel, and the people who had actually come through the worst of it and had miraculously survived—had been through a much more searing experience. They had more of a right. And while I would bear whatever witness I could, I didn't presume, say, that I would awaken the consciousness and the conscience of the wider society, because they were the ones who were already doing it, and what could I do more?

Butovsky   Do you conceive of an audience you're writing to and who might that audience be?

Kreisel   I always had a consciousness of being engaged with a particular theme and sometimes obsessed with it, so that first of all, I write because I feel I have to write, and afterwards I will try and find an outlet. That has not been too difficult for me usually, because I had my places of publication with the *Tamarack Review*, or the CBC or publishers, so I never worried about it. I was lucky that way because *The Rich Man* was immediately taken up. When I showed the first draft to Sybil Hutchinson—she was then the editor for McClelland and Stewart—she was immediately enthusiastic although she thought it needed some more work, and it did. I let it lie for a while and then I reworked it, and then McClelland took it right away. I didn't have to send it to two hundred other publishers. I was lucky that way; I **usually** could publish what I wanted to publish, and I didn't have to worry about what audience I was writing for. It didn't bother me from the start. Once I had made up my mind that I would use—as Klein had shown me you could—my full experience, then I worked and let things happen as they happened.

Butovsky   Would you say that most of your writing to date is inclined toward a subject matter that comes out of your personal experience?

Kreisel   Well, in part. It usually begins with some kind of an incident which makes—for some reason which I am sometimes not even aware of—a very powerful impression that stays with me. That has been my method of working. It stays with me sometimes for years before I begin to work with it. And, then I work it in ways that are dictated by the theme or by personalities that have obsessed me. It usually begins with some kind of experience or some kind of incident that I have known or have experienced, but then it moves from there and as I begin to work with the material I will shape it in ways that seem to make some kind of structure, that seem to make some kind of a coherent whole. So, when someone recently asked me about Klein, I recalled that incident, and I thought: this is something I have wanted to work on for some time, but, I could never quite find the right situation. And, it happened that just after I had written this down, CBC wanted to commission a story for 'Anthology' from me. So, this gave me some added impetus, but if I had not had the impetus already, I would have said no. I'm not just going to sit down and dream something up. If I have a theme that has occupied me and that I feel is right, then I will sit down and work very hard for a long time and slowly—I am a very slow writer—and do it. But, I would not have done it if they had said, 'Write a story.' What story should I write? I couldn't do that. When I've tried to do that, it never comes off. I cannot do it. It's hopeless. So, only if a theme engages me, then I work it. I won't work it autobiographically, because I always try to distance myself from the subject so that I can have an objective view of the situation itself, even though originally I may have been involved as an observer, bystander, or even directly.

Butovsky   I read 'The Homecoming' recently, and I was wondering out of what experience that emerged? Did you intend it as a novel?

Kreisel   Yes. It was originally intended to be a novel and in point of fact McClelland, on the dust jacket of *The Rich Man*, says: 'Second novel is already well under way.' They weren't lying.... That was it.

Butovsky   That notice didn't refer to *The Betrayal?*

Kreisel   No. *The Betrayal* came many years afterwards. *The Betrayal* was not written until the sixties. It referred to 'The Homecoming' which emerged immediately out of the post-War revelations, when the full disaster had become manifest. I wrote a number of chapters actually, only then to give it up because I just wasn't close enough to that experience. I felt that I was inventing things as I went on. Part of it, I think, came through fairly strongly and powerfully, but then later on the invention wasn't good enough.

Butovsky   In what years were you working on this material?

Kreisel   Around 1951, 1952. And, then I took it up later and even worked a little bit on it. I don't think that it can now be a novel, but the theme still haunts me, it didn't go away. I was just not close enough, and other people who had been there were coming out with memoirs and personal accounts. And, as I said to you before, how could I compete?

Butovsky   When you mentioned Klein earlier, were you at all aware of his journalism in those early years? Were you reading his editorials in the *Jewish Chronicle* at that time?

Kreisel   Yes. I read him then, but mostly I read his poems in the *Forum*, I think, and later *The Second Scroll* came out, and *The Rocking Chair*. I really read the books as they came out. I wasn't so fully aware of his journalism as I am now, because Miriam Waddington has been working on it and she has shown me a number of things.

Butovsky   You spoke earlier of your own consciousness of being Jewish. Could you describe what you think that consists of? When you seek to address the Jewish component of yourself, say, how would you describe that element?

Kreisel   I would describe that element in two ways. First of all, and for me centrally, there is the prophetic tradition, the tradition of Jeremiah, the real prophetic tradition of social criticism: an awareness of relationships, an awareness of the Waste Land in human relationships, the awareness that people have to make relationships all the time. You cannot take them for granted.

Relationships are not static; one always has to be conscious of one's own impact on others. One has to be conscious of how others will feel. That, I think, is the prophetic tradition which is a great ethical tradition, and I see that as central to Judaism. I am not saying that other religions or other cultures don't have it, but I think we have it in our tradition. The whole concept, then, of the responsibility of human beings, above all, to each other; through God, if you like, but basically you don't live for God, you live for other people. That, I feel, is central to the tradition.

The other major tradition is simply the historical tradition; the awareness, I think, that I have—I don't think my son has it that strongly, because we haven't kept a traditional Jewish home, but, I think, he has picked up many of our attitudes— that one comes from a long historical line, that no generation is alone, that we don't live for ourselves alone, that there is this long connection with the past. I feel the past very strongly as a part of the present, it defines the present and the present defines the past. This sense that one is not alone, that one has this long, long history and tradition to which one belongs. I think that gives strength, actually, even if one is not a practicing Jew.

Butovsky   If one speaks to a modern generation, or a Canadian-born generation that may not be that directly linked to this tradition in terms of knowledge, custom, or religious persuasion, do you think the tradition still has a vitality even where the past has become more attenuated?

Kreisel   I am not quite sure that it has the same kind of vitality for my son, for example. But at the same time, he knows the tradition because we often talk about it and our own library at home is full of books, history and imaginative literature, that deal with the tradition. One should try, in any case, to link one's self up with an historical tradition, so that one doesn't have the feeling that everything happened yesterday, an 'après moi le deluge' sort of thing.

The other thing, of course, is the awareness of suffering. At least my generation feels that and, at the same time, a certain uneasiness because one knows what has happened in history. I can never be easy. I can never feel secure because at the moment Jewish life is fairly secure here on this continent. I can never feel that this must necessarily always be so. I think my son has a stronger feeling of security than I have, and perhaps you have it too, because you were born here. I think, for me, there is always this element of doubt which expresses itself in a kind of ironic point of view, an element of doubt as to whether, in fact, this is forever. There is so much more in history that has not been that happy, so that one cannot, with absolute certainty, say that we are finished with that. So, there is the sense of being aware of human fate and of the human condition. Again, I am not saying that we are unique—other people have it as well—but I think we have a peculiar view of the human condition that is shaped by this long awareness. One could not have sat there—as I did listening to the stories of pogroms and the stories of Sholom Aleichem and Sholom Asch and others—without having the awareness that there is danger out there. It makes for a kind of wariness and it saves us automatically, I think, from sentimentality. We have sentiment, but the best writers have not been sentimental because they have been aware of the human condition. Sentiment, yes—there is a thin line between them—but not a sentimental vision of life. I take that from the tradition as well. Ultimately, I think also of the veneration for language as such. I have never seen myself as a magician of language, like a Joyce. I have not been that—and it is frustrating sometimes—but we have a sense of the word as being important and of the written word as being important. I think our tradition has taught us that the word is vital and that what you say is important: to name a thing, to say something. Our tradition has made us conscious of that. So, I have secularized the experience, in a sense, because I cannot accept the full range of Orthodox customs. I couldn't do that after 1940, 1941. So, obviously, I have had to make certain emotional adjustments around it, decide what it is in the tradition that I value. Well, I like to read Jewish writers. I like to read the Prophets and I do this all the time. I think that gives me strength.

uncollected
writings

*The drama has always been attractive to Henry Kreisel—he has
frequently acted, for example, in Studio Theatre productions at
the University of Alberta.* He Who Sells His Shadow *arises both
out of his affection for the genre and out of his post-Holocaust
need to reiterate the point that most of us have a **choice** about
the corruption of politics. The only manuscript of the radio
play he has been able to find dates from the autumn of 1956
when CBC broadcast it. That an earlier version existed is
testified to by his vigorous defense of his allegorical use of the
symbol in a 1950 letter to Robert Weaver, published in this
collection (pp. 144-45).*

'An Evening with Sholom Aleichem' was first published in
Prism International, *21, 3 (April 1983), 7-18. 'To Visit Mother
Rachel's Grave' is published here for the first time. It was broad-
cast on the CBC program 'Anthology' in the fall of 1984.*

Henry Kreisel

He Who Sells His Shadow

(A fable for radio suggested by a story of Adelbert Chamisso)

Music: Introduction to play . . . theme to background for:

Peter *(Narrates) (Softly, but with strong emphasis)* How dark, how
endless seems the night! And yet, there's barely two hours gone
since **he** sat here, and faced me, his head grotesquely poised
upon his thin, long neck. If I could have defied him **then** as I
defy him now! How readily I fell into his trap! —The dawn is
breaking. —There's still a time for thought before action. Why
should I, who have no shadow, be eager for the sun? How
unsubstantial seems the shadow? Who would not sell it, this
dark bit of nothing? And had I not crossed the sea to make my
fortune? Had I not come a thousand miles, with little money in
my pocket, in search of gold? It seems as if a hundred years had
passed since then, since I pushed my way through that huge
crowd that thronged the pier . . .

Music: Blends into:

Sound: *Crowd noises, cries of stevedores, passengers greeting each other, etc.*

Peter   *(Continuing)* . . . and turned into that narrow, cobbled street where the cheap inns and hostelries are . . . *(Fades into)*

Host   Ah, good day, sir, good day! Just off the ship, eh?

Peter   Yes, indeed. I'd like a room for a day or so. The cheapest you've got. I've got to make my money stretch a long way!

Host   I guess you do. Who doesn't, these days? I've got exactly what you want. It's a tiny room, up in the attic, but . . .

Peter   That'll do fine, thanks. Oh, there's something else. I've never been here before, but I know there's a gentleman living here, whose name is John. Thomas John. You wouldn't by any chance know how I could find him?

Host   *(Somewhat taken aback)* Thomas John! Don't tell me you know Thomas John and are putting up here in a cheap little attic room?

Peter   Well, I don't really know him, but I know his *brother*.

Host   Thomas John! The richest man in the country! *(Confidentially)* Kind of ruthless, too, they say. Drives a hard bargain; not a thought for the next man. No pity at all, they say, so long as he stands to make a profit. You can't miss his house. House! What am I saying! A regular castle it is. Just outside the north gate, built of red and white marble, and gardens and parks all round it. But you'll have to dress for the occasion, young man.

Peter   I'll put on a fresh shirt and brush my shoes. I'm afraid Mr.
-   Thomas John will have to take me as I am.

Music: *Short bridge, suggesting the passing of several hours*

Peter   Good afternoon. I wonder if I could see Mr. Thomas John.

Servant   Who are you?

Peter   My name is Peter Schlemiehl. I am a friend of Mr. John's brother. I have a letter of introduction for him.

Servant   *(Stiffly)* Mr. John is entertaining guests in the garden. You might perhaps come back later.

Peter   I'm afraid that won't be possible. *(Firmer)* Please tell Mr. John that his brother's friend wishes to call on him.

Servant   Very well, then. *(Fades with:)*

Sound: Retreating footsteps

Peter   *(Narrating)* He came back after a while, and beckoned me to follow him into the garden.

Sound: Several voices, engaged in conversation, growing more distinct as Peter approaches . . . continues in background throughout scene.

Man's Voice   Is it that hill over there?

Woman's Voice   Oh, no, no, not that one. It's too near the house.

Mr. John   *(Raising his voice above the others)* Ah! So this is the gentleman! Welcome here, Mr. —ah . . .

Peter   Schlemiehl. Peter Schlemiehl.

Mr. John   Ah, quite so, quite so. So you are a friend of my brother's. How is he? Well, I hope. *(Turning to his guests)* No, no, not that hill, the one beyond it. I'm going to build a beautiful villa there. A charming retreat. A little love nest.

Sound: Laughing

Mr. John   *(Turning to Peter)* Oh, you've brought a letter from my brother. How is he? Still writing his little verses, living in a little garret?

Peter   *(Embarrassed)* He is not rich.

Mr. John   My dear Mr. —ah . . .

Peter Schlemiehl.

Mr. John Ah, yes. My dear Mr. Schlemiehl. A man who has no money must always remain a nonentity, less than a zero.

Peter How true!

Mr. John More, a fool. That my brother could not, or would not, understand. Even though you are his friend, I hope you have sounder views. Make his reputation by his writing! *(Laughs)* Bah! Gold, sir, **gold** is the basis of all reputation. There is not a spot or a stain that gold cannot take out. The world does not care how a man has got his gold, provided he has it. It is poverty that the world despises. Tell that to my brother when you meet him again. *(Fade to crowd)*

Sound: Babble up again

Music: Softly, we hear the motif henceforth always heard when the man in grey comes into the action, a melody marred by assonances sneaks in under narrative . . .

Peter *(Narrating)* Mr. John left me and returned to his guests. It was then I noticed **him**—a middle-aged man, thin, dour, and very tall, standing behind Mr. John. He put his hand into the narrow pocket of his tight-fitting, old-fashioned grey coat, and handed the lady next to him a little package, bowing respectfully to her.

Mr. John *(Slightly off)* It is getting too hot here. A tent and some cool drinks! *(Snapping his fingers)*

Peter *(Narrating)* I could hardly believe my eyes! For barely had he spoken when the mysterious man, reaching once more into his pocket, brought out a rich, gold-embroidered carpet and a tent, and handed them to three servants who took the things, as if all this were the most natural thing on earth.

Sound: Music and conversation up briefly

Peter *(Continuing)* No one bothered with me. Mr. John seemed to have completely forgotten about me. I felt as if all this were happening in a dream, and at the first opportunity I slipped away, unnoticed.

Music: The grey motif swells . . . gradually as if in pursuit

Peter   *(Narrating)* But then I thought I heard someone following me. I turned and saw Him coming towards me.

Music: Breaks abruptly

The Man   *(Obsequiously)* My dear sir, forgive my presumption if I dare to ask a favour of you, even though we do not know each other.

Peter   *(Frightened)* What . . . What can I do for a man who . . .

The Man   *(Disregarding him)* In the short time, while I had the pleasure to be near you, I observed with great admiration—forgive me for saying so—indeed, with envy, the wonderful shadow you cast before you in the sun. No doubt you are hardly aware of it, but I assure you it is exquisite.

Music: The 'Shadow' motif, a sombre, brooding melody, is heard in the distance . . . very, very softly . . . as a temptation.

The Man   Would it be impertinent, if I asked you to let me have your shadow? I would willingly buy it.

Peter   Come, come! Haven't you enough with your own shadow? What would you do with mine?

The Man   *(Persuasive)* For such a treasure I should be prepared to pay the very highest prize. I have many things in my pocket which might be of some value to you.

Peter   I must have misunderstood you. How could you take my . . .

The Man   Let that be my concern. It is only a trifling detail, a matter of technique which I have completely mastered! Forgive me for pressing you, but I am rather short of time and I should like to conclude this deal quickly. I gathered from your conversation

with my good friend, Mr. John, that you are rather—eh—
impecunious. A word from you, and everything is altered. Look
here. This little bag. Put your hand into it.

Sound: Clinking of gold pieces

The Man *(With great emphasis)* Gold pieces! An inexhaustible
supply!

Peter Gold pieces! An . . . an inexhaustible supply!

The Man Yes, gold! Is it not splendid, sir? More dazzling than the
brightness of the sun. He who has it is accounted noble and
wise. Fame and honor are his for the asking. *(Confidentially)*
And, you must allow me to say so, with gold, even hell is made
worth heaven.

Peter *(Greedily)* It's a deal, sir. This bag for my shadow.

*Music: The shadow motif swells and grows in volume while Peter
is speaking.*

Peter And then, to my horror, I saw him kneel down before me.
Quickly and silently he lifted my shadow from the grass, rolled
it up and put it in his pocket. And when he had done that, he
made me a deep bow, and disappeared behind a hedge.

Music: Shadow motif up briefly . . . then to a quick fade out

*Sound: Street noises are now heard: cries of street vendors, rum-
bling and shrieking of carriages, etc.*

*Note: The following scene should be played with great intensity. It
could have an almost surrealistic effect. Its impact, at any rate, must
be very strong and terrifying, for the enormity of his action is now
clearly impressed upon Peter.*

Voice of an Old Woman Heh, young man! Heh, listen! Young
man!

Peter *(Walking along as if in a dream)* Hah! What is it you want?

Old Woman   *(Agitatedly)* Look! Look! You—you've lost you shadow!

Peter   Ah, never mind, never mind.

Voice of a Man   Well, well, where did you leave your shadow, young man?

A Woman   Look, Mary, look at that poor devil. He's got no shadow. How terrible! How dreadful!

Sound: A group of boys is heard storming out of a school, shouting and jostling each other. Suddenly the voice of a boy is heard above the din.

Boy   Heh, look fellows! Look at that chap over there! Look! He's lost his shadow. Heh, **you!** Heh, you there! Stop!

Sound: Peter breaks into a run. The boys run after him.

Boy   *(Shouting)* Decent people take their shadow along when they go out into the sun.

Voices   *(Calling after him)* Get a shadow! Don't come into the sun again! Every rat has a shadow!

Sound: Up loudly into:

Music: A taunting bridge leading into shadow motif played softly and sadly in background

Peter   *(Weary and slow)* Decent people take their shadow along when they go out into the sun. *(Pause)* Suddenly I was aware of the terrible thing that had happened to me. The knowledge that I would never again be free to walk in the sun came down like a cloud upon me and I wept bitterly. Henceforth, I must be a stranger upon the earth, an exile, cut off at the root from my fellow-men. For the shadow roots a man in the earth, and I had bartered away mine for a bag of gold. And it dawned upon me then that even though gold sometimes outweighs merit and virtue, a man's shadow outweighs gold. For what is a man if he is cut off from his fellows? My only thought now was to find that mysterious stranger and get back the treasure which, in a moment of greed, I had so foolishly sold him.

Music: *Up briefly to a bridge*

Sound: *Door closes with a slam*

Host Well, well. Back again! And how did Mr. John receive you? What's the matter with you? Aren't you feeling well? You look so pale.

Peter No, no, it's—it's all right. It's just that I can't stand too much sun.

Host Oh, before I forget. Someone was asking for you. He spoke to my man . . .

Peter *(Curiously)* Who could that have been?

Host I don't know. Didn't see him. I'll send my man up to you. He'll tell you. *(Shouts)* Bendel! Heh, Bendel!

Bendel *(Off)* What is it?

Host That young fellow's back. You better give him that message.

Bendel *(As before)* I'll be up in a minute.

Music: *Short bridge*

Sound: *Knock on door*

Peter *(Inside the room)* Come in!

Sound: *Door opens and closes*

Bendel Good afternoon, sir. My name's Bendel.

Peter *(Quickly)* Oh yes, you're the man who has a message for me. Who was asking for me?

Bendel   *(Hesitating)* Well, I—I don't really know. He never told me his name, though I asked him. I was just going out the door to go down to the market and get some vegetables, when I saw a man coming up and he stopped me and said: 'You work here, don't you?' and I said, yes, I do. And he said: 'Is there a young gentleman by the name of Peter Schlemiehl staying here?' and I said I wasn't sure, but I could find out for him. And then I turned to go back in and check the register, but he put his hand on my shoulder and held me back, and said, never mind, he was sure a Mr. Peter Schlemiehl was staying here and would be back in a short while. Then I said to him: 'Well, why don't you come in and wait for him?' But he said, no, he was in a great hurry. And then he beckoned me closer to him and said: 'I want you to give him a message. D'you think you could remember a message word for word?' and I said, I guess I could, but . . .

Peter   *(Impatiently)* Yes, yes . . . enough of that . . . What did he say?

Bendel   *(Slowly)* I'm coming to that, sir. 'Tell Mr. Peter Schlemiehl,' he said, 'he won't see me here again, and it's useless for him to look for me. Tell him there's a fair wind blowing and in less than half an hour's time I'll be on my way to visit lands beyond the sea. But in six months' time, on this very day, I shall take the liberty to wait on him again, wherever he may be, and that I hope then to be in a position to offer him a new, and perhaps a welcome deal. Tell him I wish him well, and only want to be of service.' He made me repeat this three times so I'd be sure to remember, and then I asked him what his name was, but he said it didn't matter. You'd know well enough.

Peter   *(With suppressed emotion, after slight pause)* What did he look like, this—gentleman?

Bendel   Oh—he was very tall and thin—about fifty, I'd say, and he wore a grey coat, old-fashioned like . . .

Peter   I know the man. Here—here's something for your trouble.

Sound: Coins clink

Bendel *(Overwhelmed)* Sir, you must've made a mistake. A—a gold piece.

Peter It's all right.

Bendel Thank you very much, sir. I—I—Is there anything else I can do for you?

Peter No thanks, not right now . . .

Bendel *(Fading)* All right, sir.

Peter Wait, maybe there is. Driving back along the quay, not far from here, I saw a young painter busily sketching away. I wonder if you'd go out and see if he's still there. If he is, tell him I want to see him. Tell him I admire his work and might want to purchase one or two of his paintings.

Bendel *(Rather astounded)* I'll see if I can find him. You're sure you—you want him to come here?

Peter Quite sure.

Bendel All right. I'll try and get him.

Sound: Door opens and closes

Peter *(Narrating)* As soon as he was gone, I sank down on the bed, exhausted. A feeling of utter hopelessness overcame me. The thought that I would have to live a hidden life, cut off and alone, was too horrible to contemplate. But then I remembered that the man in grey had said he would return, and that he would offer me a new deal. The thought brought new hope and cheered me, for my exile would be only temporary, and I had enough money after all. Perhaps the painter could do something for me. After a while Bendel came back, bringing the artist with him.

Bendel Here he is, sir.

Peter Ah, good. I'm glad you found him. You can go now, Bendel. I'll call you later.

Sound: Door closes

Peter   Sit down, please. Here—sit in this chair, and I'll stretch out on the bed, if you don't mind. I'm rather tired . . .

Painter   Thank you.

Peter   You must be somewhat surprised to be called here so—unexpectedly.

Painter   It does seem strange. And stranger still if you were actually to buy some of my paintings. Forgive me for saying so, sir, but your circumstances seem hardly to be better than mine. Indeed, my attic is bigger than yours.

Peter   *(Smiling)* Well, attics may be deceptive, and I shall certainly purchase some of your paintings. Indeed I shall pay you in advance.

Painter   You can't mean that.

Peter   I do, believe me. Here, will ten gold-pieces purchase two paintings?

Painter   Ten!—But you haven't even picked out the paintings.

Peter   I leave that to you. You send them up to me. —In the meantime there is something else I want to ask you. *(He pauses for a moment)*

Music: Sneak shadow motif softly in the background

Peter   *(A bit hesitant)* I have a very good friend who had the great misfortune to lose his shadow. A dreadful loss, as you can imagine. I am trying to help him out of his dilemma. And when I saw you painting there on the quay, it crossed my mind that you might be able to provide him with an—artificial one.

Painter   I beg your pardon. Did you say shadow?

Peter   Yes. I said shadow.

Shadow motif ends on accent

Painter   You are making fun of me!

Peter   No, I am not; I am in deadly earnest.

Painter   How could a man be so careless as to trifle with so precious a thing?

Peter   I assure you, he was quite innocent. He forgot himself in a moment of weakness. But that really does not matter. Could you, or could you not, provide him with an artificial shadow?

Painter   *(With a laugh)* Sir, you are asking the impossible. Such a shadow as **I** could paint, he must needs lose again as soon as he makes the very slightest movement—especially if he's a man who could be so careless of his **native** shadow. For a man's shadow is like his country. He who rejects his country or is driven from it cannot easily find another. And he cannot purchase one with all the money in the world.

Peter   *(Dejected)* So it seems. *(Growing very agitated)* But what is he to do? How is he to face the world and live among men then?

Painter   He had better not face the sun, if he has no shadow. That seems the most logical and safest thing to do.

Peter   But why should he have to hide, if he is innocent?

Painter   I am only a painter, sir, penniless and obscure. I observe the world and what goes on there, but I am not responsible for it. —Sorry I couldn't help you! Do you still want to buy my paintings?

Peter   *(Hardly listening)* Yes—yes, of course. Send them up.

Painter   Very well. You will have them tomorrow. Good day, sir.

Peter   Good day.

Sound: Door opens and closes

Music: Sneak shadow motif, very sombrely played

Peter   Though I had expected little from the young painter, he had shattered what hope I still thought there was. Now I began to resign myself to my fate. I would live my life as well as I could without my shadow. I would not expose myself to the sun. I would be a like a man condemned to hide by day to escape detection, though he does not know why or wherefore. I would live my life in a society which no longer accepted me, which turned its back on me and scorned me because it regarded me as different, alien—shadowless. I must live an underground existence, waiting patiently until the stranger in the grey coat came again. *(Shadow motif up and out)* I felt calmer now and more composed. At last I had faced this new and terrible situation and faced it honestly. It had lost a great deal of its terror and grimness. It would grow familiar and bearable, like a chronic disease. For no man can live in constant despair and preserve his sanity. I decided I would be better off somewhere in the country, where it would be possible to live a more secluded, unmolested life. It struck me I might take Bendel with me. He seemed a trustworthy fellow, and I liked him. I called for him.

Bendel   *(Fade in)* Is there anything I can do for you, sir?

Peter   Bendel! I want to offer you a job . . .

Bendel   A job, sir . . . but . . .

Peter   No, don't say anything until I've finished. The work would be simple. Personal service only. And I'll double whatever you're earning now. What do you say?

Bendel   *(Taken aback)* I don't know, sir . . . It's rather sudden, and . . . If you can afford to pay me twice the wages I'm getting now, why would you be putting up in this dingy little place!

Peter   *(Embarrassed)* That would be a bit hard to explain, Bendel. *(Then quickly and with a laugh)* Perhaps just to satisfy a sudden whim. But I've decided to go and live in the country, in a quiet place. I leave you to choose one. . . .

Bendel   Me, sir . . . But I can't . . .

Peter   Yes. You know this country better than I do. I am a stranger
here. I want you to choose a place, find a house and rent it. A big
house. See that it is adequately furnished. I'll leave here
tomorrow night and take a suite in one of the big hotels. There
you will get in touch with me when everything is ready. I will
provide you with as much money as you're likely to need. And
when you have selected a place, spend liberally. Let the people
know that it is a generous man who is coming to live among
them. *(Quietly, almost to himself)* I may need their good will.
(Louder) Now—will you accept my offer?

Bendel   You hardly know me, sir, and yet you're going to trust me
with money. What if I—well . . .

Peter   *(Quickly)* That never occurred to me. Perhaps that's a sign of
the trust I have in you. I don't value money. I find that I have
too much and cannot buy with it what I most need. But never
mind. I trust you. Will you serve me?

Bendel   *(Slowly)* I will, sir. But it seems strange to me—all this.

Music: A short bridge

Peter   *(Narrating)* I moved into a suite in one of the big hotels of the
city, waiting for word from Bendel. A week went by and I grew
impatient. I longed to go out into the sun, to stroll about and sit
on a park bench, but I was afraid. Then at last he sent word. He
had found a suitable house in a quiet, sleepy little village, and
everything was ready for me. I lost no time. Immediately I
ordered a carriage to be ready early the next morning, and I left
before sunrise, when it was still quite dark and therefore safe for
me to venture out.

Sound: A carriage driving rapidly on the highway

Peter   *(Impatient)* How much farther have we to go, driver? You
said we'd be there at noon.

Driver   We're almost there now. A few more minutes, that's all.
You'll get there at noon.

Sound: A crowd of people, busily talking, all in good humor. Sound grows louder, as carriage approaches.

Driver   Here you are! There's the townhall.

Peter   *(Disturbed)* Is that the place? But what are all the people doing there? Is this a holiday?

Driver   I wouldn't know, sir.

Sound: Cries of 'Welcome' and 'Long live Mr. Peter.' The carriage comes to a stop. People throng about it joyfully.

Peter   *(Who has just spotted Bendel and is very relieved)* Bendel! Bendel!

Bendel   Welcome, sir! Welcome! *(Coming closer)* I'm glad to see you.

Peter   *(Lowering his voice)* What's the meaning of all this?

Bendel   *(A bit taken aback)* Aren't you pleased to see all these people welcoming you? They're glad to see you.

Peter   Yes, yes, that may be so, but I had not expected all this. It . . . frightens me a little to see them greeting me as if I were a prince.

Bendel   Perhaps they think you **are** a prince, sir.

Peter   Bah!

Bendel   Don't let them wait, sir. Step out of the carriage, and let them see you. They're waiting for you.

Peter   *(Terror-stricken)* No, that's out of the question. Not now, not now. The midday sun is too merciless, and not a tree anywhere to shade me. No, I—I am too tired. It was a long journey, and I want to rest. Tell them I thank them. I am grateful to them for this show of affection. I'll meet them tomorrow—yes, that's it. Tomorrow night we'll have tables spread out in the open and eat and celebrate together.

Bendel *(To the people who have now grown very quiet, waiting)* Mr. Peter is tired after his long journey. He thanks you for your hearty welcome and invites you all to dine with him tomorrow night.

Sound: *The people cheer*

Peter Now get in beside the driver, Bendel, and direct him to the house.

Bendel Very well.

Sound: *The carriage drives off, amidst cheers*

Music: *A gay passage, becoming sombre and ending abruptly*

Bendel Well, sir, now that you've seen the house, are you satisfied? Have I done what you expected of me?

Peter Yes, indeed, excellently done, my dear Bendel. I'm very pleased. A perfect location. Far enough away from the village for privacy. Privacy is what I need above all. Remember that, Bendel! *(He pauses)* Why did you arrange this public demonstration?

Bendel I made no arrangements, sir. But you told me to be generous, and I followed your orders and spent gold liberally. And when they heard that their great benefactor was coming, they wanted to honor him, that's all.

Peter Bah! They honor my gold, not me. If they knew me, why . . .

Bendel There is a rumour about that you are a noble lord.

Peter *(With a laugh)* Noble lord, indeed! Well, let them. It harms no one.

Bendel Some have begun to call you **Count** Peter, and it's beginning to spread.

Peter *(Contemptuous)* **Count** Peter, then. Spend more gold, and it'll be **King** Peter. . . . *(Very quietly)*

Bendel   Very good, sir . . .

Peter   Bendel, have you never wondered who I am?

Bendel   I'd be lying to you if I said no. But it's all the same to me. You treated me better than any man I ever worked for, and that's all I care about. You trusted me with money before you really knew me, and I did appreciate that.

Peter   *(Musing)* Indeed, I did place my trust in you, and you didn't deceive me. My trust was not misplaced. I liked you from the start, for you are open and honest. *(With quiet intensity)* Look at me, Bendel. Look at this **Count** Peter, at this man whose stature has grown to that of a prince in the minds of people who never knew nor saw him. *(Very quietly)* If you could only look into my heart, Bendel, you would see such wretchedness there, such despair; it would move you to pity and tears.

Bendel   I—I—You are not well. I'll get you some water.

Peter   No, no, stay! Bendel, I trusted you with gold and you didn't disappoint me. Now I will trust you with something weightier, more secret. I must speak of it to someone, Bendel; I cannot keep it any longer or it will burst my heart.

Bendel   What is it? What's come over you, sir . . .

Peter   *(Almost beseeching him)* Bendel, don't leave me. Stay with me! You know me as a rich and generous man, and you think that all the world must honor and respect me. But no! I must shut myself off and avoid the sun. On a hot summer day like this, I must arrive in a closed carriage. I cannot show myself for fear of arousing the wrath of those who cheer me. I have been **judged**—I don't know why, or where, or by whom, and now the world has exiled me and will not let me live a normal life. Even you, Bendel, might turn from me, when you hear my terrible secret. Bendel, I am rich, generous, and kind. —But I am **a man without a shadow.**

Bendel   Without a shadow!

Peter Yes. I am marked—like Cain! Only he knew why, and I don't. *(He stops. Then with great intensity)* Well, why do you stand there gaping at me? Go on, hurl insults at me like all the people in the city. You know now who I am. Betray my secret now. Go into the market-place and bear witness against me!

Bendel *(Very calmly)* Did you really think I would? The world can hang itself and think what it wants. I'll stay with you. Perhaps I can be of use to you, help you, shield you. I'm taller and stronger than you. And there may be times when I could stand behind you, and my shadow could serve us both.

Peter *(Very moved)* Bendel. It is a rare thing in this world to see a man refuse to take advantage of the weakness of another.

Music: Plaintive melody with a touch of tenderness, becoming joyful and merry

Sound: A large group of people, talking, satisfied after a hearty meal. Clatter of dishes, etc.

Voice of a Man Quiet now, everybody. The mayor wants to say a few words.

Sound: The talk dies down

Mayor My friends! I don't want to make a long speech. I'll just ask you to raise your glasses and drink the health of our generous host. Long life to him!

Sound: Cries of 'Long live Mr. Peter!' . . . 'Long live Count Peter!' Clinking of glasses.

Peter I thank you, my good friends. And I drink to you. *(He lowers his voice)* Bendel, do you see the beautiful girl over there?—Yes, the one in the white dress—the one who's weaving a red rose into her hair now. Who is she?

Bendel *(Whispering)* That's the mayor's daughter, sir.

Mayor My dear—er—*(He hesitates a moment as if not sure whether* *to say 'Mister' or 'Count')* Mr. Peter. This is the merriest feast we've had here in many a year. And all thanks to your generosity. It was providence that sent you here.

Peter   Ah, come, come, Mr. Mayor. But nonetheless I thank you for your generous welcome. Perhaps you and your good wife would pay me the compliment of a visit some time?

Mayor   I am most honored, sir. Martha, Mr. Peter has invited us to come and visit him.

Peter   Shall we say in a week's time?

Mayoress   Oh, you are too kind, sir.

Peter   Nonsense. I shall be delighted to have your company.—I am told you have a daughter.

Mayor   Indeed, sir. There she is. Over there.

Mayoress   Our only child. Our Minna. Our pride and joy. *(Rather intimately)* Oh, I should so love to have you meet her.

Mayor   *(Sternly)* Martha, you forget yourself.

Peter   *(Quickly)* I should be delighted to meet her. Perhaps—if she is free, she could accompany you when you come.

Mayoress   Oh, how kind of you. I'm sure you'll like her.

Mayor   Martha!

Peter   *(With a touch of irony)* I'm sure that if she has her mother's charms, I shan't be able to resist her.

Music: A quick transition passage

Mayoress   *(Enraptured)* What a beautiful house! How exquisitely furnished! And these lovely paintings. How beautiful!

Peter   I am so glad all this—er—meets with your approval, madam. But it is too hot inside. Won't you come out into the garden? I think it will be more comfortable there. —I see you smoke cigars, my dear sir. Won't you have one of these?

Mayor Thank you. Thank you very much.

Peter And you, Miss Minna. You have said very little tonight.

Minna *(Startled, with a tense laugh)* Oh, but I—I—

Peter *(Playful)* Look, she blushes! —Shall we go then? After you, Madam. Sir. *(He drops his voice)* Oh, Miss Minna. I did not mean to embarrass you, but a blush does give your cheeks the color of a deep-red rose and makes your face even more beautiful. —Oh, please, stay behind a little bit. Let me have a word with you alone before we join your parents.

Minna *(Startled)* With me? Why, Mr. Peter . . .

Peter Only to tell you that—that you have quite bewitched me— ever since I saw you last week I have thought about you, and the picture of you weaving a flower into your hair will not disappear from my mind.

Minna I—I don't know what you mean. Why do you trifle with me?

Peter Oh, but I am not. You make me quite forget myself, Miss Minna . . . Don't turn away. Please.

Minna My father is looking at us.

Peter Let me see you tomorrow night, if only for half an hour. Here, in this garden. —You look hurt and angry. But you must not misunderstand me. If I ask you to come here it is because I cannot come to you. I know this sounds strange, and . . . *(Hopelessly)* Oh, I cannot possibly make you believe that I speak truly, because my truth is stranger than a thousand lies.

Minna If a man asks a girl to come to him alone and at night, then how can she believe that all he wants is talk?

Peter Perhaps because he asks so outrightly, so crudely, if you wish.

Because he does not devise stratagems to cover up his real designs. Don't hold it against me that I have spoken so brusquely to you. Only believe that I have told you the truth. — Wait. Let us walk up to the arbor together.

Music: The Minna motif, a soft and tender theme, growing livelier and breaking abruptly

Peter   What is it, Bendel?

Bendel   You're sure you want the lamp kept burning outside the house?

Peter   Yes. Someone might come to see me.

Bendel   Very good, then.

Peter   Bendel, I did a very foolish thing last night. And yet I know that I would not act otherwise if yesterday were today, though I would curse myself tomorrow.

Bendel   The mayor doesn't suspect?

Peter   No, no. I was very careful. And you have arranged the lights so well that there's no danger here. *(He pauses)* What would you say if I told you that I seized the first chance I had to declare my admiration for Minna—not in veiled allusions, but openly, directly, and in all seriousness?

Bendel   In all seriousness?

Peter   Yes.

Bendel   Perhaps that was not a wise thing to do, especially for a man . . .

Peter   . . . in my position! I know. I knew when I spoke to her, and I couldn't help myself. If you ask me what I intend to do, I can only shake my head. I cannot even wish undone what I have done. For I went further, Bendel. I asked her to come here tonight, though I hardly expect her to. So you see my reason hasn't altogether forsaken me. I am not yet foolhardy enough to barter safety for love.

Bendel Sir . . . do you know . . .

Peter Know what?

Bendel That there's someone courting the girl?

Peter *(Vehemently)* There is!

Bendel Yes. The innkeeper's son. Richard. A strong and burly fellow.

Peter *(After a pause)* I might have thought of that. *(With a laugh)* Now indeed I must seem like a love-sick schoolboy to her. —Go and shut off the light, Bendel.

Bendel Yes. I might as well.

Sound: *A bell rings*

Peter There's someone at the door! Go and see who it is, Bendel. If she has come after all, show her out into the garden. I'll wait for her there.

Music: *The Minna motif bridge*

Minna I didn't want to come here, but I could not forget your voice and your look, imploring me to come.

Peter Then you did believe me, and you did understand me. That makes me very happy.

Minna Understand you? But what do you want me to understand?

Peter Nothing—and everything.

Minna I've heard people talk, and they say you are a—a great man, and I am only . . .

Peter Don't listen to what they say. I am not what they think I am.

Promise me that you will not ask me who I am, or why I have come to live amongst you! Within six months you shall know more. Until then, certain things must be hidden as deep in my brain as I am from hope.

Minna   How can I understand you when you talk to me in riddles?

Peter   Understand only that I am unhappy. I ask very little of you. Only that you come to me sometimes, to sit by me for a little while, and help me bear the burden of my loneliness.

Minna   And if I come, must it always be like this, secretly? Are you ashamed to be seen with me among our people in the broad light of day?

Peter   Not ashamed, but afraid.

Minna   Afraid? Of what?

Peter   Of the sun.

Minna   You are the strangest man I ever knew.

Music: Minna motif rising, then slowly fading

Peter   *(Narrating)* From time to time, she came to visit me whenever she could slip away unnoticed. She never stayed long, and there were certain things which remained unspoken between us. But, oh, the pleasure to have her near me, and the emptiness when I waited for her to come, and waited in vain. And when she let a month and more go by between visits, impatience almost drove me mad.

Peter   Why didn't you let me hear from you?

Minna   I could ask the same!

Peter   Do you think that if I could, I wouldn't have come to you?

Minna   I can no longer keep up these secret meetings. My father already suspects something. And if I were seen coming here, what could I say?

Peter   Poor girl. Poor, sweet girl. What indeed could you say? —Oh,
I have been selfish. I have taken too little thought of you. I
should never have approached you. Perhaps it would be better
to end all here, now, before it's too late.

Minna   You are cruel, Peter, to talk to me like that. You want to get
rid of me. You have had enough of me.

Peter   No, no. I'm thinking of you now, not of myself. I have
thought too much of myself. Go back to your own people.
Marry a man who can make you happy. A good, honest man. A
man whose roots are solidly planted in the earth. Marry the
innkeeper's son.

Minna   *(Taken aback)* Richard! You know about him?

Peter   Yes.

Minna   He loves me. But I have never loved him. *(Slowly with
disappointment)* And I thought you loved me.

Peter   I have no right to tear you into chaos with me.

A pause

Minna   What makes you so afraid? What is there to frighten you
here?

Peter   Don't press me to tell you, Minna. There is still hope. But we
must wait.

Minna   Wait for what? If you're miserable, let me share your misery.

Peter   If you knew my misery, you wouldn't want to share it. Wait
another six weeks, until the middle of next month. By the
fifteenth my fate will be decided—if in my favour, then we can
go out into the sun together. And if not . . .

Minna   Then what?

Peter   I don't know. I would rather not think of it—now. When it is
time . . .

Minna   *(Suddenly breaks into a sob, for the strain is too great for her)* No, no . . .

Peter   *(Softly, calming her)* Minna, Minna. I promise you. All will be well. We'll look back at this moment, and you can laugh at me, and—and mock my fears, and . . .

Minna   *(Still sobbing)* I don't know why, but suddenly I felt . . . a strange foreboding, a . . . Let me go now, Peter. I must go now.

Peter   I'll call Bendel, and have him take you part of the way. And don't risk coming here again. Let me come to you. Let me take the risk now. When the moon is down, I shall come to you, and meet you in your garden, if only for a few minutes, if only to know that you are still there. You will not refuse me that.

Minna   *(Weakly)* I—I'll look for you.

Peter   Good night, sweet child . . . Watch for me when the moon is down.

Music: Minna motif and shadow motif played in counterpoint, then fading

Sound: A door softly opening

Peter   *(Roused by Bendel's entry)* Ah, Bendel. You're back.

Bendel   Yes. I took her to the fork in the road, and from there she walked on alone.

Peter   Did she say anything?

Bendel   Nothing.

Peter   Perhaps better so. *(Softly and broodingly)* Everything is dark and gloomy tonight. The air seems thick with fears and phantoms. What if he doesn't come? And if he comes, what will he ask of me?

Bendel   Oh, he'll come. Why would he have left the message for you if he hadn't meant it? And as for his bargain, I wouldn't worry about that now.

Peter He's trying to wear me down, Bendel, by this torture of uncertainty.

Bendel Not if you keep your head. —I heard you say to Miss Minna that you would come to see her. If you don't mind my saying so . . . I don't think you should. Don't take the risk.

Peter *(Narrating)* I disregarded his warning and went to her when the moon was down. We stood together for a short while in the darkness of the night. She hardly spoke at all. And I could feel an uneasiness between us, as if she suspected something, as if she knew. —Once more I went to her, one week before he was to come, and waited for her by an ancient tree, my black cloak thrown wide over my shoulders and my broad-brimmed hat pulled down into my eyes. For two hours I stood there waiting and saw the light in the house and occasionally the shadow of someone crossing by the windows, but she did not come. And suddenly the moon rose, cold and hateful to me. Frightened, I pulled my cloak closer about me, and hurried away—when all at once behind me I heard the heavy footfall of a man and stopped, terrified, turned, and saw a thickset stranger glowering at me. Panic-stricken, I ran from him and did not dare to look back until I had reached my house.

There is a pause of absolute silence

Peter It was early in the morning when voices roused me from a restless sleep.

Bendel *(His voice muffled, but in obvious agitation)* I tell you, you can't see him. He's asleep.

Richard I don't care about that. I have to see him. Now.

Bendel You better tell me what business you have with him.

Richard I'll tell him. I have a notion he'll listen to me.

Bendel   I don't like your tone of voice. I think you better go before I throw you out.

Richard   *(Laughs derisively)*

Bendel   You—

Sound: Opening of a door

Peter   *(Calling)* Bendel, who wants to talk to me?

Bendel   Oh, you're up —It's Richard, the innkeeper's son.

Richard   *(Breaking in)* Yes, it's me. I want to see you.

Peter   Show him into the study, Bendel. I'll talk to him.

Bendel   All right. This way.

Music: A short bridge

Richard   You recognized me, eh?

Peter   Let's not waste time on formalities. What do you want?

Richard   If it's all the same to you, I'd like to see your shadow. Just to make sure I didn't make a mistake last night.

Peter   You're—you're impertinent.

Richard   Not any more than a certain stranger who came where he didn't belong and with his fine manners and slimy ways forced himself between an honest man and his girl.

Peter   *(Icily)* Jealousy makes you invent things.

Richard   You waited for her to come last night, didn't you? But she couldn't because her father had at last caught on to your game. And now I know why you had to keep it hidden, why you can't show yourself where people can see you. Come out into the garden now and stand in the sun and prove me wrong.

Peter   I think you had better leave now.

Richard   *(With heavy sarcasm)* I'll leave all right, **Count** Peter! But I've called your bluff and you haven't heard the last of it yet, you—you shadowless intruder!

Sound: Door slams behind him

Bendel   There he runs. Hot as a bloodhound. Why did you have to come bursting out of your room? I could have handled him myself.

Peter   He saw me last night. You couldn't have changed that fact.

Bendel   The whole village will know by noon.

Peter   We will deal with the village when the time comes.

Music: An ominous passage

Peter   *(Narrating)* The next day, late in the afternoon, the mayor called on me. Stiff and uncomfortable, he sat down in the chair I offered him.

Mayor   *(Groping for words)* I—I come to you in a two-fold capacity—as a—as a father and as the official representative of the people of this village. *(Very hesitantly)* There are rumors about that you—eh—that you have come to live among us under false pretenses—that you are—eh—alien—because you have no— eh . . .

Peter   *(Speaking very calmly)* Because I have no shadow.

Mayor   Precisely. So the rumor has it. I have come here hoping that you can dispel it.

Peter   *(As calmly as before)* I cannot do so at the moment.

Mayor   *(Highly alarmed)* No?

Peter   No.

Mayor   *(Getting angry)* I have a daughter. A young and innocent girl. I don't know how she could so far forget herself as to . . .

Peter   *(Interrupting him)* As to follow her natural impulses.

Mayor   *(Very angry)* As to be deceived by the honied words of an unscrupulous and shadowless adventurer.

Peter   I did **not** deceive your daughter.

Mayor   No? Then why did you never tell her the truth about yourself? To think how narrowly she has escaped disaster! Every dog has his shadow, sir. What did you do with yours? Come now, where is it?

Peter   It is being repaired, sir. For an unscrupulous and ruthless fellow trampled on it and tore a hole in it. And now it must be mended.

Mayor   I will not be joked with. The citizens whom I have the honor to represent are decent and godfearing people. And we cannot tolerate strangers like you among us. Produce a shadow, sir, or else I cannot guarantee your safety.

Peter   Give me a week's time. Surely that is not too much to ask. And tell your daughter, sir, that my feelings for her remain unchanged.

Mayor   I will do no such thing. Indeed, sir, I will see to it that she is far removed from you. And look to your shadow if you want to dwell among us.

Music: Sharp bridge

Peter   *(Narrating)* I sat, counting the days, counting the hours, waiting for him, steeling myself against myself, waiting. Bendel ventured out and came back and reported that the rumors about me grew uglier by the minute, and that certain opportunists, hoping to lay their hands on my property, were rousing the rabble against me.

Music: The shadow motif well off sneaks in

Peter Then the appointed day came. Noon, then evening, then night. No one appeared. The church bell struck eleven and no one appeared. The last minutes of the last hour ran out and no one appeared. So, I thought, he will not keep his word, he will not come.

The Man Good evening, my dear Mr. Schlemiehl. I must apologize for being two minutes late.

Music: Out

Peter *(Aghast)* Ah! How the devil did you get here?

The Man *(Suavely)* Let us not be profane with one another. But, seeing that our relations have always been correct, let us continue to keep them so. I daresay you spent a pleasant and happy time since our last meeting, which, I regret to say, was far too short for us to become better acquainted. But I hope there will be plenty of time for that hereafter.

Peter *(Sharply)* GIVE ME BACK MY SHADOW!

The Man Ah, so you did miss it?

Peter As if you didn't know I would, when you drove your unholy bargain with me.

The Man Ah, come, my friend, you take things too hard. You are too sensitive.

Peter Here, take your wretched money and give me back my shadow.

The Man That, I am afraid, is not possible, for you have had the use of it for some time, and I must exact payment in return.

Peter To know that other men have shadows; that when the sun is low their shadows lengthen and proclaim their kinship with the world, and knowing all the while that I am set apart from men—is that not enough payment?

The Man However much I may sympathize with your feelings, they are of little value to me. I must be practical and business-like.

Peter   Then what must I do to get my shadow back?

The Man   Put your signature to this contract here!

Peter   *(Very suspicious)* Which binds me to do what?

The Man   To put your conscience at my disposal while you live, and to make over your shadow to me after you are dead.

Peter   *(His voice rising in intensity)* No! No! No! No! No!

The Man   We shall conclude our business more satisfactorily if you can contrive to keep your temper.

Peter   Who the devil are you?

The Man   Does that matter? I pay in honest coin. You have found it so. Primarily I am a dealer in shadows. I deal in shadows as other men deal in guns. I am sorry that I made you—unhappy. But I cannot help that. The man who deals in guns doesn't stop producing them because men are killed by them and considerable numbers made unhappy. A dealer in shadows cannot be sentimental.

Peter   But why would you have my conscience?

The Man   Because I have interests also in various enterprises spread all over this globe, not always perhaps of the most spotless kind. From time to time you shall act as my agent and collaborator.

Peter   You ask me to sell myself to you.

The Man   You put too crudely what is really done in your interest. For since some of the things I will ask you to do might go against your conscience, it is better to have none.

Peter   *(Quietly)* Why did you select me? What have I done?

The Man It is not a question of guilt or innocence. I happened to admire your shadow when I saw you by accident in Mr. John's garden that afternoon.

Peter *(With terrible emphasis)* Mr. John—Mr. John. —Did he have a beautiful shadow?

The Man One of the finest it has ever been my pleasure to see. It was superb. And he was so ready to do business. As you could see for yourself he has prospered greatly.

Peter At whose expense? And at what a price?

The Man Why don't you sign this little piece of paper and have done with questions. The yoke I impose is mild, your reward in return immeasurably greater. Principle! Conscience! Words, sir. Empty as a breath of air. Will conscience buy a hungry man a piece of bread? Will principle?

Peter No, but a man must live with himself also, and bread bought without them might turn to gall and so make life intolerable.

The Man For some men perhaps. Would it for you?

Peter I think for me!

The Man *(Blandly)* Allow me to admire the courage of your convictions, but allow me also to express my doubts as to whether a man so placed as you can afford such a luxury.

Peter I cannot afford not to afford it.

The Man *(With a touch of impatience)* Leave heroics to the faultless paragons of story books, my dear Mr. Schlemiehl. Think rather of the pleasant life that lies ahead of you. You collaborate with me, become my agent, act ruthlessly now and again. But men do, you know, men do. I return your shadow. Outwardly all's well again. Who's to know what commitments you've entered, what contracts made? —I spent all day in the village, asked questions, saw that sweet little girl—yes, yes, I did, you needn't look so surprised—saw her in tears, being bundled off by her father to some distant aunt or uncle, out of the reach of the shadowless, the alien. But there is still time. Buy back your shadow, and you may have your love again.

Pause

Peter   *(Slowly, with suppressed emotion)* I should be a bad lover if I had to barter away my conscience for the privilege of love . . . Now leave me before I add the sin of murder to all my lesser ones.

The Man   Tut, tut, my dear Mr. Schlemiehl. I cannot imagine a man of your—er—principles resorting to such crude devices. Besides, it would avail you nothing, for there will always be another like me. There are so many of me. But as for you—consider your position. You sold me your shadow. That transaction cannot be undone. You have already found a shadowless life difficult, but until now this was mitigated by the possession of money. Your obstinacy now forces me to be unpleasant. Imagine a life both shadowless and penniless.

Peter   *(Beside himself with rage and anger)* You despicable fiend! Corrupter and deceiver! I know you now, you and . . .

The Man   *(Interrupting him)* There would have been a time for such a sentiment before. But then you were blind with gold greed. And so I catch the little ones! Ah, I'm not as black as I'm painted, and I may be of service to you yet. A stroke of your pen, and all's done. Say you refuse—a bit embarrassing for me, I admit. A question of prestige, you know. But for you small victory indeed. For how will you, marked and apart, come to terms with a world which cherishes above all things conformity and hates all heresy? Think of tomorrow. In the morning, solemn and blackcoated, Mr. Mayor comes, and two of his councillors perhaps, and behind them, sullenfaced, vacant of thought, a mob of villagers, not to be halted, not to be deflected, driven only by hatred, blind and instinctive, of all men who differ from them. And the mayor says: 'The sun is up, Mr. Peter. Step out into the garden, for we should like to see your shadow and know that you belong among us.' You must face them, you with your conscience and your principles. *(A short pause)* Come now, and have done with it. Spare yourself a life of trouble and indignity. Sign.

Peter *(Who is almost exhausted, but whose mind is now made up)* No, no. Not now, and not with you. You could deprive me of my shadow, but there is yet a part of me inviolate. You cannot touch it, you cannot wrest it from me. That knowledge at least shall be a victory in my defeat.

Music: The grey motif is heard softly, grows stronger as The Man speaks, then fades to background . . . and out at end of The Man's next words.

The Man For the moment then there is no more to be said, and I can leave. I shall return hereafter. *(With grudging admiration)* You are a man of great courage, my dear Mr. Schlemiehl, but it yet remains to be seen how you will bear up. For you have elected to join the legions of the marked men, the displaced men, forever hunted and forever shunned, wandering forever like that poor and wretched Jew, and all for conscience's sake.

Peter *(Narrating, very quietly, but with strong emphasis)* With these words he left me, trembling and exhausted, and yet also feeling almost gay, as if a great load had been lifted from me. For the uncertainty and the despair are gone now, since I defied him, and conscience may yet prove stronger than the shadow. What the future holds for me, I do not know, but as long as there are men like Bendel in the world, there will always be hope for the shadowless and the alien. I know that now the struggle deepens, and I must gather what strength I have, what confidence and valour is yet left me, that my small victory may yet perhaps end in triumph.

Music: The shadow motif, played quickly, so that this usually sombre melody takes on a lilting quality and sounds almost gay.

Henry Kreisel

An Evening with Sholom Aleichem

Dear Mister Sholom Aleichem! No, that's not right. It's like I'm
writing a letter to you. But I'm not writing a letter to you. Because
where you are, there's no post office. I'm talking into this tape-
recorder, but I'm really talking to you. I have a feeling that you just
walked in the door and sat down in the corner there. You look just
like the photo I saw of you once in a newspaper or somewhere. You
were standing with a few others and you had glasses and you wore a
hat and you had a big mustache and you were smiling a little golden
smile. Just the way you look now in the corner there, in the chair.

So, hello, dear Mister Sholom Aleichem! A big hello! Maybe you
want a glass of tea, with lemon and a lump of sugar to hold in the
mouth? The way my grandmother used to drink tea. You know, it
was in my grandmother's house that I first heard about you. That's a
long time ago. More than fifty years ago. You were already dead then,
Mister Sholom Aleichem, but not too long, and they still talked about
you like you were a living man, my grandmother and her friends. To
them you were still alive, a guest in the house. Just like you are to me
now.

You're sure you don't want a glass of tea? Nowadays we drink tea
out of a cup, but my grandmother drank out of a glass. You, too, I'm
sure.

And where you are now, do they drink tea also? Out of a cup? Out
of a glass?

To tell you the truth, I didn't think about you much after my
grandmother died. In her house I used to hear your stories, about
Tevye and about Motel and about the *shtetl*, I'll tell you about that
soon, but when she died, in 1925, that was the end. I didn't hear any
more. And I'm not much of a reader. I don't have the patience. A
kibbitzer, yes, a talker, yes, but a reader—no.

So I forgot about you, Mister Sholom Aleichem—more or less. For
forty, forty-five years. I was busy making a living, bringing up a
family. Who had time for stories, especially stories that happened
such a long time ago, in a country ten thousand miles away?

Then they made a movie from your stories. A big musical. *Fiddler
on the Roof*. That's what they called it. A funny name. I don't remember no fiddlers on no roofs in your stories. Maybe you heard about

that movie? Yes, I see you're nodding your head. Good news gets around. Bad news even faster, but good news, too, thank God, once in a while.

You used to have a saying in your stories that I always liked. Two people are talking and when one says, 'I wish you a long life,' or 'May you have good health,' or 'Don't worry, everything will be all right,' the other says, 'Let it go from your lips to God's ears!' I always liked that. For a while I used to say it all the time. I even got a nickname out of it. Some of my friends used to call me 'God's ears.' How do you like that?

Anyway, I was telling about that movie they made from your stories. Everybody was talking about *Fiddler on the Roof,* and on the radio they were playing songs from it all day. I used to listen to the songs and I used to hum the melodies. Especially there was a song I liked—if I were a rich man, yabbabababababababa. That was the most popular. Maybe you heard it?

This reminds me of a story I heard once. There was this *melamed,* this poor little Hebrew teacher, he was hardly making a living, and he says, 'If I was Rothschild, I would be richer than Rothschild.' How so? they ask him. 'Because,' he says, 'if I was Rothschild, I would have all his fortune, but on top of it, I would also have my salary as a Hebrew teacher!'

So anyway, *Fiddler on the Roof* was playing downtown, and my wife wanted to go. I said, 'Sure, sure, Betty, we'll go,' but then we didn't go. I come home from work, I'm tired. I'm a salesman, Mister Sholom Aleichem. I'm a great salesman, if I say so myself. I sell men's wear in a store downtown. A specialty store—Mister Big 'n' Tall. I'm only middle-sized myself, but I can deal with a three-hundred, four-hundred pounder. He's big, he's huge, but I have a bigger mouth. I can talk. He wants a brown suit, but I haven't got no brown suit that fits him. I sell him a blue suit. That's the kind of a salesman I am.

So I come home that evening. I feel more tired than usual. Not so good, to tell you the truth. I'm hardly in the door, my wife Betty she calls out to me, 'Tonight you're taking me to see *Fiddler on the Roof.* You hear, Barnie, you're taking me tonight.'

She's always complaining I don't take her out enough, Betty, God bless her. She has a point, I have to admit. She also complains I don't talk to her enough. She has a point there, too. I talk all day in the store, I come home I'm talked out. I just want to eat and flop down in a comfortable chair, like the one you're sitting in, Mister Sholom Aleichem, look at the paper, the headlines, the sports, watch a little

TV—I always fall asleep in front of the TV—it relaxes me. If I go to the movies, to tell you the truth, I fall asleep, too. So I pay for nothing. So you can see, I'm not much of a movie-goer.

But she's been bugging me and bugging me, for two weeks already—Betty, God bless her. And now I didn't have no more excuses left. 'All right, all right,' I say. 'After supper we'll go and see *Fiddler on the Roof*. We'll make the nine o'clock show.'

We eat supper. The two of us. We have three children, bless them, but they're all married now. We have four grandchildren already, *Gott sei Dank*. We eat. Brisket she had made for supper. My favourite, Mister Sholom Aleichem. Ordinarily I would give an arm for a good piece of brisket. But this time it didn't taste so good. I felt like I had a bit of indigestion.

'Have you got some seltzer?' I ask Betty. 'Sure,' she says. 'It's right in front of you, there on the table. Are you blind or something?' So I drink a little seltzer water and it feels better—the indigestion.

After supper I lie down for an hour. I snooze a bit. Now and again a little bit of indigestion wakes me up. A sort of heartburn. But nothing serious.

Then suddenly I feel Betty shaking me a bit. 'It's a quarter past eight. We better go, Barnie, if we're going to make the nine o'clock show.'

I rouse myself up. I go to the bathroom. To tell you the truth, Mister Sholom Aleichem, I don't really feel much like going out to see a movie, even if it is a movie about Tevye and Motel and Tevye's daughters and the whole *schtick* I remember from when I was a boy and in my grandmother's house they used to hold *ein Abend mit Sholom Aleichem*, an evening with Sholom Aleichem. I'll tell you about that later.

But a promise is a promise. *Fiddler on the Roof*, here we come.

'All right,' I say, and go to get my coat. 'All right, Betty. Let's go. We'll have an evening with Sholom Aleichem.'

And just at that moment, at the very moment when I say, 'We'll have an evening with Sholom Aleichem,' a pain cuts through me like I never had before. Like a hot knife cutting through butter. Just when I say, 'We'll have an evening with Sholom Aleichem.' It's got nothing to do with you, Mister Sholom Aleichem. No, no, God forbid. I'm not blaming you one little bit, you understand, only just when I say, 'We'll have an evening with Sholom Aleichem,' the knife goes through me.

I let out a cry. It must have been a kind of a shriek because Betty comes running out into the hall, and she cries, 'What's the matter, Barnie? What happened?'

But just at that moment, a giant, one of those three-hundred pounders I try to fit into a suit, puts his arms around my waist and he squeezes and squeezes. *Oy, Gewalt!* I can't breathe. I gasp for air. But he squeezes and squeezes, and the knife keeps cutting through me.

'Barnie, Barnie,' Betty cries, 'What's happening? Oh, My God, what's happening?'

I try to say something, but I can only moan, and that roughneck keeps squeezing the life out of me. I try to hold on to something. I touch the wall, but I feel myself falling and falling, and with a thump I collapse on the floor.

The next thing I know, I am in the hospital, in an oxygen tent, with needles in my arms and tubes sticking out all over, and it's a miracle that I'm alive. In intensive care, that's where I am, and it's touch and go for three or four days.

But someone must have put in a good word for me. Betty most likely. My children. My friends. From their lips to God's ears. So maybe some big shot up there, maybe even you, Mister Sholom Aleichem, said to the angel who keeps the records, 'It's not time yet for Barnie Himmel! Put him back! Put him back!'

I see you're smiling, Mister Sholom Aleichem. Isn't that how it's done? Who decides, anyway, that this one should live and that one should die? God alone? Or does he delegate the paperwork? You know how it is said, 'On Rosh Hashanah it's entered and on Yom Kippur it's sealed—who lives, who dies, who by fire and who by water, who from hunger and who from thirst.'

One thing I learned. Everything you always think happens to other people, eventually happens to you, too.

But this time I only got a warning. I heard the knock on the door. The angel of death brushed my cheek.

After a week, ten days, they moved me out of intensive care, just on the day when I turned sixty-five. What a birthday! All my children were there. And the grandchildren. And Betty, of course. They brought a cake and flowers and they were going to have a regular party. But the chief nurse came rushing in and stopped all this *Narrishkeit.* 'No excitement!' she called out, 'No excitement! This patient is still pretty sick.'

'So take the cake home,' I said, 'and have a celebration.'

They laughed, and my son said, 'We'll drink to your health, Dad,' and I said, 'Let it go from your mouth to God's ear.'

I stayed in the hospital for another three, four weeks, and now I am home. I have a damaged heart, but I am alive, and if I am careful, and if I lose weight, and if I stop smoking, and if I do exercise, the doctor said I could live another twenty years. From his lips to God's ears. You know how it is, Mister Sholom Aleichem. You had a lot of trouble with your lungs. My trouble comes from the heart.

I've already been home for five weeks, and I have to stay home longer yet. How long? He won't tell me exactly, the doctor. So in the meantime I'm going nuts. I'm bored out of my mind. I want to get back to the store. But as soon as I mention it, Betty weeps bitter tears. 'I don't want to be a widow,' she cries. She wants me to retire. 'We'll go to Florida,' she says. 'Away from the winters in Canada.' 'I'll die of boredom,' I say. 'So you'll be a widow one way or another.' 'Don't joke like this,' she cries. It's not a joke, Mister Sholom Aleichem. It's the truth.

He won't even let me go out and play poker with my friends, the doctor. No excitement, he says, no gambling. We never play for high stakes, I tell him. But he says excitement has nothing to do with money. It's competition, he says. He says I have a compulsive personality. I'm a competitor. A compulsive personality! A lot of baloney, if you ask me. But maybe not. Maybe he's right, the doctor, maybe he knows a thing or two. Anyway, Betty wouldn't let me go out. The doctor says something, that's it as far as she is concerned.

But she's worried about me. How restless I am. How I am going nuts, sitting around doing nothing. So she talked it over with my son David, and two, three days he comes to the house and he brings me this beautiful tape-recorder.

'You're always telling stories, Dad,' he says. 'So tell your stories into the machine. Tell your life story. Then we can have someone take it off the tape. You don't have to worry about spelling the words or worry about grammar. We'll hire a secretary and she'll do it. Just tell your stories, Dad,' he says.

And here I am. A great little invention, eh, Mister Sholom Aleichem! Miracles of modern science. What you wouldn't have given to have a machine like that! Am I right? I bet you could've told twice as many stories if you didn't have to write everything out in pencil or with a pen. I don't even think they had typewriters in your day. Am I right, Mr. Sholom Aleichem?

Ah! Betty's calling me. I'm supposed to walk around a bit. Not too much. But I'm supposed to get some exercise. Then I'll have some tea. And then I'll come back and I'll tell you how they used to have an evening with Sholom Aleichem in my grandmother's house. No big fancy movies. No stars. No singing. But it was a lot of fun just the same. So don't go away. Or if you must go away, I'll call you back later.

II

Well! I never got back yesterday. I walked around a bit. I had tea. Then my daughter came with the grandchildren. So I was busy.

I was telling my wife and my daughter that I was talking to Sholom Aleichem on the tape-recorder. I thought they would think I was *meshugge*, that I had gone bananas. But Betty says, 'Talk to anyone you want, just so long as you don't go back to the store and kill yourself. I don't want to be a widow.'

I don't see you sitting in the chair, Mister Sholom Aleichem. —I'll talk to you anyway. I'm sure you can hear me, wherever you are.

You know, last night I had a dream about you, Mister Sholom Aleichem. A strange kind of a dream. You were sitting on a cloud and all around you people were sitting, also on clouds, and up above all the clouds someone else was sitting, on a big chair it seemed. Maybe a throne. I couldn't see who it was because the clouds were so thick. Maybe an important angel. Maybe—who knows?—God himself. And you were reading stories to them. From time to time there was laughter. Sometimes it sounded more like a thunderclap. The clouds shook. But you went right on reading. Then you stood up—you were standing right on a cloud, but you didn't sink in.

Ah! Now I see you again. You're back in the chair. Make yourself comfortable, Mister—. Maybe I could just call you Sholom. But no, that doesn't sound right. Not respectful. You were such a famous writer. They make movies from your stories. With big stars. And when you died, I heard, there were maybe a hundred thousand people that came to your funeral in New York. A hundred thousand people! Imagine that! So how could I call you by your first name, like you were my friend? But actually—you are my friend. I've known you ever since I was a boy. Even though I forgot about you—more or less—for forty, forty-five years.

But when I was a boy, I heard your stories every two, three weeks, on Friday nights after supper in my grandmother's house on Maria Street, here in Toronto. That's when the neighbors—ten, twelve people, sometimes more, husbands and wives, daughters and sons, even—came together in my grandmother's living room, and they drank tea and gossiped and told the news from the old country and how they were trying to bring relatives over here, and then someone always said, 'And now let's hear a story from Sholom Aleichem,' and my grandmother would bring out a book and someone would read a story, and everybody listened, and they laughed and sometimes they cried, and they made comments. They cursed the bad guys and they cheered on the good guys. It was a regular riot.

The best reader was Sam Rabinowitz. He didn't come all the time. Maybe once a month. But when he came, people used to go out and fetch other friends and neighbors. Because when Sam Rabinowitz read your stories, it was really and truly an evening with Sholom Aleichem.

Oh, could he read—Sam Rabinowitz. With feeling and with tenderness, and with humor and sometimes with sarcasm.

I remember he read about a writer who churns out plays like you churn out butter. One a month. But are they any good? Does he sell any? *A naechtiger Tag.* Don't even ask. His wife turns out babies. One a year. Healthy, strong babies. He complains. Every year a baby! *Genug!* 'I tell you what,' she says. 'I make better babies than you make plays. So let's switch. You have the babies and I'll write the plays.'

Ah, that brought applause. 'Good for her!' cried one of the women. 'How does he think the babies come?' cried another. And a third said, 'He won't leave her alone, the pig. So let him provide for the babies. He should get a job, he should.'

But best of all they liked to hear stories about weddings and marriages. Good and bad. How once seven matchmakers got into the act to arrange two matches—three and a half matchmakers per match!

I see you're laughing, Mister Sholom Aleichem. You remember the story?

How once there was a young couple, and they were already standing under the *chupah,* under the canopy, and the rabbi was just starting the ceremony, when suddenly two young women come rushing into the synagogue, screaming and cursing.

'Stop everything!'

'Don't marry him!'

'That scoundrel!'

'That robber!'

'He married me four months ago, just after Passover. He took the dowry and he left me with a child.' And she pointed to her belly.

Oh, the commotion in my grandmother's living room! Talk about audience participation! To this day I don't know how the story came out. But if he escaped with his life, that bigamist, it would have been a miracle, if they had anything to say about it.

Sam Rabinowitz was a small man. He had hardly any hair, but what he had he combed very carefully. When he sat in a big chair, his feet touched the floor, but just. He had a little pot belly. And when you looked at his tie, you could read the menu from the whole week—when he had eggs and when *borscht*, when dark meat gravy and when light chicken gravy. And when prune juice. Prune juice he liked especially because it helped him with his constipation.

But when he opened his mouth, you forgot everything. How could such a rich voice come from such a small man? But it could, and when he read you forgot everything else, and Sam Rabinowitz was like a great actor and he had the audience in the palm of his hand.

Weddings and marriages. Like I said, that's what they liked to hear most. There was another story I remember—a story about a mysterious woman with a heavy veil.

A young couple is just getting married. They're standing together under the *chupah*. A beautiful couple. The wedding dress cost a fortune. No expense has been spared. The bride's father is a big shot. And the bridegroom's father is no piker, either. The guests have come from far and wide. Reporters are here from the newspapers. And photographers, too. All is quiet. The ceremony is just about to start.

At this point, Sam Rabinowitz dropped his voice. He waited. To build up the suspense.

Suddenly she appears. A tall woman. She walks down the aisle as if she is the bride. Nobody can see her face because it's hidden behind the veil. Is she beautiful? Is she ugly? No one knows. Who is she? Nobody recognizes her. But she knows what she wants. She goes straight to the bridegroom's father and whispers something in his ear. He turns pale. He takes her by the arm and leads her outside, to a little room.

Everything stops. Panic sweeps over the guests. The bride's mother is nearly fainting. The young couple look at each other. Nobody knows what's happening.

In the little room, the bridegroom's father asks the woman behind the veil, 'What do you want?'

'I was your son's mistress,' she says. 'In Kiev. When he was a student.'

It doesn't surprise the father. Rich men's sons do these things.

'So,' he says. 'What's the ultimatum?' No fooling around for him. Right to the point.

'Let him marry me,' she says.

'Impossible,' says the father.

'Then a monthly payment,' she says. 'And a sum for the baby.' The baby? Where did the baby come from? Suddenly a baby! He'd have a thing or two to say to his son. But in the meantime, he had to make a deal.

He pulls out his wallet. He gives her money. 'Tomorrow, come to my lawyer. We'll complete the deal.'

With that, he walks out of the room. The wedding goes on.

In my grandmother's living room they could hardly wait for Sam Rabinowitz to finish. Then a big debate began. Some didn't believe it altogether. That the son had a mistress when he was a student, yes, that they believed. But she wouldn't have barged in like that. Oh, yes, she would, said others. How else could she hope to get anything? And how about the young bride? Didn't she suspect that something was not *kosher?* Sure, said one of the men, but she figured it would give her a hammer to hold over her husband's head. And if she ever wanted to take a lover, she would have every excuse. Her husband couldn't say anything. That's the way rich people do things.

Then they turned to Sam Rabinowitz. What did he think?

'It's a comedy,' he said. And that's all he said.

A comedy! All of life is a comedy. You knew that better than anybody, Mister Sholom Aleichem. Even some tragedies are comedies.

Now let me tell you about what happened once.

A Friday night again. After supper. Once again they come together in my grandmother's house for an evening with Sholom Aleichem. Sam Rabinowitz comes. He hadn't been for a few weeks because he was in the hospital for an operation. A hernia. That's what he had. They greeted him like he had just returned from the dead. Like a messiah, almost. He was just the same. His tie had a few more spots, but otherwise he was the same.

First he had some tea and a piece of honey-cake. In the meantime, several people went out to fetch others. They knew that everybody in the neighborhood wanted to hear Sam Rabinowitz reading Sholom Aleichem stories.

So more people came. The room was packed. Suddenly two new faces appeared. A mother and her daughter. Mrs. Silber and her daughter Sonia. They had just moved into our street. They lived in Mrs. Goldberg's house and they didn't know too many people yet. So they were introduced and they shook hands with everybody, and when Sonia shook hands with me and looked into my eyes, an arrow struck me in the heart, Mister Sholom Aleichem. I fell in love. Immediately. Head over heels, like the saying goes. For the first time in my life. I was fifteen years old. I had kissed a few girls, even felt them up a little bit, to tell you the truth, but never had such a feeling gone right through me, like a hot knife through butter. Never. Never before and (I'll whisper this to you) never again.

Sonia's eyes were like a deep blue lake and I fell in and drowned. Her breasts were small and round, like little oranges, and her legs were long and beautiful. She was maybe eighteen or nineteen. Maybe less.

She sat down and stretched out her long legs and put her hands in her lap, and I stood against the wall so I could see her and drink in the wonder of her, but so it wouldn't be too obvious. Maybe, maybe, I prayed, she has fallen in love with me, too. Please God, let it be so. From my mouth to God's ear.

Sam Rabinowitz cleared his throat. Someone rapped a spoon against a glass, someone else called out for quiet. They stopped talking. Rabinowitz began to read.

This time it was a story about a girl called Rayzel. This Rayzel was expecting her first child and she was already overdue. Everything was prepared. The midwife was waiting. But nothing was happening. Then suddenly the pains came. Rayzel writhed and moaned. She wanted to die. Her grandmother was standing by her because her mother was dead.

'Scream, scream!' called out the grandmother. 'One more scream and with God's help you'll make it.'

Suddenly Rayzel calls out a name. (I've forgotten the name, Mister Sholom Aleichem, but you probably remember it.) Anyway, it's the name of her husband. Where he is? It turns out he left her eight months ago. He said he was going to America to look for work. But she hasn't heard a word from him since—not a word. People were already saying that he was gone for good, that he had probably got himself another woman in America. But he left a little souvenir, and here is Rayzel struggling to deliver that souvenir.

'No, no!' she cries out, 'he hasn't forgotten about me! He'll come back to me. Where are you, where are you? God! God! God!' And the women standing around her don't know if she's crying for her husband or for God. But why not for both?

Rabinowitz read with such emotion that some people were crying. Some of the women in the room were cursing the absent husband because he could at least have sent a letter. Or even a post card.

As for me, I can't take my eyes off Sonia. I hear Rabinowitz and his powerful voice, but my heart is beating and hot flames are shooting through me.

'Sonia! Sonia!' I want to cry out to her, 'I love you, I love you!'

Now that would have been a fine how do you do, eh, Mister Sholom Aleichem?

But meanwhile Sam Rabinowitz is reading about poor Rayzel, who is moaning and crying and pushing, and calling out her husband's name.

Suddenly Sonia's face turns white. White like a sheet. She puts her hands over her ears, as if she doesn't want to hear any more. Her eyes open wide and she stares at me, but I don't think she sees me. Her body sways. And suddenly she lets out a long, low moan, 'Ahhhhhh,' and then the moan becomes a wail and then a cry.

'Mama! Mama!' she cries. 'Help me! Help me!'

'Help her! Help her!' somebody cries out. 'She's going to faint.'

Here is my chance. I rush forward. I take her hand. I stroke her hair.

Her mother starts crying. People start pushing.

'Give her some air!' someone calls out.

'Help her to the bedroom, Barnie,' I hear my grandmother's voice. 'Let her lie down. Then bring a wet washcloth and put it on her forehead.'

I didn't have to be told twice, Mister Sholom Aleichem.

'Come,' I say. 'Come, Sonia. Lean on me. Come and lie down.'

She walked slowly with me, holding on to my arm, and her mother walked behind us. And I was on a cloud. On cloud seven, as the saying goes. Or cloud nine. Whatever the number, I was on it.

Sam Rabinowitz started reading again, but I didn't go back. So that's another of your stories I didn't hear to the end, Mister Sholom Aleichem.

I helped Sonia to lie down and I held her hand—a little longer than I had to. And then I saw the wedding ring on her finger and my heart stopped beating. It couldn't be. But yes, it was.

I went out to fetch a wet washcloth and when I came back, her mother was talking to her in a soft voice and she was lying there very still, with her eyes closed.

I put the washcloth on her forehead. Then I see the wedding ring again, and I can't take my eyes off it.

I want to say something, but the words won't come out of my mouth. My voice is dry and I can't speak. But finally I manage to whisper to her mother, 'Is she married?'

She gave me such a look. I didn't know what to make of it. Then she pointed to the ring. 'You see the ring?' she asked.

'I see it, I see it,' I said.

'So why are you asking?'

I didn't know what to say.

'She has a ring,' she said. 'But where's the husband?'

Sonia opened her deep-blue eyes. 'Don't, Mama,' she said. 'Please don't.'

What I wouldn't have done to help her, Mister Sholom Aleichem, what I wouldn't have done for her!

'So what did I say?' the mother said. 'Where is he, that no-goodnik? I always knew he was a no-goodnik, but you knew better.'

I was torn in half, Mister Sholom Aleichem. I could have murdered that guy. I was so jealous. But at the same time I wanted him to come back because my beautiful Sonia was suffering. And yet—if he didn't come back, maybe there was room for me.

'Don't,' Sonia said to her mother. 'Please don't.'

'I have to say what is in my heart,' the mother said. 'I wouldn't mind so much if he had just disappeared. Good riddance. But he had to leave a souvenir.'

'Stop it, Mama! Stop it!' cried Sonia, and she put her hands over her ears. She didn't want to hear any more. Then she got off the bed, and said, 'I want to go home. Let's go home immediately.'

I was left all confused. Especially about the souvenir. Did that mean what I thought it meant? Well, in a few weeks there was no doubt. The secret was out. Up front, so to speak. But she was more beautiful than ever.

I used to hang around Mrs. Goldberg's house, where they had rented some rooms. I knew when she went to the store and I used to wait for her to come out and then I went with her and carried her parcels. I was always hoping that she would say something that showed that she was in love with me. And then I had a speech all ready. I would leave school and get a job and we would get married— her husband, if she really had a husband, was totally out of the picture. And I would accept the child as if it was my own.

Of course, she never said she loved me, and I never got to make my speech. She always treated me nice—like I was her kid brother. That bothered me a lot, but what could I do?

Soon there was a lot of talk on our street. Some said there never was a husband. And that's why they came here—the mother and the daughter. Some said they came from Winnipeg and some said from

Montreal. I asked her once and she said it wasn't true, but she didn't tell me any more.

Then one day they disappeared. She was already very big and her time was close. Mrs. Goldberg said they had gone to Montreal, where the mother had a sister. I don't know if that was true. Perhaps you heard about it, Mister Sholom Aleichem, because that's the kind of story you used to tell.

I was heartbroken for a while, but then I got over it. But I never forgot. Over the years I've often thought about Sonia because she aroused such a passion in me, but this is the first time I'm telling about it. She would be sixty-eight, sixty-nine years old if she's still alive. And the child would be fifty.

Except—for me she can never be old. She will always be the way she was when I first looked into her eyes. When I think about her it's always spring, the sun is always shining, the trees are green and the birds sing.

I'll play the tape back, and then perhaps I'll wipe it off. My son told me to tell about my life, but maybe he would be embarrassed. And Betty maybe would be jealous. But to you I can tell it. If you want, you can tell it when they all get together up there, on the clouds, for an evening with Sholom Aleichem.

And that reminds me. *Fiddler on the Roof* isn't playing in town any more. But it'll come back. And when it comes back to a theatre near us, I'll take Betty for sure this time. And we'll have an evening with Sholom Aleichem.

It's funny—you were there when I first knew what real love was, when the hot knife of passion went through me. And you were there also when the hot knife cut through me and the angel of death brushed my cheek.

Good-bye for now, my dear Mister Sholom Aleichem. I'll tell more stories some other time. And when you are back there, on the clouds, put in a good word for Barnie Himmel. So with God's help I should recover my health and have a few more good years with Betty, God bless her, and to have joy, to have *naches*, from my children and grandchildren. From your mouth to God's ears. Amen.

Henry Kreisel

To Visit Mother Rachel's Grave

How the thought occurred to her she couldn't say. It emerged from some deep region of her mind, late one afternoon during the fourth week of her illness when she lay, silent and alone, and tried to listen to the beat of her heart and imagined that she could hear its slow tattoo. She tried to hear what she thought was the blood flowing past the damaged part of the heart muscle. Her concept of the anatomy of the heart was very imprecise, a vague blur made up of dimly-remembered illustrations in magazines, coloured red and blue, strange pictures of open chests that showed how the blood circulated and how the heart (her doctor had told her it was a muscle) pumped and pumped without ceasing, endlessly. Unless the flow was blocked. And then there was pain. She remembered the excruciating pain when her attack first came. She didn't quite know what was happening to her, though she knew that it was something terrible. But she did not believe that she was having a heart attack. Women did not have heart attacks. Not often, anyway. Men had heart attacks, collapsed in the street, in their offices. She could still not really believe it, although it was now nearly a month since the attack and the doctors told her that she was making a good recovery and that she would soon be allowed to go home from the hospital.

But everything was changed, nevertheless. She felt terribly fragile, standing on the edge of a great chasm. She concentrated very hard, trying to hear her heartbeat. Sometimes she thought she heard it, but then again it seemed to fade, far away and then it seemed to cease altogether. In those moments she panicked, even though there was no pain. But she was sure that the heart had stopped beating and that she would suddenly cease to be. The thought of not-being was terrible to bear. Her hands began to tremble, she opened the two top buttons of her nightgown and placed her right hand on her breast and tried to feel the heart beating against her fingers. And when at last she felt the soft tattoo against the tips of her fingers, her hands stopped trembling, she relaxed. She was back among the living.

It was after one of those episodes that the thought suddenly occurred. She must go to visit Mother Rachel's grave, near Jerusalem, half a world away. She must go there to beseech that lovely figure to help her, to hold protecting hands over her, to heal her body and prolong her life.

The thought astonished her, though in a strange way it lifted her spirits and brought her a curious calm. It was a long time since she had felt so at peace, as if the mere thought had already brought the protecting presence close to her, here in this northern city, in the middle of the winter. In the spring, when the flowers bloomed again, she would have recovered, she would be able to undertake the long journey. With her husband. Of course. He would have to come with her. She was afraid that he would think her frivolous. She would have to use all her powers of persuasion, for he would not regard a journey to see a grave as a holiday. It was in any case always difficult to tear him away from his business affairs. His clients were always more important than she. And of course his work was important, his clients relied on him. But why was she always making excuses for him? Why did she always think that his affairs were so important that she should defer to him, that her needs must always be subordinated to his?

Nowadays young women would not stand for this. Then why should she? They had now been married for over thirty years and she had never seriously challenged the order of their relationship. In some ways she could not really complain. Theirs had been a reasonably good marriage. They had come to know each other when David joined her father's law firm as a junior partner. He was brilliant, and her father always believed that he would have a great career. It was David who had fallen passionately in love with her and he pursued her with a wild, romantic abandon. She was not in love with him at first, but he persisted and in her father he found a great ally.

She was romantic enough to allow herself to be wooed and courted and eventually she consented to marry him. Not long after the wedding his ardor cooled. He was a very conventional man and he demanded an ordered life befitting a swiftly-rising professional man. She adjusted to his demands relatively easily, especially after the birth of their son Benjamin. But in the last few years she had begun to have doubts, but she had always managed to suppress them. Imperceptibly they had drifted apart, their emotional lives no longer really intertwined. Perhaps she should have demanded more. Perhaps she had allowed her life to drain away, and only now, when death had lightly brushed against her, did she realize it.

She felt a sudden surge of irrational anger. No. No. She must not let herself be carried away. She must not get excited. She must not allow her peaceful state of mind to be disturbed. Her doctor had told her to learn to relax, to do it consciously, from the toes upwards, until all the tension had gone from the muscles. She tried now to follow that advice. She tried to call up the image of Rachel, to make it take on body, but no conventional figure appeared. Yet a curious presence was there, in her room, she could feel it. She felt herself floating in space, very calm, very peaceful, buoyed up by the unseen presence.

She closed her eyes. How long she lay thus suspended she didn't know. But when she opened her eyes again, she felt better than she had for many weeks, even before her heart attack.

She kept a little mirror on the table beside her bed, and she reached out to get it and looked at herself in the mirror. She sat up with a start when she saw how the colour had come back into her face. Was it just wishful thinking? She stared critically at herself in the mirror. Her cheeks no longer seemed sunken, there was a sparkle in her eyes. She looked again younger than a woman of fifty-three, and she thought how everyone would again remark how young she looked. Only her hair was somewhat dishevelled and the grey streaks stood out starkly. Quickly she reached for her comb and brush and began to brush her hair vigorously until she was satisfied that the grey streaks had been properly subdued and the rich dark-brown colour of her hair predominated once again. Then she realized, with a sudden and delighted shock, that she had neglected to search for her heartbeat when she woke. That had become a sort of ritual since her heart attack, a way of assuring herself that she was still alive. And now she had neglected the ritual. It was a good sign. It must be the wonderful presence that was responsible for it. She smiled, feeling a trifle embarrassed by the idea, for she did not think of herself as a superstitious person. But the conceit was so pleasant, so reassuring, that she did not want to discard it. But why did it arise in the first place? The figure of Rachel was not normally close to her consciousness. But now she remembered that in her mother's room there was a picture of the tomb of Rachel, and her mother told her that Rachel helped the sick and ailing. It was also her mother who told her the story, so many, many years ago. How Jacob had first set eyes on Rachel as she came to the well to water her father's flock. How he had fallen in love with her (she was shapely and beautiful, her mother told her) and how he had served her father for many years in order to have her. How many years? Was it seven years? Or was it twice seven years? She couldn't quite remember. The story was complicated. There was another sister. Yes. There was another sister, and Jacob married her first, and then had to serve their father another seven years before he could have Rachel. What was the father's name? She couldn't recall it, nor any other details of the story. Except Rachel's death. She had died young. Was it in childbirth? She searched her memory. Jacob buried her at the place where she died. Yes. It was after Rachel had given birth to Benjamin. Benjamin! The name gave her a start, for it was the name of her own son. Her own Benjamin. And she remembered how hard a birth it was. She had almost died. Was that why the figure of Rachel had suddenly come to her, why her presence had so suddenly manifested itself? Who could say? But why the strange thought that she must go and visit the grave of the beautiful woman who had died in childbirth?

She made an impatient gesture with her hand, as if she wanted to have done with the whole matter. She put the mirror, the comb and the brush back on the little table by her bed. She didn't want to speculate any more. Perhaps she should get up and walk about a bit. In a while, she thought.

She picked up a magazine and began to leaf through it, but she couldn't get very interested. Nothing seemed to register. It all seemed unimportant, overwhelmed by that strange feeling of an unseen presence in her room. However hard she tried to put it from her mind, it would not be shut out. And even though she decided, quite deliberately, not to search her memory for any more details of the story of Rachel, she could not banish the almost palpable sense of a presence, though she could not give that presence any tangible form. She decided not even to try. It was better so. She did not want to see a conventional picture of a pale, long-robed woman, beautiful, aetherial. That would be banal. No, no. Let the presence remain. She would try to accept it, quite simply, quite naturally.

Then later in the evening when David came (for he came every day, he was very concerned about her) and perhaps Benjamin also (he tried to come every day, but couldn't always make it), she might tell them what had happened to her this afternoon.

Should she tell them that she must visit Rachel's grave? The mere thought gave her pause. What would happen if she simply said, 'I must go and visit Mother Rachel's grave?' Come to think of it, she didn't even know exactly where the grave was. Somewhere in Israel, she thought. They had never been there. So she would look foolish if she said, 'I must go and visit Mother Rachel's grave.' Neither David nor Benjamin would understand. They were very practical men, not much given to introspection. But then neither was she, and that's why the sense of an unseen presence was so disturbing, even though it had brought her a moment of peace and of calm. And for that she was grateful. No doubt when the right time came, she would know what to say.

Outside it was getting darker and her room was in twilight, but she didn't want to turn her bedside lamp on. She wanted just to lie there peacefully. It was almost time for one of the nurses to come and take her temperature and give her her pills. Until then she would lie quietly. Her body felt relaxed. Outside, in the corridor, people were walking past her room, the sound of voices came drifting in, brief snatches of conversation. But it all seemed a long way away.

Sooner than she had expected, the cheerful voice of Patricia, her favourite nurse, roused her. 'Why so quiet, Mrs. Larkin? Are you feeling all right?'

'Oh, yes, yes,' she said quickly and raised herself against her pillow.

The nurse turned on the light and walked over to the bed, holding out the thermometer, but she stopped abruptly before she had quite reached the bed and stared at Mrs. Larkin, as if she had suddenly become aware of something that was out of the ordinary.

'Why, Mrs. Larkin,' she said, 'you're looking different. You're looking so much better than you did last evening when I came on the shift.'

Mrs. Larkin sat up. She broke into a smile. 'Do I really? Do I really?' she cried out. She knew of course that she was looking better, for she had closely inspected her face in her mirror. Only she might have been deceiving herself, it might all have been wishful thinking. But now it was confirmed. Patricia had confirmed it, without any prompting, quite spontaneously. 'What has changed since yesterday?' she asked eagerly. 'What's different?'

'You look so much younger,' Patricia said. 'Your colour's come back. You look so much—so much—alive. . . . Perhaps that was the wrong thing to say.'

'Oh, no, no. Not wrong. No, no. Thank you for saying that. You've made me so happy. I feel more alive.'

The young nurse smiled. She placed the thermometer in Mrs. Larkin's mouth, under the tongue.

Mrs. Larkin took the thermometer out of her mouth. 'You weren't saying that only to please me?'

'No, no. Why would I do that?'

'Oh, because you wanted to make me feel better, perhaps. You've always been so nice to me. I always feel nice when you come into my room.'

'I wouldn't lie to you,' said the young nurse.

Mrs. Larkin gave her a long look. Then, without quite wanting to, she said, her voice low, almost whispering, 'It's Rachel's doing.'

The young nurse looked puzzled, as if she hadn't quite grasped what Mrs. Larkin had said. 'Rachel?' she asked. 'Who is she?'

'Oh, you know. She's a character in the Bible. A beautiful young woman. She was bringing her father's sheep to the well when Jacob saw her. And then he had to work for seven years for her father before he could marry her.'

'Oh,' said the nurse. She didn't know what to make of this. There was a tone of impatience, even of irritation, in Mrs. Larkin's voice. She had never been conscious of it before, even during the early days of her illness.

'Don't you know the story?'

The young nurse hesitated. 'Well—not really,' she said then. 'I don't really remember hearing the story.'

'Not even when you were a child?'

'Not that I remember. We were never great Bible readers in my family.' She began to feel uncomfortable, because the conversation was taking such an unusual turn, and it seemed to her suddenly as if she were being interrogated. 'What of it anyway?' she said sharply. 'What difference does it make? What's it all mean?'

Mrs. Larkin shrank back defensively. 'Nothing really,' she said hesitantly. 'Nothing at all.'

'But then what did you mean when you said it was Rachel's doing?'

'It was all so very strange,' said Mrs. Larkin. She hesitated, not knowing quite how to put things without making herself look ridiculous. 'I—I can hardly believe it myself. It's not as if I'd been thinking about Rachel a lot. On the contrary. I don't ever recall thinking about her at all. I barely remembered her story when I thought about it afterwards.' She paused for a moment, aware that what she was saying must seem confusing to Patricia. Or else it would seem ridiculous or far-fetched at best. Especially if she were to tell her about that sudden and overwhelming desire to visit Rachel's grave.

The young nurse didn't say anything, though she was genuinely intrigued by whatever it was that Mrs. Larkin had experienced.

'How—how can I tell you what happened?' Mrs. Larkin continued. 'It's very strange.' She hesitated, then decided to say nothing about visiting Rachel's grave. That might seem altogether too ludicrous. 'Well—I—I had some kind of feeling of a—of a presence in the room. Not that I could see a figure—I mean there was no person in the room. I wasn't hallucinating or anything like that. But I was quite sure and I relaxed and sort of dozed off—I didn't fall asleep. I was always quite conscious, but I felt suspended, almost weightless. It was a wonderful feeling and all the time I knew that there was something in the room. No—not something. Someone. And then I knew that it was Rachel. And I knew that she had come to help me.' She felt herself being carried away and she stopped. She didn't want to lose control. 'Does that seem weird to you?' she asked.

The nurse shrugged her shoulders. 'In a way, yes, it does,' she said. 'But then, you get used to some strange things in a hospital.'

Mrs. Larkin didn't like that. She had hoped that Patricia would be sympathetic. But then, hadn't she herself invited such a response by her question?

She continued, in a much quieter tone of voice, a bit embarrassed even, because she could sense Patricia's scepticism, but she felt that she must bring the matter to a close. 'When I returned. . . .' She paused for a moment, surprised by the word she had used. Had she been away, then? And if so, where?

Patricia was looking at her quizzically and so there was no time to stop and consider the question. 'When I returned,' she repeated, this time more deliberately, 'I felt that I had—recovered. I felt better than I had for months—long before my attack. And—do you know?—I didn't put my hand on my heart to feel the beat with my fingers. I used to do that, you know, automatically when I woke from a sleep and often during the day as well. And this time I didn't do it, didn't even think about it until long afterwards. It was such a wonderful feeling. And then I looked in my little mirror and I could see that I looked better, and when you came in, you confirmed it. Without any prompting from me. You said I looked younger. You said my colour'd come back. You said I was more alive.' She dropped her voice. 'Something extraordinary was going on,' she almost whispered. 'I'm sure of it. There was—someone here. Some power. . . .' Her voice trailed off.

'You better take your temperature now,' said the young nurse very matter-of-factly, almost as if she were talking to a child.

Mrs. Larkin was annoyed. 'Don't treat me like a little girl, Pat,' she said. With a sharp, deliberate motion she put the thermometer into her mouth and glowered at the young nurse. Her feeling of well-being was almost gone, the tranquil glow spread by that unseen presence now replaced by the mundane routine of the hospital, where patients had their temperature taken and where soon a tray of bland food would be deposited by her bed.

'I'm sorry,' said the young nurse. Patients who'd had heart attacks often had strange reactions. She should have shown more understanding. Perhaps there was something in all that. Mrs. Larkin did look a lot better. Did it matter what had brought about the change? If Mrs. Larkin thought it was because of some presence and gave that presence a name, why shouldn't she have the right to believe that? 'I didn't mean to upset you,' she said, 'but I've got to hurry. I'll see you in a little while.' With a slight pat on Mrs. Larkin's arm (again she treats me like a child, Mrs. Larkin thought, still somewhat annoyed), the young nurse turned and walked quickly out of the room.

Mrs. Larkin tried to compose herself. In a way, she thought, this was a kind of rehearsal. Patricia was usually so understanding, so sympathetic, and if Pat thought that what she heard was strange (weird even, though to be fair, this was a word that she herself had used and so had in a way suggested it to Pat), then what would her husband and her son think of that outlandish story? Especially if she were to mention a visit to that grave! She was glad she hadn't mentioned that part of the happening to Patricia. Yet in a way it was the most important part of the whole experience, it was the trigger, it was what had so suddenly, so unexpectedly occurred to her. The sense of a presence in the room came later. Perhaps, she thought now, that had been a more conscious evocation on her part. Perhaps it was her attempt to give substance to what was an evanescent feeling, to force a revelation. That must seem strange to people. It had seemed strange to Pat and would seem even stranger to her husband and to her son.

Perhaps it would be best not to say anything, to keep the sense that something extraordinary had happened to herself. Yet there were results. She felt better and looked better. Pat had noticed it. Her husband would, too. Perhaps. He was not always very observant. She wouldn't say anything. Not right away. But when the proper moment came, she would know, and she would say simply, 'I must go and visit Mother Rachel's grave.'

Why 'Mother' Rachel? She didn't know. She only knew that that was the way the thought had first presented itself. Something incongruous there. For when she imagined the figure, it was a young girl she saw, radiant, bringing her sheep to the well. Yet when the thought had first risen in her mind, it was 'Mother' Rachel's grave she was to visit. A strange paradox. She was too tired to try and unravel it.

After a while the young nurse returned and Mrs. Larkin took the thermometer out of her mouth and gave it to her.

'I'm sorry I was a bit snappish before,' Mrs. Larkin said.

'Oh, that's all right. I was also a bit snappish, as you call it.' They both laughed.

'Your temperature's been quite normal now for the last few days,' the nurse said, noting the reading on her chart. 'They'll let you go home pretty soon.'

'I hope so,' said Mrs. Larkin with a sigh. 'I've been here too long. Perhaps that's why I've gone a bit soft.'

'Oh, no, no, no,' said the young nurse quickly.

'So you don't think I'm weird, after all?'

'I never did. People do have strange experiences.'

'I suppose so. It was very real, though.'

'Is it still real?'

'You mean—is it—is she still here? Rachel?'

'Yes.'

Mrs. Larkin hesitated a moment. 'No,' she said then. 'No. I—I don't think so. I can't feel her presence any more. Not right now. . . . Could you hand me my robe, please? I think I'll walk about a bit before they bring the supper tray. Not much to look forward to. I'm getting tired of the wonderful cuisine here.'

'I can hardly blame you,' said Pat. She helped Mrs. Larkin out of bed and held her arm lightly as they walked out of her room. Then Mrs. Larkin went over to the lounge where a television set was turned on and a few ambulatory patients were watching. Mrs. Larkin nodded a greeting to them and sat down. She watched for a few minutes, but the images on the little screen hardly registered. She felt irritated and impatient and she went out of the lounge and walked up and down the hallway a few times, feeling curiously uneasy and restless. Again and again the figure of Rachel imposed itself upon her. She tried to dismiss its presence and that curious thought of visiting her grave. It was a dream, she told herself, and one could dismiss dreams. One didn't have to tell dreams to anyone. So when her husband and her son came to see her later on, she would say nothing. In that way she wouldn't expose herself to ridicule.

At the end of the hallway she saw the orderlies push the carts with the supper-trays and she walked slowly back to her room. She turned the overhead light on and when her tray was delivered she sat down on a chair beside her bed and began to poke at her food. She wasn't very hungry and the food didn't look very appetizing.

But suddenly she was sure that someone was standing behind her, though when she quickly turned her head to look, there was of course nobody. How her mind was playing tricks on her. How tenaciously it held on to the sense of a presence in her room.

She left the food on her tray half-eaten and poured herself some tea, very strong, but lukewarm and bitter-tasting.

'Will it really help me if I visit your grave?' she suddenly heard herself saying, and was surprised, even shocked, to hear the words issuing from her mouth and addressed obviously to Rachel whose presence in her room she now seemed to take for granted. So her attempt to banish the figure from her consciousness had come to nothing. Indeed, Rachel had now become a familiar, intimate friend to whom one could turn for advice and comfort. She waited, almost as if she expected an answering sign from the presence she knew to be in the room, but no sign came. She was disappointed, but not surprised. She knew that she was being watched over.

No, no. This was ridiculous. She must tear herself away from this fantasy, she must shut it out. She must prepare herself for her visitors, who would be here in an hour or so, and she must not give them the impression that she was out of her mind.

A few minutes after seven her husband came. Tall and rather heavy-set, he hesitated a moment by the door, then said, 'How are you, my darling?' and walked slowly over to her bed, bent over and kissed her lightly on the forehead and on her hair, and then touched her gently on her cheek and gently stroked her arm and then took her hand into his and held it.

'I—I feel quite well,' she said. 'Really quite well.' She looked up at him, into his eyes. Would he notice that she looked much better, that colour had returned to her face, that she looked younger? He was not given to extravagant compliments, though on occasion he would be charming and even romantic.

'That's nice,' he said. 'That's very nice.'

Was that all he was going to say? She looked at him, as if willing him to go on, to say something more. He was still handsome, did not look his age—nearly sixty—though his face was fleshier than she would have liked, and he had allowed his body to become a bit flabby around the waist. But his elegant, well-cut grey suit, beautifully draped, concealed a lot of his bulk and made him look like an athlete just beginning to go to seed, but still muscular. His grey hair, still full and carefully combed, gave him the professional air that he cherished and cultivated.

'Don't you notice anything?' she asked.

He looked puzzled. 'Notice? What should I notice?'

She was shattered. Her lips began to tremble. But she would not allow herself to cry, though she felt the tears beginning to come.

'Yes,' he said. 'Yes. Your hair looks beautiful.'

She brightened. 'And my face?' she asked. 'Has the colour returned to it?'

'Yes,' he said. 'Yes. How could I not see it?'

'Because your mind was elsewhere. On your clients. On your cases.'

'Perhaps. Forgive me.' And he leaned over the bed and kissed her, on the cheeks, on the lips. 'How lovely you are. And how I love you.'

Could she dare to tell him about the presence of Rachel in the room? She felt strangely excited and she felt she needed time to compose herself.

'I'd like to sit up in a chair,' she said.

'Of course,' he said. He helped her to get out of the bed and held her robe for her and she settled herself in the chair.

He pulled his own chair close to hers and reached out and took her hand. They sat like this for what seemed a very long time. Then she looked away, towards the window and the winter darkness outside, and said very quietly, 'When I woke up from my afternoon nap, I felt a presence in the room, as if someone was watching over me. And then I was sure that it was Rachel.'

'Rachel?' he said, puzzled. 'Who is Rachel?'

'The character in the Bible. The wife of Jacob. The mother of Benjamin.'

He didn't know what to say. He wanted to make a joke of it, but her look was so intense, as if a fire burned inside her, that he thought better of it. 'Tell me more,' he said at last.

He could see that she was pleased, and then she began to tell him, and as she spoke her face lit up as if the presence had returned, and he felt eerie, a powerful emotion gripped him. He had never experienced anything like it, he had never, in all the years of their marriage, heard her speak so passionately. He saw her as he had never seen her before, he loved her as he had never loved her before.

'You don't think that what I'm saying is ridiculous?' she said abruptly.

'No, no,' he said. 'No, no. It is strange, but it is not ridiculous.'

'There's something else I want to say. When I am better, when the spring comes, I want to visit Rachel's grave. Will you take me?'

This he had not expected. It seemed a bizarre request.

'Where—where is the grave?' he stammered.

'I don't know exactly. Somewhere near Jerusalem, I think. We can find out. We can look it up.'

'Why do you want to go there?'

'To see the grave and speak to her.' The words came in a rush. 'To thank her for coming to me, for encouraging me to live. She died young. We both have Benjamin. I am getting old. But I don't want to die yet.'

'Don't talk nonsense,' he said sharply. 'You are getting better. You cannot die. You cannot leave me alone.'

'My dear, dear David,' she said, her voice tinged with irony. 'Always thinking of yourself. But what of me? What of my needs?'

'Forgive me,' he said. 'I only wanted you to know how much I need you. That life without you would be a desert.'

'Will you take me, then?'

'I will take you.'

'Perhaps that's why she came to me,' she said. 'To let me know that because I was so close to death I can desire life as I never could before.'

He got up and reached his arms out towards her, then pulled her gently up and embraced her. Tears ran down his cheeks. She returned his embrace, passionately, full of life. Only their full awareness of how close she had been to death could charge their kisses with such a deliberate affirmation of life.

Neither of them heard Benjamin, their son, come into the room. Neither of them saw him, they were so absorbed in each other.

He stood for a moment, astonished by the passion that radiated from them. He felt like an intruder, seeing things too private for him to see, and then he tip-toed out of the room, to wait in the hallway until calm returned and their passion was spent.

writings about henry kreisel: essays and reviews

Michael Greenstein's 'The Language of the Holocaust in The Rich Man' *was first published in* Etudes Canadiennes, *4 (1978) and is used by permission of that journal and the author. His* 'Perspectives on the Holocaust in Henry Kreisel's The Betrayal' *and his review article,* 'Close Encounters: Henry Kreisel's Short Stories,' *are reprinted by permission of the author and of* Essays on Canadian Writing *where both were first published (23 [Spring 1982] and 26 [Summer 1983] respectively).* 'Henry Kreisel: A Canadian Exile Writer?' *by Karen Gürttler is reprinted, by permission of the author and of the University of Toronto Press, from* The Old World and the New: Literary Perspectives of German-Speaking Canadians, *edited by Walter E. Riedel (Toronto, Buffalo: University of Toronto Press, 1984). Robert Lecker's 'States of Mind: Henry Kreisel's Novels' was first published in* Canadian Literature, *77 (Summer 1978) and is used by permission of the author. The articles by Carol Hlus and Thomas E. Tausky are published here for the first time.*

Neil Besner's review of The Almost Meeting and Other Stories *appeared in* Canadian Literature, *94 (Autumn 1982); W.J. Keith's review of the same collection appeared in the* Dalhousie Review, *61, 4 (Winter 1981-82), and Stephen Scobie's was first published in* Queen's Quarterly, *89, 3 (Autumn 1982). All are reprinted here by permission of their authors.*

All references to Henry Kreisel's work in the essays which follow are to the following editions:
The Almost Meeting and Other Stories. Edmonton: NeWest Press, 1981;
Another Country: Writings by and about Henry Kreisel, *edited by Shirley Neuman (Edmonton: NeWest Press, 1985).*
The Betrayal *(1964; rpt.* Toronto: McClelland and Stewart, *(1971);*
'The Prairie: A State of Mind' [1968], *in* Contexts of Canadian Criticism, *edited by Eli Mandel (Toronto: Univ. of Toronto Press; Chicago, London: Univ. of Chicago Press, (1971). pp. 254-66;*
The Rich Man *(1948; rpt.* Toronto: McClelland and Stewart, *(1961).*

Michael Greenstein

The Language of the Holocaust
in The Rich Man

In his 'Introduction' to Henry Kreisel's somewhat neglected first novel, *The Rich Man,* John Stedmond tends to underplay the importance of the historical background: 'the story in a sense exists independent of its time and place' (viii). Although the holocaust is not as overt in this novel as in Kreisel's second, *The Betrayal,* nevertheless, given the facts that he wrote it immediately after World War II, set it a decade earlier, and personally escaped the horrors of the concentration camps only to be detained in the internment camps of the new world, one cannot accept the opinion that the events of the thirties are merely peripheral. To comprehend Kreisel's fictional approach to the historical events in *The Rich Man,* the reader needs to examine the problematic nature of language exhibited in the novel's voices, gestures, crowds, quarrels, and aesthetic symbols.

George Steiner's theory about language and silence in response to the tragic genocide in the Second World War provides some assistance when applied to Kreisel's work: 'Nazism found in the language precisely what it needed to give voice to its savagery. Hitler heard inside his native tongue the latent hysteria, the confusion, the quality of hypnotic trance. He plunged unerringly into the under-growth of language. . . . And instead of turning away in nauseated disbelief, the German people gave massive echo to the man's bellowing.'[1] This confusion of language, the voices of both vic-timizer and victim, and the mesmerized crowds are all in evidence in *The Rich Man.* Tassigny's description of his painting, *L'Entre-preneur,* the novel's central symbol that refers to Hitler, resembles Steiner's comments: ' "It means a man, who . . . who . . . how shall I say, *Monsieur,* who . . . who has something to show off and he shouts and screams so people will hear and come and pay to see. They come, they pay, sometimes only money, sometimes more, the whole body and the soul" ' (36). Stammering through this explanation to an uncomprehending Jacob Grossman, Tassigny reveals the difficulties of linguistic expression experienced by most of the characters as he continues to describe the hollow, megaphonic voice on the canvas: ' "But the man cares nothing, for he is full of falseness. And more and more people come, *Monsieur,* because his voice is so . . . so powerful

and loud. . . . They are caught by the voice. . . . The people seldom see
the face, most of the time they only hear his voice—from the radio,
from loudspeakers" ' (36-37). Kreisel's emphasis on 'voice' is not
merely an artistic and dramatic end in itself, but is also a means of
conveying the modern barriers of communication erected by despots
like Hitler, manipulating language. In addition to the tormentor's
abuse of language, the victim's attempt to convey his experience of
the ineffable is of equal importance to gain a fuller picture of the
complexities of language related to the holocaust.

Some of the earliest voices in the novel are broadcast on the faceless
radio with a Negro quartet singing 'Swing Low, Sweet Chariot.'
'Their voices were deep and infinitely sad. "Coming for to carry me
home." One by one the voices fell away until only a full-throated bass
voice was left' (10). Following this song that prepares for Jacob's
return home to Vienna 'is a modern arrangement of that old
favourite—The Blue Danube Waltz' (10), the jazz version of the old
tune pointing to the differences between the new American world
and the old European. As soon as the music is over, the 'suave voice'
of the announcer reports the news of Goering's statement of
Germany's rearmament. Every time Jacob listens to his favourite
melody, 'The Blue Danube Waltz,' the illusion is shattered. On the
ship Jacob's pleasant reverie is interrupted by the reality of
seasickness: ' "Even the music is sick",' announces Tassigny (31). In
Vienna Jacob soon discovers that the musicians in the street are
beggars: ' "I am only a poor street singer, searching somewhere for a
bit of luck".' Jacob cannot hold on to his dream for long when he asks
them for the 'Waltz': 'They were not even pretending to play in
harmony any more. Each man played the tune himself, as if he were
playing a slow solo.' The music which had earlier been sick now
'sounds like a funeral march' (142).

Hollow music and empty voices form part of the problem of
communication within Jacob's experiences reflecting the breakdown
of meaningful language in the international arena. A procrasti-
nating Prufrock with a bald spot on the pate of his head, the middle-
aged presser plans to ask his employer for a leave of absence: 'How
would he go on? It was difficult to find the right words. Ah! If he
could talk to him in Yiddish, everything would be fine. But in
English!' (9). But his handicap in expressing himself is more than a
matter of the immigrant's lack of fluency in the new language, for he
cannot capture the right word to depict his own appearance: 'How
would he look coming into Duncan's office in these old pants with

the patch on the left knee so clearly visible? Like a nobody, like a . . . like a . . . He couldn't think of another fitting term' (9). Paralleling Tassigny's struggle with language, Jacob's ill-fitting terms, like his clothes, accompany him to Perfect Clothes where he goes through the interview with Mr. Duncan, seeking to suggest through manual gestures what his mouth is unable to utter. 'He was thinking hard, trying to find the right beginning. He stammered a few words and then he was quiet. He fumbled about in his pockets for nothing in particular and brought his hands out empty. Twice, without opening his lips, he began to talk with his hands, but dropped them again' (17). Jacob longs for the historical tongue to express his needs: ' "I vished I could talk in Yiddish mit you, Mistah Donken. It is not good for me to talk in English over serious t'ings. English is all right to make a joke or kibitz wit' the boys. But over serious t'ings it is good to talk in the modder language" ' (17-18). Jacob's pursuit of the mother language complements his quest for the old country.

As the interview progresses, the tension between voice and gesture builds:

> He did not use his hands. They lay stretched out on the desk now, rough hands, hands tired after a lifetime of labour. And now they looked like strangers because he was expressing something in which they had no part. . . . He tried to make his voice sound impersonal, casual, cool. His hands strained to take part in the talk. . . . "I marry here. We live quietly, we have children. . . ." He could no longer treat his hands as strangers. He drew them to him and they joined in the conversation. "I have a son a doctor, Mistah Donken!" The pride nearly burst him. His voice took on an almost unearthly tinge of happiness. It was a cry of joy, an expression of a supreme achievement (18).

Like Sherwood Anderson's grotesque Wing Biddlebaum, Jacob summons his hands in the conversation from crescendo to climax. Most interesting of the immigrant's solecisms is his use of the present tense merging successes and failures of the past with great expectations in his son's future. What the voice fails to express, the synecdochic labourer's hands add when they respond with their own language; in this fusion of gesture and accent the aging anti-hero in the new land finds self-expression as Kreisel exploits dramatic dialogue with supporting action. But Duncan's curt allusion to the Nazis' murder of Dollfuss undermines the foundations of the elaborate structure and style of Jacob's performance.

The contrast between the old and new worlds, between Europe and North America, between the grandfather and child in Grossman, and between an Orthodox Jewish past and an assimilated present emerges in Jacob's use of language, especially in the pun on his favourite word, the Yiddish equivalent for *so, alors,* or *n'est-ce pas:* 'The word *Noo* was the richest and most expressive word in his vocabulary. He could play with this little word like a virtuoso. He could thunder it in a loud bass, and he could whisper it softly, drawing it out gently. He could pronounce it sharply, almost threateningly, like a stab, and he could speak it lightly and playfully, modulating his sing-song, his voice wavering and trembling until it died away like the closing notes of a sad aria. In the mouth of Jacob Grossman this little sound was capable of expressing the profoundest emotions and the most delicate shades of meaning' (16). Since this passage occurs during a discussion about money and work with the 'rich man,' facetiously referred to as J. Rockefeller Grossman, 'richest' acquires a double meaning while the operatic metaphor anticipates Tassigny's painting. The last word the protagonist utters at the end of the novel as he iconoclastically throws his albatross out of the train window is not an affirmation like Molly Bloom's 'yes,' but his favourite ambiguous sound, the only possible articulation from the 'entrepreneurial' megaphone: ' "Noo?" he said in bitter exasperation, glaring at the picture. And in final despair, "Noo?" ' (207).

On the *Ile aux Noix* which Jacob mistakenly calls the *Illinois*— another linguistic lapse pointing to the distinction between Europe and North America—the language barrier continues between the French artist and the Jewish gesturer. 'Soon they were deeply involved in conversation, chiefly distinguished by the fact that neither understood the other's English. Tassigny tried French, but that didn't work, and he switched back to English. They made some progress, although for the time being they communicated more by sweeping, expressive gestures than by words' (27). 'They gesticulated together for a short time, somehow understanding each other' (29). When Jacob is invited to join in a game of cards, 'With a politeness that was alien even to himself, and a conscious effort to speak flawlessly, he informed the gentleman, punctuating his remarks with large, apologetic gestures, that he did not know how to play bridge' (28). Jacob's response to Tassigny's *pictura poesis* of the waves demonstrates again the failure of language: 'Nobody had ever talked to him like that. . . . He felt the limitations of the foreign language, the limitations of any language, even his own, to express the phenomenon of a turbulent sea. . . . Jacob was at a loss for words' (32).

The difficulties in communication multiply when the two men argue about painting, the artist advocating form while the simplistic viewer opts for representational content even though he carries optical illusions with him wherever he travels. Language frustrates both of them in their debate: ' "But I [Tassigny] cannot explain to you in words." . . . He [Jacob] did not know what to say. . . . Jacob did not seem to comprehend anything he said' (35). Explaining his cubistic canvases to Jacob, 'Tassigny grew irritated, and talked more rapidly. He talked with his hands, gesticulating wildly' (35), but all of his theorizing about design, form, and feeling means little to Jacob whose hands grope for words. After Jacob purchases the painting, he has a surrealistic nightmare about a monster: 'The voice grew louder and more insistent and more threatening' (39). Jacob is plagued by many voices, including his own. Like most of the relationships in *The Rich Man*, the friendship between Jacob and Tassigny deteriorates and they soon part company.

In Europe the voices become more threatening, for to get to Austria Jacob must first traverse the inferno of Germany where a Nazi officer examines his passport. Ironically, Jacob, who has had so much trouble communicating with other characters, understands the Storm Guard Officer easily. No sooner does he arrive in Vienna, however, than meaningful dialogue is defeated: 'They were all talking mumbled sentences and nobody made an effort to understand what was being said' (44-45). They stand 'in silence,' for they 'had so much to tell each other that nobody said anything. . . . They were for the moment isolated within themselves, alone among the multitude' (46). The same silence and isolation reappear at the circus when Jacob informs Koch of the family's tragedy, 'expressing himself more by gestures than by words': 'The two men looked at each other in silence. They were now an island within themselves, isolated and far away' (158).

During the ride to the Grossmans' home when the two young nephews ask their uncle about anti-Semitism, a 'thick cloud of silence fell into the car and settled' (50). At home the naive, inquisitive family asks their visitor from the new world about Niagara Falls: ' "It is so big . . . I can't tell you in words. The noise from the falling water is so powerful, you can't hear even your own voice" ' (60). And later, when Jacob accompanies his nephews to their secret cave, comprehension between characters becomes perplexing. 'The boys

walked on either side of him, talking rapidly, and both at the same
time, so that Jacob had a great deal of difficulty understanding what
they said, and no chance at all of saying anything himself. His
difficulty was further increased by the fact that they began talking in
the broad Viennese dialect as soon as they were in the street, and
Jacob could only get every tenth word or so' (109).

Amidst this confusion of language among the Grossmans, the
language of Albert Reich (whose name means ironically both *rich*
and *empire* in German) stands out, setting him apart 'from the rest of
the family. For the first time, too, Jacob noticed the quality of his
language. He could not easily fit him into the picture' (63). Like
Tassigny, Albert 'paints a black picture': 'His voice, when he was
agitated, had the same driving intensity as the Frenchman's' (65). In
this sequence of 'voices' Albert describes Hitler's voice, 'loud and
strong, and it kept on getting more powerful' (64-65). These voices
recall the symbolic megaphone of *L'Entrepreneur* and the demonic,
Babel-like abuse of language in propaganda. Albert remains an
outsider in the eyes of the rest of the family: 'but he didn't speak so we
could all understand what he said, but he was talking with big words
and nobody knew what he was saying. How can you like a man when
you understand some of the things he says, only they are like poison
to you, and other things that you would like to hear he says in a way
you cannot understand?' (98). The voice of reason in characters such
as Albert, Koch, and Tassigny penetrates the facade of false rhetoric
while innocent victims like the other Grossmans remain deaf to the
language of reality.

Once the truth of Jacob's financial status is divulged, his other
brother-in-law, Reuben, exclaims his impatience with the impasse of
language: ' "But what is the use talking? Words, words, words" '
(191). And Jacob once again fails to express himself when he writes to
his son. 'All these things he wanted to say, speaking from a full heart,
but the words were cold once he put them on the paper, and when he
read over what he had written, he was dissatisfied and tore up the
letter, stuffing the pieces into his pocket. He could not express in
writing what he wanted to say . . . perhaps it would be better not to say
anything to anybody' (198). Lost in the labyrinth of language,
struggling through futile gestures to tell their story, Jacob and his
family are forced to confront the impending doom of Nazi
persecution.

Besides the perplexities of language, voice, and gesture, several
scenes and episodes in the novel are related directly to the historical

background or indirectly through their symbolic association with *L'Entrepreneur.* Tassigny's impressionistic description of the waves, for example, carries the same prophetic implications as his painting:

"The water changes all the time. It is never the same. Never for one minute. The colour is different every second. A thousand different shades. But the most interesting of all are the waves. Sometimes you see the wave come slow, as if she is afraid, and is not sure what will happen when she hits the ship. She waits there on the top, trembling a little, and then, suddenly she rushes down like mad and breaks herself against the ship. Sometimes the waves come quick, so quick you cannot see, one behind the other as if they cannot wait, as if they have lived enough, and now want only to destroy themselves. And it seems as if each wave wants to be the first to die" (32).

This rather pessimistic interpretation not only contrasts with Jacob's sanguine expectations of gay Vienna, but acts, as well, as one of the many adumbrations in the novel that point to the current political situation with the rise of Fascism leading to mass destruction. The waves represent both fate and its victims when Jacob tells Koch in the middle of the circus about Albert's death: 'the noise which raged all about them came to them, muffled and indistinct, like the sound of the waves lapping and breaking themselves against a desolated shore when the sea is calm' (158).

Another example is Jacob's demonic dream recapitulating images from his past alongside the cubistic *L'Entrepreneur.* The price he pays for the painting is not merely thirty dollars—a materialistic reduction of the aesthetic artifact—; rather, as with Frankenstein, Promethean *hubris* exacts a haunting monster. First he sees a huge pile of white suits in contrast to the jet-black megaphone of the face in the painting. 'Suddenly a faceless giant with enormous legs came stalking through an open window. . . . The monster came closer and closer, walking very slowly. . . . He could not take his eyes off the giant. Looming behind his right leg there was a thin, mask-like face, and when Jacob looked closer he saw to his amazement that it was Sam Silver. Now the ghoul was within arm's length, and he could feel its breath, and he wondered where the breath was coming from since there was no face. Two powerful, hairy arms reached out and grabbed him, and the last thing he saw was Tassigny sitting on the window-sill, eating a corned beef sandwich and laughing' (39). The nightmare provides the subconscious language for conveying what ordinary language fails to express[2]; the confused identities of Sam Silver and Tassigny parallel the confusion of language. Silver, the aspiring capitalist who plays a Sancho Panza to Grossman's Quixote, replaces the original painting's female face representing the women who control Jacob's life, while Tassigny replaces Jacob at the delicatessen prior to his departure.

This interchanging of identities occurs in other relationships and forms part of Jacob's illusions about himself and the rest of the world. Jacob's son becomes a surrogate for the father who has denied himself and his daughters some of life's pleasures in order to provide for David's education. Thus, Jacob boasts first to Duncan and then to Tassigny, 'I have a son a doctor,' a pet phrase showing where the rich man's fulfillment lies. Similarly, he distorts his relationship with Tassigny to add 'I have a friend an artist' to his collection of delusions. Falling prey to the enchantment of music, an international language, Jacob takes pride in the Frenchman's piano playing and confuses him with his son. 'Jacob felt his heart swell with pride. He felt as if he personally had something to do with Tassigny's playing. It had been like that . . . when he had sat in Convocation Hall that day David received his degree of Doctor of Medicine. . . . He remembered the deep and solemn swellings of the organ . . . and when his son kneeled and the purple hood was placed over his head, a part of it belonged to him and to Malke. Had they not deprived themselves of many things that they might live to see this moment?' (29). Jacob also associates Tassigny with Albert, who is also interested in art: 'Jacob's eyes were glued on Albert. There was something about him that reminded Jacob of Tassigny. His voice, when he was agitated, had the same driving intensity as the Frenchman's' (65). And Albert and Jacob mirror each other on the question of Jacob's supporting the family: Albert tries to ask for a loan, but 'the words stuck in his throat' (141); Jacob wants to help, 'but the words stuck in his throat' (176), for the paralysis of silence afflicts all of those unemployed during the thirties.

The first of the diabolic visual symbols Jacob encounters after L'Entrepreneur is the deep red band with the black swastika in a white disk on the German Storm Guard Officer. Then 'Jacob saw the strange and ominous insignia on his cap—two crossed bones and a leering death's-head' (43). The next visual representation, a sculpted variation of L'Entrepreneur, is a landmark in the centre of Vienna. 'They had almost reached the end of the long Praterstrasse where it gets shabbier and is suddenly redeemed by the huge, obelisk-like monument of Admiral Tegetthoff. The monument fills a big square into which flow five long avenues. Steps lead up to it, and its wide base is covered with straining figures of warriors and foaming horses, writhing wildly against the harnessing bridles. A thick, marble, pillar-like column, adorned with beaked prows of warships, shoots out against the sky, and on top stands the admiral, gazing far out into space, his hand gripping a telescope' (49). The nineteenth-century heroic warrior contrasts with the modern anti-hero, Grossman; the sole instance of the historical present tense in the narrative underscores the antithesis between the heroism of the past and the barbarism of the twentieth century; the monument, nevertheless, is a reminder of war and is therefore a sculptured presentation of Tassigny's abstraction with a telescope instead of a megaphone.

From this monument Kreisel turns to a description of the murals in the steam chambers, grim reminders of the gas chambers: 'The walls were covered with frescoes, depicting the part that water had played in the progress of the human race through the centuries. Not all the frescoes were of equal artistic merit, but a few were executed with a magnificent, sweeping power, and the painter's brush had caught a moment of man's gigantic struggle to wrest energy from the roaring masses of water and had given it form and substance on the wall' (95). Aesthetic parallels of *L'Entrepreneur*, these artistic creations change to destructive 'execution' of 'roaring masses' of mankind.

Another part of Jacob's initiation into the old world is the cave episode where he and his nephews can view the world from a Gygean vantage point as Kreisel invokes Columbus' discovery of America in their pursuit of primitivism. In an adventure worthy of Huck Finn, the *rite de passage* involves an oath not to reveal the location of the Platonic cave; they join hands in a symbolic gesture and Jacob becomes a true confederate: ' "Now you're one of us" ' (114). In the cave Bernhardt repeats his history lesson, ' "*Patria nostra olim provincia Romana erat*" ' (114), a reference to the contemporary Austrian servitude. When the two brothers begin to argue and wrestle furiously, 'straining like wild horses' (115)—the same image as in the militaristic Tegetthoff monument—Jacob calms them by reminding them of their federation in language reminiscent of the European alliances. ' "A fine pair of partners you are. . . . What kind of a federation have you got? You make a federation and then you fight" ' (115). Indeed, the cave becomes a microcosm for the events to follow internationally, for not only do the boys discuss the arguments and anger of their parents, but more crucial is the confrontation with the anti-Semitic gang. The pacifist Bernhardt suggests, ' "Let's make a pact with them",' whereas the militant Herman responds, ' "Le[t]'s fight them" ' (117).

Having escaped from this cave of the Cyclops, they head for the Circean enchantment of the circus at the Prater and in so doing they move from isolation to crowds and music. The decadence portrayed in the film *Cabaret* or the propaganda in Leni Riefenstahl's work is analogous to Kreisel's implicit suggestion about the manipulation of the irrational crowds by Wagnerian sensationalism: 'From all sides came the tin-clang of weary Wurlitzers, accompanying the endless circles of merry-go-rounds. In the beer-gardens and in the open-air cafés loudspeakers blared out the latest jazz hits, newly imported from America. It was a mad, whirling, strident cacophony' (120). Old and new worlds meet through the medium of jazz, the musical counterpart of the cubistic *L'Entrepreneur*, which echoes the jazz version of 'The Blue Danube Waltz' at the beginning of the novel. For the diabolic undertones associated with the illusory circus world, one need only think of Coketown in *Hard Times*, Archibald MacLeish's sustained metaphor in 'The End of the World,' and Robertson Davies' Faustian troupe in *Fifth Business*—indeed, the star of the show, *Die Dame ohne Unterleib*, would fit well in Dunstan Ramsey's crippled world.

The merry-go-rounds in the circus form part of a circular movement reflecting the general confusion of language and identity. Jacob's voyage ' "has been going around and around" ' (13) in his head for many years. After Shaendl's accident, Albert's 'head began to spin, slowly at first, round and round, in large circles, and then faster and faster, with the circles narrowing until his head seemed to revolve around a tiny axis at fantastic speed' (152). This vertigo leads to his death and is soon followed by Jacob's dizziness when he thinks of Shaendl's need for money: 'Endlessly revolving like the needle of a gramophone caught in the spiral groove of a record' (175). Jacob's 'head was reeling' (177). The novel comes full circle when he remembers the Kafkaesque factory clock near the beginning of the novel: 'The illusion, the wonderful illusion of the past few weeks had now suddenly come to a shattering, painful, ugly end. He was an insignificant, poor presser again, No. 1003, pushing his way into crowded streetcars every morning hurrying to punch the time clock, and all the grandiloquence, all the splendour, all his luxurious pretensions had now quite fallen away, and from the recesses of the past mocked at his pitiable nakedness' (177). The wheel of fortune turns, leaving a fallen Lear ragged and exposed.

At the circus the bugler and the barker, yet another in the list of *les entrepreneurs*, draw the unsuspecting masses as if by dictatorial suasion. 'The crowd gathered round the platform, giggling and talking, shuffling impatiently, like a lowing herd of cattle waiting to be led to pasture' (120). The pathetic pastoral simile is a repetition of Tassigny's image of the people who see *L'Entrepreneur:* ' "One goes and all follow, like a herd of sheep" ' (36-37). The victims of this mesmerizing propaganda become the tormentors who seek other victims, the innocent scapegoats. The political parallels in mob psychology are too evident when all the world's a circus: 'The clown kept on making jokes which were ancient and bad, but he had a receptive and very uncritical audience, ready to laugh at anything, and thankful that they were being entertained free of charge' (121). The standard joke about the dead father prepares for the visit to Solomon Grossman's grave and the death of Albert while recalling Jacob's favourite biblical story about Joseph and his brothers, especially the part when he asks if his father is still alive (104). The deluding circus, effete yet childish, ends with *Die Dame ohne Unterleib*, the lower half of the distorted legs of *L'Entrepreneur*. 'The fact that the wheelchair was not of the orthodox kind, but looked rather like a big wooden box on wheels, seemed to trouble few of the spectators' (122).

The loss of individuality in the midst of the crowd may be seen at the circus or in the mass political rallies of the period. After Shaendl's accident the curious crowd gathers and the interne in the ambulance shouts, ' "This isn't a circus" ' (148), Kreisel displaying a Swiftian aversion to these onlookers. Yet Jacob feels the need of losing himself in these crowds. 'And suddenly, as he walked, alone and unable to escape from his own thoughts, he felt the desire to mingle with a large crowd of people, to disappear in it, and thus perhaps to escape from himself' (155-156). In this act of bad faith and disengagement Kreisel explores the universal theme of the individual shirking responsibility in the lure of the anonymous, dehumanizing crowd.[3] 'He knew the cruelty and the indifference of a great city. He knew how utterly alone a man can be even among a million other men. The crowd pushed and pulled about him, hundreds of men and women, out to amuse themselves and have a good time, but he was not a part of them. That was the way he had felt, walking the hot pavements of New York and Detroit and Toronto with Sam Silver' (156).

Poverty, unemployment, visual and aural symbols, arguments within the family, the motif of the crowd, the difficulties in the exchange of language from character to character, the decadent world of illusions closing its eyes on unbearable realities, lengthy political debates—all of these render the events of the 1930s more than peripheral. Albert's statement applies to the Jews as well as to Austria: ' "And to us here who had to look on helplessly it seemed that nobody in the whole world cared. This is such a little country. Only six million people. We don't matter" ' (63). And Koch's prophecy demonstrates the explicitness of the holocaust in *The Rich Man:* ' "I feel that out of all the agony, out of all the suffering, a new state of mind, a new world-spirit will eventually be born, even though I will probably not survive the holocaust" ' (133).

---

[1]George Steiner, *Language and Silence: Essays 1958-1966* (1967; rpt. Harmondsworth: Penguin, 1979), pp. 140-41. For another theory of *l'univers concentrationnaire,* see Lawrence L. Langer, *The Holocaust and the Literary Imagination* (New Haven: Yale Univ. press), 1975.

[2]Albert's feeling of guilt is another manifestation of *L'Entrepreneur:* 'a monster without a head, lurking on the fringes of his consciousness' (150).

[3]For a discussion of the 'crowd' see Walter Benjamin, *Illuminations,* edited by Hannah Arendt; translated by Harry Zohn (New York: Schocken, 1969), pp. 166-76.

Carol Hlus
He Who Sells His Shadow

Kreisel's radio drama 'He Who Sells His Shadow' considers a theme which dominates his later work: the dilemma of the individual irreconcilably exiled from the majority of mankind and confronted by the insoluble frustrations of alienation. Inherent within the play, too, are direct or indirect references to isolation, powerlessness and self-estrangement, adjuncts of alienation. An adaptation of Louis Adelbert von Chamisso's fantastic tale *The Marvellous History of the Shadowless Man* (Germany, 1813; London, 1913), the play suggests Kreisel's respect, at this early stage in his career, for continental Europe's literary tradition to which he has strong personal links.

' "[A] man who has no money must always remain a nonentity, less than a zero," '[1] remarks the rich man, Mr. John, and provokes the play's protagonist, Peter Schlemiehl, to sell his shadow to the mysterious The Man for a bag containing ' "an inexhaustible supply" ' (*Another Country*, 211) of gold pieces. The barter sends Schlemiehl into exile and demonstrates that his name aptly describes his character. The thoughtless sale of the shadow places Schlemiehl at the mercy of his shadow's new owner who, before Schlemiehl discovers the folly of his actions, leaves for an unspecified destination with the shadow in his possession. Schlemiehl seems destined to spend the rest of his days in well-shaded locations, indoors, or in well-lighted places where shadows do not form. A shadow, Schlemiehl learns, guarantees man physical and social presence, and a man without one is vulnerable to every possible kind of abuse. All but the faithful servant, Bendel, reject Schlemiehl as he encounters the adversities generated by the absence of a shadow. On returning, finally, The Man offers to give Schlemiehl the shadow in exchange for his conscience. Schlemiehl is plunged into an existential conflict: he must either remain shadowless and join 'the legions of the marked men, the displaced men, forever hunted and forever shunned, wandering forever like that poor and wretched Jew, and all for conscience's sake' (239) or regain his shadow but surrender his soul. Either choice portends a dismal future. Schlemiehl refuses to bargain. He insists on living, not in Sartrean Bad Faith, but as a being-for-itself. Because of his initial greed, however, he is left to live his life in exile. What he admits early in the play proves true: ' "I must be a stranger upon the earth, an exile, cut off at the root from my fellow-men. For the shadow roots a man in the earth, and I . . . bartered away mine for a bag of gold" ' (212). Schlemiehl's experience instructs the reader to value the substantial, that which has solidity—the shadow—over the insubstantial, that which has no solidity—money.

Peter Schlemiehl is powerless before The Man who trades him gold for his shadow. Schlemiehl learns too late the falsity of The Man's argument that ' "with gold, even hell is made worth heaven" ' (211); however, he adheres to his principle, ' ". . . a man must live with himself also, and bread bought without [conscience and principle] might turn to gall and so make life intolerable" ' (237). Although Schlemiehl stands steadfast and proves that there is a part of him ' "inviolate" ' (239), after The Man reminds him of his future, eternally marked and apart from the world, Schlemiehl has only a superficial power. The Man controls Schlemiehl's soul; therefore, Schlemiehl remains self-estranged from his true self.

The source, as well as the existential content of 'He Who Sells His Shadow,' attests to Kreisel's indebtedness to the European literary tradition. Kreisel eliminates some of the romantic elements of Chamisso's tale, his drama's direct source; each story, however, has the same moral: learn to value one's conscience more than gold. The roots of both stories, undoubtedly, are in the Faust legend which recurs in a variety of European literary works.

Kreisel's choice of stories for adaptation is not accidental. Like Chamisso, a Frenchman destined to live in exile in Berlin during the French Revolution, Kreisel experienced exile, first, in 1938, when he left Austria after the *Anschluss* and took refuge in England, and then, from May 1940 to November 1941, when he was interned as an enemy alien in England and Canada. His diary entry describing the transfer of interns from Camp 'B' in Fredericton to Camp 'I' in Quebec expresses his alienation: 'As I watch the people through the windows [of the train, in Edmunston, New Brunswick], I must think that they can not be less dangerous or more innocent than I and many more. Yet we are treated like this. It is enough to make any body lose faith in the world and in mankind. In Edmunston we can see the U.S. border-house about 200 yards away, just across a river that runs parallel with the train. What an irony! The land of liberty and freedom so near and yet so far' (*Another Country*, 36). Kreisel's interest in a story of an exile by an exile evolves, undoubtedly, from his own alienating experiences.

Because 'He Who Sells His Shadow' is a radio drama and an adaptation of an earlier writer's work, it cannot be considered on the same level as Kreisel's novels and short stories. Appearing as it does, however, early in his career, it is interesting because its themes of alienation and exile correspond to the themes he concerns himself with in his novels and short stories.

---

[1]*He Who Sells His Shadow*, a radio play produced on 'CBC Stage,' 1956, suggested by Adelbert von Chamisso, *The Marvellous History of the Shadowless Man* (Lodon: Holden & Hardingham, 1913).

Michael Greenstein

Perspectives on the Holocaust in Henry Kreisel's The Betrayal

Speculating on the problematic nature of rendering the Holocaust in fiction, A. Alvarez writes: 'The difficulty is to find language for this world without values. . . . Perhaps the most convincing way is that by which dreams express anguish: by displacement, disguise, and indirection.'[1] Henry Kreisel, who fled from his native Vienna in 1938 and thus avoided the fate of millions of European Jews, uses the techniques of dream, displacement, disguise, and indirection in *The Betrayal* both to distance himself from the subject matter and to involve the Canadian reader who seems so far removed from the European tragedy. To gain this double perspective of distance and involvement for himself and his readers, Kreisel displaces space and time, and disguises the experiences of his characters.

Spatial perspective enables Kreisel to distance the story geographically from the stage of European tragedy by contrasting the guilt of the older civilization with the innocence of the new world. Not merely the Atlantic separates the two worlds, but in addition thousands of Canadian miles, the metaphoric sea of the Prairies.[2] In choosing Edmonton as the setting for this novel, the author emphasizes the vast differences between Western Canada and Europe. The narrator, Mark Lerner, whom Kreisel uses to distance himself from the story, comments on the sheltered life of Canadians removed from wars and revolutions: 'It is hard, for instance, to walk the streets of this growing, unself-conscious western city, where I have now been living for two years, teaching the turbulent history of Europe to young Western Canadians, and to realize that elsewhere the past is not merely history but something that touches sensitive nerves, evokes powerful responses' (2). He immediately qualifies this generalization to demonstrate the universal implications of evil whose tentacles span even the greatest distances: 'For here, too, in this western city, so peaceful, stodgy even, in spite of all its activity, its growth, its feeling that the world has only just begun and history is a tomb, a collection of dry bones, here too the old ghosts stir, walk beside many a man or woman on the crowded, peaceful pavements or stand beside them as they look down into the river valley and see the great Saskatchewan River flowing dark-grey in the summer or lying stiff and white and frozen in the long winter' (2). The recurrent image of the 'old ghosts' in the novel reminds the reader not only of the nightmarish quality of the experience, but also of the impossibility of escape from mankind's universal guilt.

Reflecting the paradox of aesthetic distance and existential *engagement*, the ever present Saskatchewan River becomes the spatial backdrop of everywhere and nowhere, as well as the temporal symbol of arrested history, the flux of events frozen for scrutiny. Moreover, the Saskatchewan resembles the Danube, for Theodore Stappler, the second narrator and Lerner's double, links the force of liberation between the two rivers with his father's drowning: ' "There are some pretty treacherous eddies in the Danube. But people swim in the Danube, anyway. They also drown, some of them" ' (154). Lerner's attachment to the river demonstrates the extent to which it participates in the lives of the two narrators: '. . . I look down on the magnificent river winding its way through the city, and watch the changes of the seasons as they reflect themselves in the mirror of the river, until I think that I could not live without the river' (205). The Saskatchewan accepts and conceals the evidence for Held's suicide, thereby completing the Held-Stappler-Lerner axis of guilt, betrayal, and involvement.

The Chinese restaurant beside Stappler's hotel also divides the city and suggests a meeting between the oriental and the occidental, the everywhere and nowhere of universal nothingness: '. . . right on the dividing line between what seemed to be two different parts of the city, a green and red neon dragon above what appeared to be a Chinese restaurant' (59). In a reversal of the St. George legend, Stappler sleeps there 'protected by the dragon!' (60). Like the magnetic force of the river, the demonic and apocalyptic attraction of the dragon works on Lerner and Stappler: 'The neon signs were already on, and the green and red dragon, of whose splendour Theodore Stappler had spoken the night before, now beckoned to me' (142). Kreisel develops the religious implications of the protecting dragon during Lerner's and Stappler's ' "last supper" ' as they discuss crucifixion, martyrdom, and an Austrian Corpus Christi parade (155-56). ' "And then Kretschmar, the lover of the saints and of the martyrs, forgot all about love and everything else the saints and martyrs might have taught him, and became the soldier of his lord, just as many years afterwards he became the loyal servant of his earthly Messiah, Adolf Hitler" ' (157). The evils of the past with their global consequences invade the purity of Edmonton: Kreisel is not simply accusing the Catholic Church for its complicity with Nazism; rather, he is implying the universal guilt of mankind as victimizer.

Like the river and the dragon, Emily Carr's painting of a British Columbia forest scene lures both characters. The painting resembles the river in its paradoxical combination of stasis and flux; further-more, both represent spatial perspective, the vanishing point for the winding water and tangled trees reflecting internal, psychological depths. For Stappler the canvas expresses ' "tangled emotions" ' as he analyzes the subtleties and ambiguities: ' "Everything seems quiet. . . . But that is only on the surface. Below, everything is in motion. The landscape is static, but the colours are dynamic. So everything is still, and yet everything moves" ' (33-34). As spatial symbols of displacement and indirection the painting, the Chinese dragon, and the river serve a twofold purpose: first, like the two narrators, they mediate between Kreisel and the Holocaust; second, they include the Canadian audience by associating the West with the evil of the Third Reich.

Aside from these specific instances of spatial dislocation, a general sense of the Canadian vastness emerges in Stappler's Arctic quest. The liberating, infinite Canadian space stands in marked contrast to his earlier European experience of persecution where space contracts in pursuance of the victim. The perspectives of time and place converge, approaching the infinite: ' "... you are really close to the absolute elemental quality of nature. It takes some time before you become aware of any variation in the landscape at all. After a while you see that the surface of the ice is constantly changing. So all is movement and yet all is still. . . . Time and silence acting together have produced a no-time" ' (217). Thus, the paradoxical landscape parallels Emily Carr's sylvan stasis and kinesis as well as the movement of the Saskatchewan River with the repeated 'no-time' and no-place of existential nothingness of *l'univers concentrationnaire*.

Stappler's eternity and infinity at the novel's close provide a culminating vision of history or meta-history appropriate for the education of Lerner, the historian, for Lerner's academic discipline presents the major temporal perspective in *The Betrayal*. If Canadian space is played off against European territory, then the French Revolution as studied and taught by Lerner in Canada is compared to the more contemporary history of the Holocaust. The betrayal of Jean-Paul Marat and Charlotte Corday is juxtaposed with the Held-Stappler betrayal and the murders of World War II. Lerner's narrative roams from the betrayals in Sicily where he was wounded to the impact of history on Western Canada: 'But history has a way of exciting even those students who have grown up here, in the West, who are conscious of little turbulence, and are no longer much aware even of the war so recently past. It seems strange that soon, for many of them, the names of Hitler and Mussolini, Stalin and Roosevelt, Churchill even, will be names only dimly attached to living men, who gave commands, inspired and terrorized, and in one way or another affected all our lives' (2). Shifting to the present tense, Lerner teaches his students about the complexities of the Revolution, concluding with a moral contrast between the leaders of the French Revolution and the Nazis: 'I attempted to draw a distinction between the violence unleashed by the French Revolution, which, however destructive, also released positive forces, and the violence of the Hitlerite movement in Germany, which was essentially negative and nihilistic. Marat, I said, like Robbespierre, like Danton, was an idealist. But his idealism, turning into a kind of fanaticism, consumed him. He lacked self-knowledge. Perhaps all fanatics lack it. They do not understand the action of time . . .' (4). Like his double, Stappler also expounds his own theories of history; when asked about his Austrian background, he replies: ' "That's such a long time ago. Some things in the past seem so long ago that they're no longer real. Others, mind you, that happened long, long ago are very real. They dominate the present. The past is a curious phenomenon. I have lived in Austria and in Italy and in France and in England and in Canada. When a man moves about constantly, as I've done, time and places begin to play tricks. . . . my youth . . . seems lost in a prehistoric fog. It's not real to me any more" ' (28). This confusion of time and place is, indeed, a curious phenomenon rendered more complex by the overlapping territories of reality and fiction with the Holocaust assuming the metaphoric form of a nightmare.

The counterpart to Stappler's quest for the infinite and eternal at the end of the novel is the 'moment'—the heroic moment of action when he could have saved his mother. Stappler first introduces the word, Lerner repeats it, and Stappler re-examines it dialectically as time outside history: '. . . speaking very slowly, as if he were revolving something in his mind, "the moment. If I could only have it again" ' (91). He tells Lerner to look at his watch and observe the second hand go round five times, an act that he has performed many times. Trapped by his memory, unable to escape the rotations of the clock, Stappler struggles for temporal comprehension after having lost all sense of time. And Lerner shares this temporal confusion with his confrère as the novel reaches its climax: 'Everything seemed jumbled; event melted into event. I no longer knew where dream ended and reality began. . . . I could no longer differentiate the past from the immediate present. Everything was now, and yet everything seemed to have happened somewhere in the distant past' (195-96).

The breakdown and restructuring of spatial and temporal perspectives manifest the third and most important perspective—the phenomenological. The process of adjusting perspectives, the education of Lerner and Stappler viewing the same events through opposite ends of a telescope, occupies most of the novel and constitutes Kreisel's phenomenological approach to the Holocaust. Bruno Bettelheim recommends phenomenological involvement as one solution to facing the survivors and victims of the Holocaust: 'If, with empathy and compassion, we dig towards those who have so completely given up all hope . . . , this will bind us together . . . and we both will awaken: they from their living death; we from apathy to their suffering.'³ Intersubjective consciousness revolves around the triangular axis of Lerner, Stappler, and Held with each character representing a different symptom of and response to the Holocaust: Lerner is distanced innocence, Stappler the victim, and Held the victimizer. The kind and degree of involvement of the characters rest at the heart of the matter. This existential *engagement* appears in the opening sentence, '. . . it seems strange that I should have got involved with Theodore Stappler at all,' and *involve* recurs throughout the novel along with the verb *betray* which connotes a demonic form of involvement.

The *Doppelgänger* motif linking Lerner and Stappler implicates the Canadian in the Holocaust by shrinking the phenomenological distance. Lerner and Stappler are identified through their acting abilities, and dramatic metaphors run through the novel underlining simultaneously the relationships between reality and illusion, and between involvement and detachment. Both the content and the style of Lerner's lectures reflect his double identity: his academic interest in the French Revolution contrasts with his existential implication in recent history, while stylistically Lerner sees himself as an actor whose *persona* in the lecture hall disappears in his extracurricular life. Lecturing about 'the high dramatic moments' of the Revolution, Lerner values his experience with undergraduate drama societies at the University of Toronto which has taught him 'that there is such a thing as an audience, and that this audience needs to be captured and held' (1).

Just as Lerner's acting instinct arouses in his students a sense of participation in the past, so Stappler, like Kreisel, is 'a very effective teller of stories': 'At one point I asked him if he had ever been an actor . . . there was no doubt that he had a fully developed sense of the dramatic, and he could project the personality of others, mimic their speech and imitate their mannerisms' (53-54). And Lerner records both the events of Stappler's story and the Holocaust in a theatrical metaphor: '. . . having anticipated the catastrophe, the final act of a tragedy, I was glad it had come at last. . . . Held, though one of the chief figures in the affair, had nevertheless receded into the background for the time being, and Theodore Stappler himself had taken the centre of the stage' (90).

Lerner's involvement in this drama represents the attachment of all those who consider themselves innocent—whether Canadians or the majority of mankind who remain neutral, blind, or indifferent, acting in bad faith by not combating evil. That the dramatic parallels afford one perspective for historical phenomenology may be illustrated in an example which acts as an ironic, though tragic, play within the play. When Stappler's middle-aged father ' "became involved with a young actress",' the son watches her in the roles of Desdemona, Ophelia, and Gretchen. ' "I used to sit there in the theatre and feel myself torn in two. Because I identified myself with my mother. . . . I felt that my father had betrayed her. . . . And I used to sit and watch that young actress going through the agonies of betrayal and despair on the stage" ' (159). The constant repetition of the words *involvement* and *betrayal* serves as a linguistic trap from which character and reader never escape, while Stappler's split indicates the shifting identities between actor and audience. The affair ramifies beyond the subsequent suicide of Dr. Stappler: his widow ' "mourned also a lost world, until she herself was lost in the chaos and in the total corruption of that time".' Thus, the individual story forms part of the larger history immediately preceding the war; furthermore, the post-war continuity appears immediately when Lerner says that Stappler is leaving Ophelia to which he replies, ' "Horatio will be kind to her" ' (160), thereby extending the full range of the dramatic allusion.

Lerner's suitability for this role of Horatio, the confidant, arises partly from the fact that he is a Jew, whereas Stappler is only half-Jewish. His relationship to and awareness of the Holocaust precede his encounter with Stappler; he remembers his grandfather who had come to Canada from 'the Warsaw ghetto—the same that during the war was to be so completely, so tragically annihilated. There, but for the grace of God, might I have been' (9). After this statement there follows the interview with Katherine which draws both student and teacher into the vortex of the concentration camps. A refugee, Katherine echoes Lerner's earlier thoughts: ' "I could have been there myself. More likely I would have been one of the dead" ' (14). These words give Lerner a jolt because he knows that he too has escaped the Holocaust in a physical rather than phenomenological sense.

> Her words sent a shudder through me. Because what might have been was more than a mere abstraction. I felt suddenly as if a sombre reality, the spectre of Auschwitz, had invaded my office. I felt all the more uneasy because I was taken by surprise. I don't usually wish to avoid facing unpleasant realities, but nothing had prepared me for the turn our conversation had taken. The murder of Marat was far enough in the past so that the blood had had a chance to dry. But the bones that had been here evoked had not yet crumbled. (15)

The dualism within Lerner between his academic and existential selves acts as a counterpoint to his doubling with the Helds and Stappler. He manifests a rather naive pride or complacency in his university life, considering himself an effective lecturer: 'I would feel my ego rising and a flush of satisfaction mounting into my cheeks' (1). He rationalizes his physical attraction to Katherine Held, the one who leads him across the academic boundaries of his office toward the more human settings of his apartment and the Victory Hotel. 'Outwardly I keep a stern, impersonal demeanor, befitting a man solely concerned with academic questions and wholly involved in his own little corner of his subject' (8). But to be 'wholly involved' he must include his other self in the fates of Stappler and Held. Lerner's linguistic categories reveal this rather simplistic outlook: he constantly labels 'academic exercises' or 'romantic' impulses. He and other characters distance themselves through ironic manners or an ironic tone of voice. As Lerner becomes more involved in the lives of the Helds and Stappler (which means the Holocaust), the phenomenological distance contracts: '. . . the distance that separates professor from student seemed to have narrowed, indeed to have disappeared altogether' (19-20).

The first stage of Lerner's participation occurs in his office with Katherine's introduction of the Holocaust; the second stage takes place with Stappler in his apartment: 'Here it was, the whole horror of the recent European past, in this apartment, where on the whole I live a peaceful, contented, relatively happy life. Here now were the old ghosts, and I was, whether I wanted it or not, involved' (43-44). This intrusion of the Holocaust firmly cements the *Doppelgänger* as does the repetition of *whole* and *involve:* 'Somehow, though I had resisted it, a bond had unquestionably been established between us. . . . That was ironic, since my intention had been quite the opposite. For I had no wish to become involved with him. . . . The truth is that I resented having become involved . . .' (46).

The divisions within Lerner match those within Stappler whose Jewish mother, Protestant father, and Catholic teachers make him ' ". . . a little bit of everything. Everybody and nobody. Everything and nothing" ' (60-61). Like the spatial and temporal extremes of everywhere and nowhere, eternity and the moment, this Existential paradox underlines the dualisms within *The Betrayal* and the universality of extremity outside the novel. In addition, both brothers share a dream that can be interpreted as an unconscious reaction to the horror of the Holocaust. Stappler dreams of a man (obviously himself) wandering through a desert in search of water and seeking refuge in a cave where he soon observes his mother approaching. He tries to follow her through this surrealistic landscape:

> Then suddenly he found himself by the shore of a stagnant lake. Along the shore stood petrified trees, and from the lake itself gaseous fumes arose and poisoned the air. And he saw his mother in the middle of the lake, and he cried out to her.
> Only the wind answered, and the fumes from the lake enveloped him, blinding and choking him, and, like a drowning man coming up for air, with arms flailing, he awoke from his dream. (63)

The nightmare refers to the fate of Mrs. Stappler in the Nazi gas chambers and reappears later in Lerner's sleep: 'By a stagnant lake I lay entangled in roots. I struggled to free myself. On my left and on my right there were two men whose faces never came into clear focus, although I kept looking at them, staring and staring. . . . They stretched their arms out towards me, as if beseeching me to help them, to get them out of the bog, to free them from creeping roots that were threatening to strangle them. But how could I help them? I was myself entangled' (194). This entanglement, like the one represented in Emily Carr's painting, relates to phenomenological involvement: 'The more I tried to detach myself, the more involved, the more entangled, I became' (196). Ultimately, Kreisel is caught in his phenomenological labyrinth among racial roots in his attempt to comprehend the Holocaust through fiction.

These dreams, along with the paradoxical treatment of time and space, fulfill the criteria of displacement, disguise, and indirection by which Kreisel confronts the Holocaust. Likewise, the dual narrative mode of the *Doppelgänger* provides the author with the necessary distance while approximating the sinister events in Europe with the seeming Canadian innocence. What Lawrence Langer says of Holocaust literature in general applies to *The Betrayal*, particularly with respect to the role of Lerner: 'The reader is temporarily an insider and permanently an outsider, and the very tension resulting from this paradox precludes the possibility of the kind of "pleasure" Adorno mentions, while the uncertain nature of the experience recorded, combined with the reader's feeling of puzzled involvement in it, prohibits Adorno's fear that the reader may discern in the inconceivable fate of the victims "some sense after all." '[4]

---

[1]A. Alvarez, 'The Literature of the Holocaust,' in *Beyond All This Fiddle: Essays 1955-1967* (London: Allen Lane The Penguin Press, 1968), p. 26.

[2]Kreisel's article 'The Prairie: A State of Mind' develops this image and is used by Robert Lecker as a basis for discussing the novels in 'States of Mind: Henry Kreisel's Novels,' *Another Country: Writings by and about Henry Kreisel*, pp. 304-316. Lecker examines spatial confinement, but does not attempt to relate the novels to the historical context in general and the Holocaust in particular.

[3]Bruno Bettelheim, 'The Holocaust: Some Reflections, a Generation Later,' *Encounter*, 51, 6 (Dec. 1978), 19.

[4]Lawrence Langer, *The Holocaust and the Literary Imagination* (New Haven: Yale Univ. Press, 1975), p. 3.

Karin Gürttler
Henry Kreisel:
A Canadian Exile Writer?

Henry Kreisel, professor of English and Comparative Literature and author of two novels and short stories, all written in English, was born in Vienna in 1922. He fled to England in 1938, was arrested in 1940 as enemy alien, deported to Canada, and held in internment camps in the eastern part of the country for almost a year and a half. He is primarily known for two novels, *The Rich Man* and *The Betrayal*, published in 1948 and 1964 respectively. If Kreisel's life and *oeuvre* are examined within the context of the generally accepted time-frame of (German) exile literature, that is, the period between 1933 and 1945, he can hardly be classified as an exile writer. Nevertheless, a case can be made for examining his novels within this context, since in both novels the writer's exile experience is of central importance. *The Rich Man* and *The Betrayal* reflect the transformation into literature of Kreisel's personal exile experience; significantly, this extends in Kreisel's case far beyond the actual period of exile and points to a more general connotation of the term 'exile.'

The case for examining the two novels within the context of exile literature could be made on the basis of a biographical approach. The novels in question contain numerous references to Kreisel's personal experiences in exile: he gives the names of the various internment camps; he refers to his mother's arrest on a train and her subsequent commitment to a concentration camp; he reminds the reader of his (Kreisel's) deportation from the Isle of Man to Canada; he refers to his work in a textile factory and mentions a number of other biographically verifiable details and events connected with his exile experience. In order to answer the question 'Is Henry Kreisel a Canadian exile writer?' a biographical approach might therefore be justifiable, especially in view of what Peter Laemmle aptly points out when he writes: 'What really connects the exile writers to each other is the mutuality of their biography: the experience of the exile situation.'[1] The exile experience common to all exile writers is undoubtedly an important aspect. However, the question arises to what degree the exile experience was really relevant to their creative process. There are some examples of writers in exile whose experience was not transformed into art. Within this context Jost Hermand's typological classification of exile literature according to the degree of political engagement against the Third Reich—he refers to 'resignedly escapist, consciously humanistic and actively antifascist currents'[2]—is of somewhat limited use; it seems a somewhat too convenient makeshift formula. It is, after all, possible to include under the term 'resignedly escapist' almost anything which does not fit into one category or the other. A typology of exile literature, in my estimation, is of questionable value, since the process of transforming the exile experience develops along different lines and manifests itself quite differently in individual authors. For this reason, I consider the suggestion of Egon Schwartz, who proposes a phenomenology of exile as reflected in the work of art itself,[3] to be more appropriate. Under this definition, I consider the exile experience as the generative principle in text production, whereas exile structures make up the operational model within the different levels of the text. Within this context of exile structures I should now like to focus on Henry Kreisel's novels *The Rich Man* and *The Betrayal*. The emphasis will be on the following particularly relevant aspects: 1) the narrative structure of *The Rich Man;* 2) the narrator in *The Betrayal;* 3) the symbolic use of paintings in both novels. Although models may be different, a comparative analysis of exile novels could discern a recurrence of narrative patterns; similarities in the function of the narrator may become evident and might lead to establishing distinct analogies between, for example, Joseph Conrad, Thomas Mann, and Henry Kreisel; likewise, similarities in the author's use of mythological patterns or in polyphony could become evident.

The Narrative Structure of The Rich Man

The Rich Man, first edition 1948, is the story of Jacob Grossman, who when nineteen years of age leaves his home in Galicia and departs for the New World. After several unsuccessful starts, he attains a modest livelihood through diligence, tenacity, and thriftiness, raises a family, and provides a reasonable education for his children. At the age of fifty-two, after thirty years of monotonous and hard work at the ironing machines of a Toronto clothing factory, he decides that he now, at last, can do what he had dreamed of all his life: return to the Old World and to Vienna, which rises in his fantasies of imperial Austro-Hungarian grandeur. He fantasizes a cheerful, carefree Vienna, singing and dancing to the waltz-strains of 'The Blue Danube.' It is the Vienna of glittering Hollywood sets and screen illusions. Jacob Grossman does not return to the Old World as a simple factory worker, who has put years of his savings into this trip, but rather as a man of success, as one who has made it, who has come to money and prestige, and who now enjoys abandoning himself to the pleasure of being gaped at and admired by his relatives during that short, immensely expensive period of a few weeks. He, Jacob Grossman, is the only one in the family who has achieved something, and the only one to have brought honour to the name Grossman.

This is the narrative model, which develops between the opposite poles of the Old World and the New World. It is the centuries-old myth of setting out for a new world and then returning to the old. It is the myth of the fairy-tale hero as well as of the Arthurian knight, and it is also the myth of the modern success-hero. In this case, it is the myth of the rich uncle from America, but the myth has undergone a significant modification in its traditional narrative structure. The New World does not fulfil the expectations of wealth and success, and, correspondingly, the expectations of refuge and salvation in the Old World also remain unfulfilled. The myth crumbles before the reality of down-to-earth everyday life, which is common to both worlds, and levels them down to a single world governed by the same laws. The myth becomes the anti-myth at the moment when the protagonist, moved by a false self-assessment, in his vanity and hubris attempts to appropriate to himself the behaviour and action patterns of the mythical hero, thereby violating the law of his own mediocrity, and thereby assuming a wishful identity and status which are not meant for him and cause him to fail.

The Old World-New World polarity appears continuously in a two-fold refraction, in the refraction of fiction and reality. On the manifestative level we are dealing with the categories of space, motion, and outwardly visible living conditions. Jacob Grossman's New World, Canada, is portrayed in his stories as a wide, open, and free space, as a country of unlimited opportunity, of success and of wealth. Indicators of this New World are given: comparisons of size (the Great Lakes area, Niagara Falls, population density in relation to the size of the country, and so on), geographic distances (a four-day trip from coast to coast), unrestricted freedom of movement (no compulsion to carry a passport, no controls), the outward appearance of the protagonist (a white suit made of sleek alpaca wool, white soft-leather shoes, the presents for his relatives, the Tassigny painting). All these indicators are façades and status symbols of an imaginary self; they are the wishful projections of his own mediocrity. Jacob Grossman's true living space in the New World is that of lower-middle-class restrictedness and modest living conditions. His outward appearance is in inverse proportion to his financial means, to his lifetime position as a simple factory worker, and to his condition of dependence on his employer, his wife, and his daughter.

Jacob Grossman's image of the Old World is limited to the city of his dreams, to nineteenth-century Vienna, to the imperial Austro-Hungarian monarchy, the waltzes of Johann Strauss, magnificent, ethereal, and full of *joie de vivre*— nothing but wishful projections of someone returning home. The living space of his relatives, however, the Vienna of 1935, manifests only restrictedness, seclusion, need, and poverty. It is not the city of the Hollywood movies, but a city of mass unemployment, of political assassination, and of the coming dictatorship along with its concomitant phenomena: secret police, arrests, newspaper bans, and underground activity. The Vienna of 1935 does not sing and dance; even the street musicians who roam the impoverished quarters, begging for a few pennies, are dispersed by the police. 'The Blue Danube' waltz only resounds like a dissonant funeral march. The indicators of the real Vienna in the novel are underground activity and concealment (the storeroom in Albert Reich's bookstore, the cave in the Prater: 'It was almost like being in a small, windowless room, pressed against a narrow corner' [118]), as well as restrictions on the freedom of movement, on the freedom of speech (the impossibility of travelling out of the country, the necessity of holding political discussions behind closed doors), and, finally the economic decline, and with it the loss of the basic necessities of existence.

The worlds of fictions disintegrate. Jacob Grossman's fiction of the Old World has been shattered, along with the imaginary role he intended to play in it, namely the realization of every immigrant's dream: to return home as 'a settled, prosperous-seeming man' (31). His relatives reject the fiction of the New World, a world full of false promises and unfulfilled hopes. On the level of human values, it is not only Jacob Grossman who fails—Grossman who has been induced by his craving for recognition not to destroy the image his relatives have made of him, but instead to try to preserve it with

complacent lies. Along with Jacob Grossman it is the New World
that fails. Solidarity, the readiness to help, self-denial have become
empty phrases. Confronted with the manifest indifference of the so-
called Free World, and with the hopelessness of evading the
catastrophe by emigration—' "For people who have no money the
doors of foreign countries are barred with steel" ' (67)—Jacob
Grossman is left with nothing but the bitter feeling of being given
up.

The Narrator in The Betrayal

The Betrayal, Kreisel's second novel, published in 1964, carries
into the present the theme of guilt and complicity during the
persecution of the Jews in Vienna, a theme which is preluded in the
last part of *The Rich Man.* Once again the two poles of action are
Canada and Austria, this time Edmonton and Vienna.

The young Canadian history professor Mark Lerner, whose name
can be interpreted to mean 'teacher' as well as 'learner,' becomes
inextricably involved in a whirlpool of moral conflicts, in which he
is successively called upon to be a witness, a judge, and finally a
counsel. He acts his part with reluctance and from the loftier view of
the university professor, keeping his distance and avoiding rash
conclusions. At the same time, Lerner represents the Canadian
mentality vis-à-vis the stunning and irrational events in Europe's
recent history. Canada is a young country, still in the state of
innocence, as it were, a country that still believes in moral integrity. It
is a country in which law and justice, though often misused, have
never been shaken to their very foundations. Canada's standards of
value are still intact, her historical consciousness is aimed at the
future, unencumbered by a past filled with national catastrophes,
which would have corrupted and perverted her at the very core.
Canada is the outside spectator of world history—' "you Canadians
have it so easy, so cosy, so rich, so beautifully settled in soft chairs to
watch the world's drama" ' (150). Canada, full of self-reliance and
trust in the orderly course of things, is self-confident and possesses a
kind of naive self-righteousness. When Canada does intervene it is
only in the role of a mediator avoiding implication, of a neutral
referee looking for balance. In short, this is the Canada of the Lester
B. Pearson era.

Lerner is also the narrator of the events. In his whole bearing he strives towards objectivity and respectful distance. He acts as the catalyst of passionate outbreaks and self-destructive moral conflicts. He is a narrator in the tradition of Thomas Mann's Serenus Zeitblom and Joseph Conrad's Marlow, but differs from these two in his personal detachment. At least one Canadian critic has noticed this: 'Professor Lerner . . . is somehow too calm, too comfortably ensconced in his world to communicate powerfully the passions he has glimpsed. His aloofness is perhaps characteristic of the winterbound Canadian consciousness—an irony of which Mr. Kreisel is undoubtedly aware.'4 The impact of the plot of treachery and retaliation, of escape and persecution, is neutralized by means of the objective narrator. The dynamic force of the confrontation is reduced through reflection and self-analysis, and the plot is dissolved by argumentation. The novel thereby becomes a thesis novel. We may justly assume that this narrative attitude has as its underlying cause the author's own endeavours to distance himself from events which reflect his own bitter experiences, and to unravel the complex of inextricable involvement with guilt by means of an almost surgical analysis of the motives of human actions. By means of a reflective-analytical process the author attempts to shed a new light upon, and to make comprehensible, the phenomenon of the breakdown, under the pressure of violence and terror, of the moral principles governing human actions, and to set new standards of assessment. After all, the incomprehensible forces of a dehumanized time, when everything is out of joint, lie beyond the conventional norms of valuation. The monstrosities have assumed, in all their irrationality, such proportions that the categorizations of guilt and innocence, responsibility and irresponsibility have been invalidated, and in consequence, one can, at best, only inquire about degrees of guilt and responsibility. Only different shades of grey remain; there is no black or white.

The narrative scheme is quite simple: 'the hunter becomes the hunted and at last the victim' (3). Joseph Held, who has helped escapees, becomes a traitor when he delivers a group of Jewish refugees to the Gestapo in order to save the life of his wife and daughter. Theodore Stappler, Held's pursuer and the only survivor of this group, has had the opportunity to warn his companions, one of them his own mother, but he fails. All of them die in a concentration camp. At the end of the pursuit, the pursuer stands before himself: pursuer and traitor, Stappler and Held become one person.

The vicious circle of entanglement with guilt is finally complete. The one seeking retaliation is now being accused, revenge makes no more sense, Held commits suicide, Stappler dies in an avalanche during a rescue mission in Canada's far north.

This narrative scheme is projected in the parallel of the Marat-Charlotte Corday episode in Mark Lerner's lecture on the French Revolution. Although personally dragged into the conflict of guilt and retaliation, Lerner does not undergo any significant change, and faithfully carries out his role as chronicler. He has become a bit more pensive, but he has not given up his Canadian attitude of non-involvement and non-commitment. He has, however, learned what it means when history lives up to its claim of being relevant to the present, by moving out of the secured zone of its historicity. He has learned that the answer of the succeeding generations turns out to be no different from that of the generation affected. 'I had often asked my students how we are to judge extreme situations and the reactions of fallible human beings to them. And now, asking myself the same question, my mind simply refused to come to grips with it. That was in a sense cowardly, an evasion of responsibility' (182).

The Symbolic Use of Paintings in the Two Novels

The significance of the paintings in these two novels is particularly great, first, because of their distinctive character within the novel's discourse, and second, because of the various levels of meaning that they connote. The ways in which these paintings and their meanings are transmitted to the reader are indeed complex. On the one hand, we are dealing with a fictional objective language, that is, the sign-language of the painting, which in itself has a connotative character. On the other hand, this objective language does not appear in its original form, that is as an image or a visible sign, but rather as a description in words, whereby this description itself is connotative, since it does not merely confine itself to a simple denotation of the elements of the pictures. Furthermore, the reader will also complicate the procedure by his or her reactions to the images connoted by the words. And finally, the painting in the text is a recurrent symbol that relates to all the other images and symbols and thereby attains a variety and multiplicty of meanings.

Now the fact that paintings or pictorial elements are mentioned or described in a literary text is not unusual. Their function, however, is

normally limited to contributing to the frame of reference of a
particular person, that is his social class, his education, his material
situation, and so on. In short, the painting is used as a symbol of a
socio-cultural framework. The Tassigny painting in *The Rich Man*
also fulfils this function by helping to expose the incongruity
between semblance and reality in Jacob Grossman's life, and in this
respect it has the same symbolic function as the alpaca wool suit and
the white soft-leather shoes. Significantly enough, this same
discrepancy can be observed in Jacob Grossman's attempt to
interpret the picture: his interpretation of Tassigny's *L'Entrepreneur*
remains at the level of naive analysis, that is, it does not go beyond a
simple enumeration of the individual elements of the painting. All
his analysis achieves is a literal description of the picture; it comes
nowhere near attaining the connotative level of the symbolic picture.

This symbolic connotation is achieved on two levels in the text:
first, through the reactions of the journalist Koch and the statements
of Tassigny himself, and second, through the recurrence of the
painting as symbol throughout the text and through its association
with other symbolic elements. Both levels of connotation are
selective, they evoke more than they explain, and thus they are open-
ended: the reader has to fill in meaning for himself.

L'Entrepreneur shows, in the style of Expressionism, the figure of
a man without a face, or, more precisely, with a black megaphone-
like something instead of a face. His legs are oversized, taking up
about three-quarters of the whole painting. A woman's face, thin and
distorted, is partially obscured by the man's right leg. The
predominant colour is a glaring green-yellow. These are the literal
components of the painting.

On the second level of meaning the painting and its title connote a
multiplicity of things. The title *L'Entrepreneur* refers to the man's
function in society: the solicitation and exploitation of the masses by
means of advertising. The painting further symbolizes his attitude
and position, as exemplified by the relation of the man to the female
figure: he is erect and dominating, whereas she is lying down and
dominated. His nature is also symbolized by his anatomy: the
oversized legs stand in sharp contrast to the absence of a head, which
is represented merely by the neck. In other words, the intellectual and
moral forces are subjugated by physical strength and brutality. The
megaphone-like object in place of the head points to the excessive
volume of the human voice caused by mechanical means of mass
communication such as megaphone, loudspeaker, and radio, which

reduce the human voice to nothing but screaming and thus annihilate the human and spiritual qualities of communication. In this context it is interesting to note that in modern art the existential crisis of our time, the loss of individuality and of human values such as character and integrity, is often represented by the symbol of the mechanical puppet. The distorted female face in *L'Entrepreneur* denotes this lack of individuality, and it also symbolizes the crowd, a seduced and subjugated mass condemned to woe and misery. In keeping with all this is the colour combination green-yellow-black, which in its ecstatic disharmony works as a cry of despair. As Koch comments: ' "All the agony and the torture . . . God damn it" ' (164).

The terminology used by Tassigny belongs to the religious mythical world, and we thereby attain a further level of connotation, namely the artist Tassigny's apocalyptic vision of the modern seducer of the masses and of the mass exterminator. It is not reason that rules, but rather the diabolic voice of the modern propaganda machine, the incarnation of evil and dehumanization. This connotative level is complemented by the context into which the painting of *L'Entrepreneur* fits: it is the political and historical context of the year 1935, with the German Nazis threatening to annex Austria, an annexation that finally took place in 1938 with terrible consequences. The Tassigny painting thus symbolizes the tyrannical rule of the Nazis: Tassigny, the artist, has transformed the threatening signs of the times into a vision of the coming inferno, and he thereby fulfils his role as prophet and as soothsayer in the original sense of the word: ' "I think that a painter, an artist, must be a fighter and a prophet. . . . If people do not understand, I cannot help it" ' (37). Every prophetic language is enigmatic, and the process of cognition implies at the same time a process of decision. In Jacob Grossman's case both take a negative course.

Just as in *The Rich Man,* a painting is also at the centre of *The Betrayal.* Very much as in the first novel the painting here brings into focus and symbolizes personal character traits, actions, and events in a compressed, symbolic language. The painting is an Emily Carr: a scene of the British Columbia forest, with its mighty tree trunks looming out of an impenetrable maze of intertwined roots and creeping vegetation. We are dealing here with two levels of connotation. With regard to the elements of the painting and its composition, the first level refers, speaking temporally, to the past, while the other indicates the potentiality of the future. One level refers to the gyratory principle of the vicious circle, the other to the dynamic principle of ever-present life. The polarity we encounter here is between two principles of life, between on the one hand the irrational and subconscious principle of the matrix, of chaos confined within the eternal circle of being and passing away, of birth and destruction, and on the other hand the rational and conscious principle of logos, of order, decision, and liberation. The jungle of intertwined roots and creeping underbrush symbolizes the impossibility of escaping the central conflict, as well as its disastrous effect, the moral entanglements and their inherent insolubility. The vertically rising tree trunks symbolize the young generation, in particular Katherine Held, who from the quagmire of past involvements with guilt and failure finds the straight path that leads to a bright future. Finally, this woodland scene of Emily Carr's is also a symbol for the Old World and the New.

Lawren Harris's painting *Snow Mountains in the Arctic Ocean,* with its powerful yet simple form and colour scheme, appears at the end of the novel as a complement to Emily Carr's woodland scene of British Columbia. As a symbol it is associated, in this context, with Theodore Stappler's last phase of life, thereby symbolizing death, but also purification and catharsis.

In retrospect then, the question 'Is Henry Kreisel a Canadian exile writer?'—asked at the outset and dealt with above by analysing his two novels with respect to the structure of *The Rich Man,* the attitude and the function of the narrator in *The Betrayal,* and the symbolic use of the paintings in both—can be answered positively. Besides the numerous autobiographical references to his own personal exile experience the novels contain clearly discernible exile structures. Kreisel is personally aware of the fact that the transformation of his exile experience is central to his writing, as is evident in his own statement: 'I would agree that, although I consider myself a Canadian writer, I belong (in the sense in which you have defined the issue) to a certain category of "Exilliteratur." I can even say that I was conscious of this fact, and it was because I wanted to explore . . . the psychological and literary conditions of exile that I proposed (and wrote) my doctoral dissertation, which has the title "The Problem of Exile and Alienation in Modern Literature".'[5]

---

[1]Peter Laemmle, 'Vorschläge für eine Revision der Exilforschung,' *Akzente,* 6 (Dec. 1973), 512 (my translation).

[2]Jost Hermand, 'Schreiben in der Fremde,' *Exil und innere Emigration,* edited by Reinhold Grimm and Jost Hermand (Frankfurt a.M.: Athenäum Verlag, 1973), p. 16 (my translation).

[3]Cf. Egon Schwarz, 'Was ist und zu Welchem Ende Studiern wir Exilliteratur?' *Exil und innere Emigration II,* edited by Peter Uwe Hohendahl and Egon Schwarz (Frankfurt a.M.: Athenäum Verlag, 1973), p. 158.

[4]Hugo McPherson, 'Betrayal, Desertion, Atonement,' *Tamarack Review,* 34 (Winter 1965), 108.

[5]Letter from Henry Kreisel, 7 Nov. 1980.

Robert A. Lecker

States of Mind:
Henry Kreisel's Novels

In his essay entitled 'The Prairie: A State of Mind,' Henry Kreisel examines the relation between the prairie environment and the prairie consciousness as it is manifested in writing. Significantly, the essay takes as its point of departure Kreisel's own response to a landscape which he came gradually to know in the first years he spent in the Canadian west. Kreisel is at pains to point out that the assimilation of the prairie consciousness frequently precedes the objective recognition of the forms that consciousness can take and their deliberate expression in writing. For example, a short story Kreisel published in 1966, 'The Broken Globe,' is full of the images of prairie man that he only later recognized as recurrent in prairie literature: 'These were in fact the images that came to me and I should myself have regarded them as purely subjective, if I had not afterward in reading encountered similar images in the work of other writers who write about the appearances of men on the prairie at certain times' ('The Prairie,' 255). As the essay makes clear, Kreisel had come under the prairie influence almost immediately upon going west prior to 1948. Even then, he was 'awed' by a letter to the *Edmonton Journal* 'in which the writer . . . asserted with passionate conviction that the earth was flat' (254). In the 1968 essay, Kreisel notes that 'Even as I write these lines, the emotion evoked in me by that letter that appeared in a newspaper more than twenty years ago comes back to me, tangible and palpable' (254).

The prairie which has had so potent an effect upon Kreisel is of course real, but it is also the author's metaphor. He is more concerned with a state of mind than he is with a specific place. He implies that we are all prairie men who carry within us the prairie consciousness. Above all, it is Kreisel who displays that consciousness—the men he writes about in his essay are very much a part of himself. The critique is as much a 'romance' as his novels, a theoretical formulation of his own quest fictionalized in his work. Thus the essay functions as a displaced example of his deepest themes imaged in terms of the prairie landscape. As he studies other prairie fiction, Kreisel finds the symbols of his own sense of self. In turn, he transforms the prairie into a field of symbolic images which comes to represent the landscape of the modern mind. Thus the essay actually serves as a key to Kreisel's own novels, for it provides us with a statement of the images, themes, and archetypes that reappear in *The Rich Man* and *The Betrayal*.

Kreisel likens the prairie to a sea: 'Only one other kind of landscape gives us the same skeleton requirements, the same vacancy and stillness, the same movement of wind through space—and that is the sea' (258). In actual fact, Kreisel connects not one but three landscapes with the prairie. He refers to Ross's Philip Bentley drawing scenes of the prairie as a desert, 'scenes that mirror his own frustration' (264). The 'barren sea' which Philip Grove's horses hurl themselves against is synonymous with 'those drifts of snow' (266) characteristic of arctic desolation. The prairie, the sea, the desert, the arctic—for Kreisel these 'lonely and forbidden spaces' (260) combine to form a metaphorical modern waste land, a moral wilderness devoid of signposts and heedless of individual identity.

Kreisel also sees man's response to the waste land in metaphorical terms. He becomes the archetypal wanderer 'driven to follow a dream' (260) or the mythical frontiersman 'pitted against a vast and frequently hostile natural environment that threatens to dwarf him' (256). Man the conqueror-explorer is frequently a victim, both of the elements and of loneliness. Again, the 'extraordinary sensation of confinement' (259) which plagues the prairie settler takes on universal significance; 'the theme of the imprisoned spirit' (265) is the theme of modern literature.

Kreisel reminds us that the fate of the individual usually represents the fate of society at large. In its search for security, the prairie community often shuts out the world, but in so doing shuts itself in. The settlements become 'islands in that land-sea, areas of relatively safe refuge from the great and lonely spaces' (259). Ideals and dreams are constantly thwarted by the presence of the real: 'Man, the giant-conqueror, and man, the insignificant dwarf always threatened by defeat, form the two polarities of the state of mind produced by the sheer physical fact of the prairie.' As Kreisel says, 'There are moments when the two images coalesce' (256). The result may be a *doppelgänger* motif, the ultimate expression of alienation. Or the divided spirit may be confused and self-deceiving, an escapist living in a private dream and pretending that the outer world is absent. Another may be an actor performing on a private stage—his artificial interior reality. A third may venture boldly into the wilderness to defeat the ambiguity of fate. Clearly, these are all attempts to deal in some way with the surrounding sea. Kreisel is writing about a quest for order, stability, and reason. He is describing the tactics men employ to guarantee their very existence. Kreisel presents the same themes and characters in his novels.

The Rich Man tells the story of Jacob Grossman, on older Jewish man confined for thirty-three years to the routine job of a clothes factory presser. In order to visit the family he has left behind in Europe, Jacob decides to leave work and the daughter he lives with for a six week trip to Vienna. Squandering his meagre savings, Jacob manages to impress his relatives as a wealthy man by their standards. But when a desperate situation forces the family to ask Jacob for financial help, the truth comes out. Jacob returns to Toronto shaken, unhappy, and exposed for the poor man he really is.

From the beginning of the novel, it is clear that Jacob remains an imprisoned spirit, an alien in his adopted homeland. The Toronto which Jacob has lived in for more than three decades is presented as an essentially barren urban wilderness. The more we follow Jacob in his movements at home or overseas, the more we realize the extent to which he has either denied his environment, or coloured his view of it so as to reinforce a contrived sense of security. The first scenes of the novel are interesting in this respect. We are introduced to Jacob as he emerges from the cocoon-like safety of his bed. Before the first line of the book is completed Jacob is not only awake but already seeking out the clock which will assure him that events are still well organized and proceeding on time as planned. In the first paragraph Kreisel is careful to emphasize the extent to which Jacob's survival depends upon organizing the day to come. Repeatedly we are told that Jacob's existence is a matter of what 'should have been,' what 'he would say,' how he 'would . . . go on,' how he 'would get down to the factory' (9). The obsession with maintaining a sense of time and place continues throughout Jacob's day, magnifying the significance of his need for an almost hermetic isolation. Leaving his own room, Jacob makes his habitual moves from the kitchen, to the tramcar, and into the factory. Although Jacob has decided to upset the order of the day by speaking to the factory manager, he reassures himself by entering through the workers' side entrance. Before the door has even closed Jacob begins to look for the familiar symbols of stability: 'He swung open the door. There, against the walls, were the time clocks, and instinctively his eyes wandered to the rack where his own time card was. It was there, No. 1003, standing lonely in the left-hand rack beside one of the clocks' (15). Clearly, Jacob is firmly entrenched in that neo-Calvinist 'work ethic' framework that Kreisel refers to in his essay. Having laboured for more than half his life in the same building, Jacob has managed to insulate himself completely from life in the open. It is important to note that Jacob's alienation is chosen as much as it is imposed—it is essentially a means of defence.

When Jacob moves from the safety of Canadian enclosures to a European setting, absolutely nothing changes in terms of the exterior landscape. Overseas, as in Toronto, Jacob is equally at odds with everything outside. He (as well as every other character) does all he can to block out the surrounding world. After leaving the ship, Jacob completes the route to Vienna by train. Later, when he 'tried to recall what the Belgian countryside looked like, he found that his memory was blurred and hazy' (42). In actual fact, Kreisel informs us, 'He paid no heed to the beautiful scenery. . . . Jacob saw nothing' (43). Indeed, Jacob sees little during his entire visit. Retreating with his family from the atmosphere of anti-Semitism and political repression which surrounds them in the European city, Jacob's stay in Vienna becomes a series of interior adventures designed to deny the real hostility of the environment beyond the doorway. Correspondingly, spatial structures generally describe hidden, withdrawn, or highly enclosed areas. Upon his arrival, Jacob hustles the family into a taxi which in turn moves swiftly to their meagre rooms. The next day, Jacob visits the public bath. The image of the tomb is obvious here, for 'the semi-darkness in which it was shrouded and the beckoning couches gave to the atmosphere an extraordinary degree of restfulness and peace' (96). Another excursion brings Jacob to Albert's bookshop, 'wedged in between a grocery on one side and a butcher shop on the other' (128). The culminating enclosure scene, and the novel's finest representation of the attempt to retreat from a disordered world occurs when Jacob accompanies his nephews to the 'cave' they have discovered in a nearby area. In their naiveté, the children give voice to what Jacob is reluctant to admit: 'when you're in the cave you can see everything that's going on outside, but anybody that's walking around outside can't see you at all when you're hidden inside' (107).

Jacob's ideal world is described in the child's words about the cave. Throughout the novel Jacob is concerned with establishing a selective vision, one which will enable him to recognize the 'outside' only when he chooses to, and even then, only from a governing perspective. At the same time, the cave metaphor is appropriate to Jacob because it represents his own need to hide from the outside at will, simultaneously substituting for exterior reality an artifical interior milieu. Kreisel underlines the negative qualities of such a synthetic existence. No sooner has man framed himself within protective boundaries than those boundaries begin to weigh him down. What was to be a zone of freedom is transformed into a narrow cell. Jacob's sensations at the close of the cave scene make this view explicit. He felt that 'All the air seemed to have been cut off. It was almost like being in a small, windowless room, pressed against a narrow corner' (118).

Life in *The Rich Man* may be generally described as windowless. Here, man is not interested in the true picture so much as in imposing his own picture upon the landscape, altering it to suit his needs, and refusing to recognize it except within the framework he himself has chosen. It is for this reason that Jacob's rare glimpses of Vienna tell us much more about Jacob and what he refuses to see than they do about the city itself. His first impressions, caught from the security of the taxi, are revealing: 'The streets were alive with people; old men and women promenading slowly up and down, sitting on benches in the mellow evening air, young couples walking arm in arm. The cafés were full of patrons, some sitting outside in the improvised gardens and vine-hung terraces, chattering and drinking coffee' (46). This is the romantic Vienna that Jacob has always dreamed of. Only later do we realize the extent of Jacob's self-deception. The streets are full of people, Reuben explains, because in a city of two million, three hundred thousand are unemployed. The men sit drinking coffee because ' "as long as they have a few groschen left they would rather do this. This way at least they save their shoes" ' (94). Even the music performed by the street singers ' "is only another way of begging" ' (94).

It is appropriate that the most important pages of *The Rich Man* should be those devoted to the actual voyage from Canada to the Old World. The sea Jacob crosses is metaphorically that 'vast land-sea' which Kreisel spoke of. Upon this featureless expanse, Jacob sets himself as the explorer in search of his past and the innocent values associated with childhood. He has yet to learn that the age of innocence is irrevocably lost. In his own eyes, and in the white alpaca suit he has purchased for the occasion, Jacob becomes the mythical rich man of stature and strength—a transformed conqueror, the physical sign of his country's growth and prosperity. Jacob finds himself in pursuit of a dream, but he is repeatedly forced to confront the futility of his ideal and the reality of his own spiritual isolation.

In an interesting way, this dichotomy has been foreshadowed from the first scene in Jacob's bedroom. As he shaves, 'The Blue Danube Waltz' plays over the radio, but the waltz is preceded by a recording of a Negro quartet singing 'Swing Low, Sweet Chariot.' Throughout the novel, we find Jacob searching after the lost ideal of the waltz: 'He wanted a lot of violins, hundreds of them, the way it was always done in movies about gay Vienna' (10). Again and again Jacob asks to hear the piece, but never does he hear it properly. The music is always disrupted by some intrusion of the real. The Negro song is in fact much more suited to Jacob than the waltz—the never-changing form of his employment amidst 'the steam of the Hoffman presses and the sweat of hundreds of workers' (15) marks him as enslaved to a system that reduces men to strictly mechanical activities.

The ironies of Jacob's position are readily apparent: while he may be a big man in his own eyes, and perhaps a giant in the eyes of his European relatives, he is in fact a dwarf, a victim, not a victor. To survive, Jacob must involve himself in a dangerous game of role-playing. He can maintain himself only by assuming a false front that gives him a controlling sense of power. As Kreisel tells us, 'there was indeed a great deal of the showman in Jacob Grossman.' However, there is a very serious aspect to Jacob's acting, one which is crucial to the sea experience in general, for Jacob's quest for an appropriate identity coincides with his search for values, for an acceptable frame of reference though which he can see an unexplored world. Repeatedly in *The Rich Man* Jacob tries to find or purchase physical objects which act as co-ordinates in relation to which he can place himself and his attitudes. Nowhere is this more apparent than in the meeting on board the ship between Jacob and the French artist Tassigny. Tassigny has completed an abstract painting entitled *L'Entrepreneur*, 'remotely suggesting a human figure, though this was not at first easily apparent because a geometric construction built up of spheres and rectangular planes obscured it. The figure had a long, fleshless neck, but no face. Where the head should have been, there was a thick, cylindrical, megaphone-like contraption, painted jet-black, and pointing sideways' (36). The picture suggests Jacob's own adopted role as the entrepreneurial gross man. As his exaggerated stories and countless lies make clear, Jacob is all voice, but faceless.

In contrast to Jacob, Tassigny maintains that whether or not his expressions are understood is inconsequential, ' "So long as I have always told the truth, the way I see the truth" ' (37). Tassigny's reasons for creating the painting are therefore diametrically opposed to Jacob's reasons for purchasing it. The canvas gives Jacob a false sense of power and wealth. He almost begins to like the painting, 'not because he came to appreciate Tassigny's art, but because he fancied that with the purchase of the painting he had become, not only Tassigny's equal, but even his superior. He felt his ego grow, and become inflated like a balloon. For was he not now a patron of the arts?' (40).

When at the story's end Jacob comes face to face with the futility of his own self-deception, it is appropriately Tassigny's painting which is angrily discarded; for in casting away the image of the entrepreneur, Jacob symbolically kills the myriad impressions which have governed his overseas life. Although the novel may seem to describe a progression from innocence to experience, or from falsity to truth, it is clear that in the end, by rejecting the painting, Jacob symbolically rejects any truths he has discovered in his journey through the external world. Having experienced the hostility of the wilderness around him, Jacob retreats to the safety of a framed lifestyle—he returns to that windowless complacence which blocks out the violence of the real. We are left with the nagging sensation that for Jacob, very little has changed.

Kreisel's second novel, *The Betrayal*, also deals with a man who attempts to deny the threat of external experience by entrenching himself and his perceptions in a well-ordered but narrow sense of place. From the comfort of his high-rise apartment living-room in Edmonton, Mark Lerner, a Canadian-born professor of history, recalls the story of Theodore Stappler, who has relentlessly pursued to Canada Joseph Held, the man responsible for his mother's death ten years earlier in Auschwitz. Through their mutual interest in Held's daughter Katherine, Lerner finds himself involved with Stappler and playing the role of his confidant, constantly asked to judge and identify with Stappler's need for revenge and the potential guilt arising from Stappler's own inactivity in the face of Held's betrayal of his family.

Like Jacob, Lerner is confined within a punctual routine and imprisoned by his lifestyle. The habitual reading of essays merely replaces the endless pressing of garments that Jacob devotes his life to—both duties are the rituals around which these men structure their daily experiences. Lerner is a bachelor living alone two thousand miles from 'familial love' (10). Daily, he moves from his snug apartment ('though the sound-proofing could be somewhat improved' [8]) to a university office equally removed from life in the streets. Outside, there is always snow, or the frozen river, or 'a light wind which made it seem much colder than it was' (23). Lerner himself is antiseptically intellectual, as cold and sterile as the environment he shies away from. But he is not immune to the sense of prairie loneliness described in Kreisel's essay. As he emerges from the Victoria Hotel towards the end of the novel, the landscape presents itself to him thus:

> Whiteness in darkness. It had very nearly stopped snowing. Only a few perfunctory flakes were still drifting down from the black invisible sky. . . .
> For a moment I felt as if I had stepped out onto a strange and unknown street. The landscape seemed curiously unfamiliar, like a landscape in a dream. The buildings were sombre, forbidding shapes, rising from the white pavement into the darkness above. There was very little traffic on the road. I did not know what time it was. It seemed the dead end of the night. (192)

The disorienting landscape which Lerner confronts reflects his own inner confusion. Lost in a timeless foreign world devoid of human fellowship, Lerner experiences the dead end vision of existential despair which marks him as a modern man. In his response to this metaphorical glimpse of the desert Lerner is identical to Jacob. He reveals his desperate need for stability and control by becoming a collector of paintings, seeing himself as one who can frame experience by purchasing it pre-framed and pre-packaged. Considering the three 'distinguished' oils in his possession, particularly a scene by Emily Carr, Lerner boasts proudly that 'I rather fancy myself a patron of the arts' (8). The painting is indeed valuable, for it provides us with a key to Lerner's personality. By using the painting we can open those doors that Lerner has tried so firmly to bolt. Lerner's approach to the canvas is similar to his appreciation of history—what the professor wants is an intellectualized existence, the vitality and dynamism of life without its pain, its involvements, or its crises. Repeatedly he returns to the question of Charlotte Corday's potential guilt, presenting it as a universal example of the need for moral choice. But never does Lerner apply the problem to his own very questionable acts. He admits that he is 'prepared to grant . . . a certain validity' to his colleague's suggestion that 'I like the study of history because it involves me in the acts and sufferings of humanity but at the same time allows me to keep involvements at arm's length' (46). Although Lerner might try to convince himself that in the course of his encounter with Stappler he manages to shed this protective intellectualism, it is clear that he remains forever preoccupied with rendering the fluid static and with containing the shifting sea. We need only observe Lerner at the end of his story, as he continues to sit behind that ever-present living-room window which acts as his frame around the world. There, in silent isolation, he can 'look down on the magnificent river winding its way through the city, and watch the changes of the seasons' (205). Instead of participating in the exterior flow of nature, Lerner remains content merely to view life from a distanced and controlled perspective.

In keeping with this attitude, it is only natural that for Lerner, human action itself is denigrated to the status of an *objet d'art*, something to be toyed with and forgotten. The 'meaning' of Joseph Held's life can therefore be consigned by Lerner to some dingy corner, out of the way, but available should the occasional need for it arise: 'Sometimes, wrestling with some intractable moral problem that history raised for me, I thought of Joseph Held and tried once more to come to terms with his action, but I could never settle the matter in my own mind, and it remained one of those loose ends which dangle somewhere in the attic of one's mind, untidy and uncomfortable, but fortunately out of the way, safely hidden amid the other bric-à-brac that gathers dust there' (209).

Just as *L'Entrepreneur* in *The Rich Man* was an abstract representation of Jacob, so in *The Betrayal* the Carr painting describes the real Mark Lerner who hides within a deceptively stable frame—a violent, terror-stricken individual torn by moral ambiguity and fear of an irrational universe. When Stappler comments that the work ' "expresses tangled emotions" ' (33), he speaks unconsciously about Lerner's essence. Yet Stappler must still grasp the fact that those emotions are skilfully hidden. Within a page, he understands the relationship between surface and content characteristic of the book at large: ' "Everything seems quiet," Theodore Stappler said. "But that is only on the surface. Below, everything is in motion. The landscape is static, but the colours are dynamic. So everything is still, and yet everything moves" ' (34). In stressing the fact that everything **seems** quiet, Stappler touches upon what is perhaps the most important feature of the painting: it is deceiving, and it demands a second viewing. Again, the emphasis upon deception must be applied to Lerner as well, and we find, not surprisingly, that he is in another way very much like Jacob Grossman—he is an actor, and the classroom is but one of his many stages. From the very first page of the novel, Kreisel asserts this fact. 'There is something in me, I think, of the actor' (1), Lerner confesses. He complains when 'the high dramatic moments' (1) of his lectures fail to excite the entire student audience. Later, speaking in his role as narrator, Lerner makes it plain that given the chance, he would cast himself as the hero of his play: 'We are all heroes in our mirrors, or think at least that, when our moment of testing comes, we would not miss the chance to give a true, perhaps even heroic, account of ourselves' (90). Lerner's mention of the mirror is interesting on another level. His inability to effectively isolate himself from his surroundings is signalled by the fact that regardless of his will, he begins to take on and reflect the qualities of everything that is put in front of him. Thus he tries in futility to stop the 'tangled roots' of Carr's painting from 'coming out of the canvas and spreading into . . . [his] brain' (193). In a similar manner he attempts to detach himself from the events of Stappler's life, but is eventually forced to admit that 'The more I tried to detach myself, the more involved, the more entangled, I became' (196). The 'entanglement' metaphor begins on the canvas and spreads right through the theme of the story. Both Lerner and Stappler are caught between the image of what they should be and the image of what they are.

In this respect, perhaps the most interesting feature of the novel centres on the way in which Lerner and Stappler subtly exchange roles as the narrative progresses. Stappler, the encyclopaedia salesman, becomes the giver of knowledge, ironically replacing the professor, who in time becomes a true learner, the recipient of Stappler's 'lesson of life.' Early in the story, Stappler's own words anticipate the *doppelgänger* motif. Realizing that he and Lerner were fated to meet, Stappler cries out Baudelaire's phrase, ' *"Mon semblable! Mon frère!"* ' (52). It is primarily in their approach to existential responsibility that Lerner and Stappler are twins. For Lerner has consistently refused to act for the benefit of anyone but himself; he is guilty of complacence and apathy. His selfishness and lack of commitment make him a fine example of Sartre's *mauvaise foi*. Stappler's story attracts him because it is so like his own. Lerner would prefer to resist the truth, yet he is perversely fascinated by what is essentially the story of his own acts of betrayal: 'For he had involved me, subtly and in a sense against my will. He had disturbed the order of my life, and I found myself once again resenting his intrusion. Then, too, a part of my consciousness whispered to me that the events of the past had perhaps best be forgotten. . . . Yet there he was, this stranger who had suddenly burst in on me, and he wouldn't allow it. He dug it all up, like a dog suddenly uncovering a mouldering bone' (141).

Lerner's academic study of *Intellectual Cross Currents* in European history represents his own attempt to place his life in a rational well-defined context. He is fearful of the chaos implied by any form of ambiguity. In this respect, Stappler's tale appears terrifying: 'I found myself reflecting that the most terrible thing about the kind of situation he was describing—complete social upheaval and the tearing away of all moral sanctions, a situation not unfamiliar to me from my own study of European revolutionary history—the most terrible thing about such a situation was that simple, black and white distinctions between good and evil were all blurred. There was just a grey range of evils, all of them morally corrupting' (73-74). Stappler's 'situation' forces him to flee from a twentieth century reign of terror in search of a more tranquil place. In the Arctic wilderness he eventually finds 'a kind of peace, and a sense of unity with elemental forces' (216). His descriptions of the Arctic make it clear that he found Kreisel's prairie. Stappler was 'struck by the immensity of the landscape, by its great silence, by its timelessness' (217). In his letters to Lerner he noted that ' "It takes some time before you become aware of any variation in the landscape at all",' and he added that 'time does not exist. Particularly here, in the great silence, in the great stillness' (217). For Stappler, the frozen wilderness represented an ideal freedom because it existed beyond time—only in timelessness could he liberate himself from his past. However, Stappler's ultimate 'freedom' led him only to death. As the victim of an Arctic avalanche he surrendered to an environment whose desolation overcame him. This final encounter with external reality cannot help but remind us of similar confrontations described by Kreisel in his discussion of the prairie man as the conqueror and the conquered. Stappler has always been the uprooted wanderer of Kreisel's essay. Throughout the novel he follows the dream of an ideal community secure from exterior threats. Soon after we meet him, he relates to Lerner a dream which effectively restates many of the images which Kreisel mentions in his critique. The dream itself is such a potent metaphor for Kreisel's view of the human condition that it deserves to be quoted in its entirety:

The landscape was always the same, strange and yet familiar. It was evening, always evening, and there was something baleful about the evening. A deep red sun poured heat down upon a barren landscape. There were rocks like massive obelisks, and dried-up cactus plants, but also, scattered about here and there, a few green trees, like weeping willows. Suddenly huge black clouds appeared in the sky, like the outstretched fingers of a gigantic hand, and advanced towards the sun and threatened to engulf it. In this desolate landscape the figure of a man with a knapsack on his back and an alpenstock in his hand was stumbling from rock to rock. And as if, like Moses in the wilderness, he were looking for water, he struck each rock with his alpenstock and turned away again each time, for there was no water. He looked up into the sky and was terrorized by the cloud that was moving slowly towards the sun, and in his terror he sought refuge in the shadow of a red rock, but the rock threw no shadow, and so, stumbling on, at last he found a cave and crawled into the darkness of its black, gaping hole, and there squatted on the ground, his knapsack still on his back, his alpenstock still in his hand. Thus squatting, he pondered, but without any real hope, how he might ever get out of this desert, live again like a human being in a rational society, stop being agitated and terrorized by weird manifestations, cease to flee from rock to rock, grow roots anew, like the willow tree, and have his place again among men, in a universe that was not entirely unfriendly. (62)

Stappler sees Eliot's symbolic waste land, and it is this 'desolate landscape' which he must traverse in search of permanent values. He becomes the mythical explorer in search of the promised land, just as he is the original settler seeking out shelter and food. Like a primitive, but also like Jacob, the man of Stappler's dream is drawn towards the safety offered by the cave. Most important is the profound sense of isolation which permeates Stappler's dream. To 'live again like a human being in a rational society' would be to construct amidst the wilderness the social domain of the prairie community or homestead, it would be to find 'a little schoolhouse standing lonely and defiant in a landscape that is like a desert' ('The Prairie,' 264).

The vision which appears to dominate Stappler's life also affects Lerner. He consistently looks for signposts which will direct his journey into the unfamiliar territory of Stappler's tale, and in response to the perils of that journey, he too hides in a series of well-structured cultural retreats. Eight years after his first contact with Stappler, Lerner is still collecting art. Of his recent acquisitions, the most valuable is a Lawren Harris, 'one of those silent peaks, all white, rising out of a blue sea, all still, serene, and yet curiously tense, as if at any time the white mass would shatter and break itself' (205). The Arctic which Stappler managed to confront in the raw is imported by Lerner in the form of a painting. Again, the canvas reflects Lerner's personality, also 'curiously tense' and close to its breaking point. He admits that 'In a way which I find hard to express, this painting seems to go together with my Emily Carr' (205). Accordingly, he hangs them side by side facing the bed, so that they can be seen in the morning and just before sleep. The final position of these paintings signifies the fact that for Lerner, nothing at all has changed—the original vision is fundamentally the same as the vision which completes the book, and so the two paintings, like the novel's beginning and end, can be put side by side. Lerner remains in his rooms, trying to convince himself that life can be purchased and the real world denied. He tells us that 'the walls of the apartment are glowing and alive' (205) with art. But we know that these walls are the barriers which he has erected to shield himself from the universe beyond the high-rise. Although he hides in a kind of paralysis from life, when it comes to his paintings Lerner believes that he 'responded to them immediately, spontaneously' (205). Unlike Jacob, he cannot cast away the art which enables him to feel secure, yet the fate of all these paintings makes it clear that life in *The Betrayal* is no less futile than it is in *The Rich Man*. Both novels describe a failed quest for freedom. In the end, the actors return to the physical and mental fortresses they have been building all along.

Kreisel maintains in his essay on the prairie that 'the knowledge of the vast space outside brings to the surface anxieties that have their roots elsewhere and this sharpens and crystallizes a state of mind' ('The Prairie,' 260). The critical statement reflects upon Kreisel himself and also upon his fiction. His characters are filled with a deep sense of *angst* about the irrational world around them. They are intensely conscious of their loneliness and their need for a genuine friend. The question is not so much whether they are prairie men, salesmen, or professors, but how they are human in every modern sense of the word.

Thomas E. Tausky

Under Western Canadian Eyes: *Conrad and* The Betrayal

In a 1958 article on 'Joseph Conrad and the Dilemma of the Uprooted Man,' Henry Kreisel remarked that 'The facts which form the background of his [Conrad's] fiction were of course based on his own experience. What Conrad knew was what it meant to live in a country dominated and oppressed by foreign powers, but also what it meant to break away from the country of one's origin. . . .'[1] In choosing to write fiction drawn from the social reality he himself experienced, Kreisel has followed Conrad's example. Kreisel has also taken Conrad's subject—the 'uprooted man'—as his own, and his treatment of that subject is enriched by an acute awareness of Conrad's dramatic situations, his methods of narration, and his understanding of ethical crises.

We may look most confidently for the imprint of Conrad in *The Betrayal* (1964), a novel Kreisel published some years after both his Ph.D. dissertation (on 'The Problem of Exile and Alienation in Modern Literature') which included a discussion of Conrad's work, and the article on Conrad already cited. A connection between this novel and Conrad has previously been made by three other critics. In a review, John Carroll comments that 'it is to the credit of Kreisel . . . that he can recall Conrad so often in this novel without damaging comparisons.'[2] Hugo McPherson, in another review, says that 'Both his narrative technique and his choice of situation recall the intensity of Joseph Conrad,' but goes on to suggest that 'if Theodore Stappler is a plausible brother to Lord Jim, Dr. Lerner is no substitute for Conrad's narrator Marlow.'[3] In his introduction to the New Canadian Library edition of *The Betrayal*, Sidney Warhaft agrees that 'Lerner is no Marlow,' but argues that 'there are many signs that he is designedly made different from Marlow' (viii). He finds, however, 'a host of Conradian touches' (vi).

Warhaft goes on, very plausibly, to find parallels between Kreisel's academic narrator, Mark Lerner, and the academic narrator of Thomas Mann's *Doctor Faustus*. It is possible, however, to find another model for Kreisel's narrator and for significant aspects of his plot without venturing beyond Conrad: if we contemplate *Under Western Eyes* as well as *Lord Jim*, we may find a context which serves to illuminate Kreisel's considerable, and still undervalued, achievement in *The Betrayal*.

An affinity between *Lord Jim* and *Under Western Eyes* was perceived many years ago by Conrad's friend and fellow novelist, André Gide. Gide's journal entry might also be applied appropriately to *The Betrayal:* 'Much interested by the relationship I discover between *Under Western Eyes* and *Lord Jim*. . . . That *irresponsible act* of the hero, to redeem which his whole life is subsequently engaged. For the thing that leads to the heaviest responsibility is just the *irresponsibilities* in a life. How can one efface that act?'⁴ (emphasis Gide's). In each of the three stories, the protagonist has a crisis of 'irresponsibility': Lord Jim jumps into a lifeboat, leaving hundreds of Arab pilgrims to their fate; Razumov, in *Under Western Eyes*, betrays a revolutionary acquaintance to the Czarist secret police; Stappler, in *The Betrayal*, fails to rescue his mother, in five minutes' failure of nerve, when she could have been saved from the Nazis. Each of these central figures is closely observed by a first person narrator who guides the reader while attempting to grapple with the meaning that the action has for his own character and situation.

In outline, each protagonist experiences a roughly similar psychological development. The initial period of failure is brief (the word *moment* is used frequently in both *Lord Jim* and *The Betrayal*) and an explanation for his own inadequacy eludes the character. Thereafter, a much longer period (months in *Under Western Eyes;* years in the other two novels) of mental bewilderment and ineffective activity ensues. Finally, a conscious decision is taken which represents a new departure in both self-understanding and contact with others: Lord Jim finds a primitive society, Patusan, where his virtuous acts bolster his self-esteem; Razumov confesses his betrayal to the victim's fellow revolutionists; Stappler becomes a doctor in the Arctic. Each protagonist then faces a seemingly tragic end: an outsider intrudes upon Lord Jim's peaceable kingdom, and eventually he feels compelled to sacrifice his life; Razumov is crippled in a brutal beating that follows immediately upon his confession; Stappler is killed in an avalanche. In each case, despite the sombre conclusion, what Conrad in another novel calls 'victory' is achieved. As Kreisel says about Conrad's exiles: 'There are ways, to be sure, in which the dilemma of the uprooted man can be mitigated. There are values like loyalty and honour and duty that can give direction and purpose to a man's life.'⁵ Each narrator remains as a witness to the successful self-transformation each protagonist has made.

It will be apparent that Stappler's final phase is closer in character to Lord Jim's choice of a new field of action than to Razumov's deliberate martyrdom. Razumov achieves a curious sort of social role when he is frequently visited by radicals who feel guilty about the unauthorized punishment he has suffered, but he does not become involved in the fate of a primitive community as the other two do. Razumov is also the odd man out if we consider the characters as they appear at the beginning of the stories: he is the illegitimate, and barely acknowledged, son of a nobleman, whereas the other two have more respectable but less aristocratic origins; he is industriously laying the foundation for a life as a bureaucrat, whereas the others do not have such limited and carefully calculated goals.

Central to the youthful characters of Lord Jim and Stappler is a vague but exalted concept of self. It is this tendency that causes both characters to be called ' "romantic" ' —Lord Jim by Stein in a famous passage,[6] and Stappler by Lerner (92). In the judgment of the narrators, each viewed himself as a potential hero: Marlow tells us that Lord Jim 'saw himself... always an example of devotion to duty, and as unflinching as a hero in a book' (5), and to Lerner, 'It was clear. He wanted to be a hero' (91). The unheroic subsequent behaviour of the protagonists constitutes an ironic contrast with their expectations, but also the unrealistic ' "illusion" ' (to use Conrad's own term in *Lord Jim* [79]) seems in itself to be an underlying factor in the sudden and unexpected moment of cowardice. This relationship is made explicit in *Lord Jim*—the passage just quoted is said to be Jim's state of mind immediately before he misses an opportunity to effect a glorious rescue, in an episode obviously foreshadowing the pilgrim ship catastrophe.

When the irresponsible moment comes, the reader of both *The Betrayal* and *Lord Jim* is left with a delicately poised balance of evidence with which to contemplate the question of moral responsibility for inglorious conduct. The protagonist's response to a crisis is disastrous, and associated with a flawed character, but the circumstances which thrust the crisis upon the character are not of his doing, and make honourable action extremely difficult. One's instinct to condemn 'irresponsibility' is tempered by an awareness of the mitigating factors often insisted upon by the narrators. As Marlow reminds another observer who stresses the loss of honour, the European officers aboard the pilgrim ship offered no example to Jim except for the vilest cowardice and self-interest. When Jim challenges Marlow to state what he would have done if placed in Jim's circumstances, Marlow can only reply that he does not know, and even implies that he might well have jumped. Marlow frequently denies an ability to comprehend Jim's character, with the result that the reader is less tempted to condemn Jim; these comments range from the simple assertion ' "I don't pretend I understood him" ' (47) to the eloquent conversion of Jim's mysteriousness into a general principle: ' "It is when we try to grapple with another man's intimate need that we perceive how incomprehensible, wavering, and misty are the beings that share with us the sight of the stars and the warmth of the sun" ' (109). Also, of course, all of Jim's subsequent actions speak in his favour: his manliness in facing a legal inquiry, his burning sense of shame, and his wisdom and courage in handling the affairs of Patusan.

The setting for Stappler's betrayal bears some resemblance to the background in *Lord Jim* in that the protagonist's lack of nerve seems more forgivable when measured against the darker deeds of others. Though Stappler fails to save his mother, Joseph Held, a Jewish lawyer who arranges their escape, acts with more cruel deliberation in betraying a group of Jews to the Nazis in order to protect his family. Stappler's moment of crisis also has a significant parallel with Razumov's plight—in each case, the agony of the choice facing the character is magnified by the fact that a whole society has made evil its good.

At first glance, Razumov would seem to be less deserving of pity than the other two central characters. Whereas the other two risk death if they were to act honourably, Razumov seemingly has an alternative open to him—to avoid choosing sides by dismissing his revolutionary acquaintance without turning him in. Razumov commits what might be thought of as the most inhuman act, in consciously choosing to sacrifice an individual for the sake of a dubious idea, the notion that 'absolute power should be preserved... for the great autocrat of the future' (37).[7] Yet, as Conrad himself remarked in his Author's Note, 'Razumov is treated sympathetically' (8). The narrator very explicitly portrays him as the victim of a peculiarly Russian disease: 'It is unthinkable that any young Englishman should find himself in Razumov's situation. This being so it would be a vain enterprise to imagine what he would think. The only safe surmise to make is that he would not think as Mr. Razumov thought at this crisis of his fate. . . . He was a Russian; and for him to be implicated meant simply sinking into the lowest depths amongst the hopeless and the destitute' (28-29). Similarly, soon after Stappler tells Lerner about his failure of nerve, Lerner excuses him on the grounds that the time is out of joint: 'it seemed to me . . . that both Held and Stappler were themselves victims, as much indeed victims of the affair as the people who had actually been arrested. That observation, I thought, ought to be recorded, ought to be made clear. For that situation, in which the victims themselves are made to seem responsible for their fate, seems to me one of the really obscene corruptions of our brutal century' (92).

If the three narrators can find cause to forgive the protagonists, the protagonists cannot easily forgive themselves. Stappler seems at times more able than the other two to wrestle with his failure on the level of conscious intellectual introspection. Yet he is plagued by vivid nightmares, feelings of acute loneliness, and even (as Razumov is) by a hallucination, and in these respects Kreisel has, to a considerable degree, successfully followed Conrad's example in probing the psychology of unresolved guilt. When Stappler explains the scene of betrayal to Lerner, his disturbing agitation causes Lerner to reflect on the true source of his anger: 'his finger jabbed the air and pointed towards me, as if he were trying to accuse me, as if I, in fact, were Held, although it was also clear to me that his fury was really directed against himself as much as against Held' (87). One is reminded of Lord Jim's bitter anger towards Marlow when he thinks Marlow has called him a ' "wretched cur" ' (43), and of Razumov's bitter denunciations of the inoffensive narrator of *Under Western Eyes*.

At one point in *The Betrayal*, Lerner compares Stappler to 'The ancient mariner . . . pouring out his tale' (108). All three of the protagonists resemble Coleridge's model in undergoing psychological torture for having committed what they feel to be an unforgivable sin; all three feel that 'till my ghastly tale is told,/This heart within me burns.'

The need to confess overcomes the more prudent desire to conceal. Jim's customary reaction is to run away when his cowardice is uncovered, but he unburdens himself to Marlow; Razumov confesses to Natalia and then to the assembled revolutionists after he has been cleared of suspicion; Stappler risks forfeiting the respect of both Lerner and Katherine Held by the frankness of his explanations. In each case, the trust and affection the protagonist feels for his interlocutor cause him to cast aside his mask. As Ian Watt has said, the relationship of Marlow and Jim is that of a parent and child[8]; Razumov's confession to Natalia comes after he realizes he loves her; Stappler, much to his surprise, is greatly attracted to Katherine Held after he locates her father in Edmonton, and repeatedly is linked with Lerner as a brother.

If, each protagonist feels, the crime is comprehended, it may be forgiven, both by the world at large and by its perpetrator. Lord Jim ' "would like somebody to understand—somebody—one person at least!" ' (50); Razumov 'felt the need of some other mind's sanction. With something resembling anguish, he said to himself—"I want to be understood" ' (39). Stappler has a somewhat more active role planned for his listener. He wants ' "one other man to know. . . . If possible I want that other man to confront Held" ' (50) and later he enlists Lerner as his spokesman in explaining his actions to Katherine. But a more fundamental motive is apparent when he tells Lerner that ' "unless I can talk it out . . . I'll go out of my mind" ' (45). In seeking the approval of the ' "man of conscience. Of conviction. Of principles" ' (108) he has selected, Stappler is looking, in the words of Ian Watt's comment about Lord Jim, for 'someone who can grant him the absolution that is supposed to follow confession.'[9]

Mark Lerner, Stappler's confessor, does not on first acquaintance seem better equipped for that role than the Wedding Guest to whom he compares himself. Indeed, if he is like the Wedding Guest at the beginning of the narrative in his complacency and self-absorption, it is less certain that he emerges from his involuntary exposure to a haunted tale-teller as 'a sadder and a wiser man.' In congratulating himself about his scholarly work on the French Revolution ('I have something of importance to say, I think, about the impact of extreme situations' [204]), he is ludicrously unaware of the inadequacy revealed by his inability to have anything definitive to say about the extreme situation in front of his nose. His indecision about Held's culpability is not even cause for much soul-searching; it is merely 'one of those loose ends' which remain 'fortunately out of the way' (209).

Flaws such as these have made Lerner an unattractive character in the judgment of some critics. In the most whole-hearted condemnation, Robert A. Lecker finds Lerner 'antiseptically intellectual, as cold and sterile as the environment he shies away from,' 'a violent, terror-stricken individual.'[10] For other critics, Lerner's defects are linked to alleged defects in the novel: in Hugo McPherson's view, Lerner, unlike Marlow, is 'too comfortably ensconced in his world to communicate powerfully the passions he has glimpsed.'[11] F.W. Watt suggests that Lerner, 'for all the freedom of entry into his consciousness we are given, is a static and restricted character.'[12] Without denying an element of truth in these uncomplimentary opinions, one can still seek to find a Lerner who commands more sympathy both for himself and for the fiction in which he is so prominent.

Like the narrator in *Under Western Eyes* (and indeed, like Stappler) Lerner often seems unable to intervene decisively in crucial situations. Yet it would be unwise to accuse him of mere callousness or indifference: he is simply too torn between contrary impulses to be able to appear firm-minded. The two words *involvement* and *judgment,* which are used over and over again in the novel, come to define Lerner's areas of divided feeling.

Lerner is not always introspective, but he is very conscious of the ambivalence he feels towards involvement with others in general, and involvement with Theodore Stappler in particular:

> I cannot, in all conscience, deny that part of me does not like to become too involved with others. Brian Maxwell once suggested that I like the study of history because it involves me in the acts and sufferings of humanity but at the same time allows me to keep involvements at arm's length. I refuted his analysis at the time, but I am now prepared to grant it a certain validity. But it is also true that I shrink* from involvements because, once involved, I am too involved. My whole being becomes involved; my nerves become frayed, my body tense. I sensed, sitting there and facing Theodore Stappler, that he would demand such an involvement. I therefore resented him, yet I could not, even at the moment, deny that a bond had been created between us. In an obscure way I identified myself with him. (46)

This response to Stappler, stated at an early stage of his confession to Lerner, persists throughout the novel. One might think, from the number of occasions upon which Lerner feels 'irritated' (45) or 'annoyed' (51) or is overcome by 'a sense of outrage' (151) that Lerner's chief aim is to resist the emotional claims Stappler makes upon him. He does in fact balk at Stappler's specific demands for the very reason he gives in the extended passage just quoted: he fears becoming 'too involved.' When he is called upon by Stappler to tell Katherine of her father's misdeed, the reader observes a concrete instance of the tension which Lerner had already outlined in

---

*Henry Kreisel confirms that the text's reading of *shirk* is a misprint for *shrink*. S.N.

principle between the effort to retain detachment and the instinct to yield to emotion: 'I said to myself that I would try to speak as drily, as dispassionately, as nearly without any intonation even, as possible— almost, I thought, as if I were a judge summing up a case. But when I actually began to speak, my voice trembled and my heart was beating so strongly that I had trouble keeping myself under control' (169).

Despite the qualms and misgivings just noted, at every stage of the novel Lerner's resistance to involvement is matched by surrender to it. Subsequent events are foreshadowed in the first chapter, the first and last paragraphs of which contain the phrase 'involved with Theodore Stappler.' By p. 44, Lerner is forced to acknowledge that 'I was, whether I wanted it or not, involved.' In the final confrontation with Held, he acts as Stappler's ' "representative" ' (173) and ' "witness" ' (51, 67, 175, 177). It is as a 'witness' once again, one 'who had inexorably been drawn into the circle' (184; one of several allusions to Dante's *Inferno* in the novel) that Lerner decides, just as the Helds leave Stappler's hotel room, to 'set all this down' (184). When Lerner meets Stappler for the last time, years later, he is still inclined to be resentful of Stappler's 'summons,' but once again allows his emotions to take control: 'I was so excited, so shaken, so consumed by sheer curiosity that work was impossible for me' (210).

Lerner is no match for Marlow in the depth of his psychological and humanitarian involvement with the protagonist, but there are similarities in the origins of the two narrators' emotions. In his penetrating study of *Lord Jim*, Ian Watt argues that Marlow can, on occasion, resent Jim instead of sympathizing with him: 'By the time the two men actually meet, then, the reader knows that Jim arouses a highly complicated and unstable assortment of personal and moral problems for Marlow; and this puts the reader in a position to appreciate the tensions and hostilities in Marlow's subsequent behaviour.'[13] Marlow finds it disturbing that Jim, who is ' "one of us" ' (i.e. an Englishman; 27, 48, 57, 65) should fail in a test of honour: Marlow's own moral code of 'solidarity'[14] is called into question. Lerner, too, feels a powerful sense of kinship (in his case, a feeling literally of brotherhood), but is disconcerted by the challenge to his pre-existing values. Like Marlow, Lerner has a racial bond with the protagonist: he is Jewish and Stappler is half-Jewish. Lerner is, however, the second generation of his family to be born in Canada, and this factor is one essential cause of his tendency to resist Stappler while still simultaneously identifying with him. The basis for Lerner's attitude is indicated to the reader very early in the novel, when Katherine Held reveals that she is a European refugee: 'I felt suddenly as if a sombre reality, the spectre of Auschwitz, had invaded my office. . . . The murder of Marat was far enough in the past so that the blood had had a chance to dry. But the bones that had been here evoked had not yet crumbled' (15). When Lerner later is forced to contemplate Stappler's share in the European horror, he still finds that identification with a Jewish victim is painful, if inevitable: 'Yet if my grandfather had not come here, then I, too, would have been caught up in the European holocaust and I, too, might have fled desperately from country to country, as Theodore Stappler had done. And so, even as I resented his being here with me, disturbing the peace of my existence, causing old ghosts to walk here, I had also to accept him as if he were my more unfortunate brother. Part of me rejected him, but part embraced him' (46-47). Lerner's reluctance is effectively signaled by the diffidence of 'had also to accept him' and 'as if he were' instead of the more whole-hearted 'as my unfortunate brother.' The situation is analogous to the relationship between the narrator of Conrad's famous 'The Secret Sharer' and his more unfortunate brother, but Conrad's character 'identified with my secret double'[15] in a steadily progressive way that is opposite to Lerner's persistent ambivalence of feeling.

If Lerner remains uncertain about the degree of involvement he will permit himself, he is also tormented by the issue of the judgment to be made upon Stappler's and Held's European drama. Like Marlow, he finds the situation presented to him is too complex to be judged decisively; like the narrator of *Under Western Eyes*, he tends to excuse rather than to blame. We cannot, of course, entirely separate the question of judgment from the question of involvement: Marlow's compassionate judgment is a measure of his involvement with Jim; the narrator's apparently sympathetic judgment of individuals in *Under Western Eyes* reflects his earnest desire to dissociate himself from Russian thought and life. Lerner's judgments, when they are wise, show that he can, on occasion, choose to involve himself in the fate of others, but his characteristic refusals to judge sometimes serve to bring out the squeamishness which Stappler attacks as being either professorial (49, 101, 118, 178) or Canadian (150).

Throughout the novel, Lerner alternates between the willingness to judge and a disavowal of judging, just as he alternates between involvement and resentment against involvement. He is most unequivocal as a judge when Stappler tells him of his strategy of using Katherine as a tool against her father; in this situation, moral outrage is not difficult, and Lerner tells the reader that he 'was physically revolted' (121). He even offers a firm piece of advice, that Stappler should stop pursuing Held. More commonly, the pattern of a scene is that Stappler pauses in his narration, and the two 'brothers' discuss the moral implications of an incident. Lerner either refuses to judge, or offers a judgment that Stappler considers to be too lenient, and after a brisk discussion the narration resumes.

Since Lerner's attitude changes so frequently, and the situation he is called upon to judge is so complex, the judgment we pass on his judgments cannot be simple or one-sided. Two examples may serve to illustrate. Near the end of his tragic final appearance, Held asks Lerner the inevitable question, postponed until that point, ' "What would you have done?".' Lerner's answer does not appear to be very adequate:

> Challenged directly by Joseph Held, I pondered the question again, and in absolute honesty I could not answer it. So I took refuge in evasion, all the while aware of my cowardice.
> "That all depends," I said.
> "Aha!" Like acid, Theodore Stappler's voice cut through my careful and deliberate words. "The *Herr Professor* is taking up his position on the fence again."
> "I'm not a judge," I mumbled. (178)

Lerner's reply, and the fact that part of it is 'mumbled,' do not make him appear very heroic; Stappler would certainly have made a more forceful response. Some mitigation of Lerner's 'cowardice' may be found, however, if we ask ourselves the same question and realize its difficulty, a reflection the scene is designed to prompt. Also, Lerner, like Stappler in his moment of crisis, is very much 'aware' of his own deficiencies, and the reader is therefore more willing to indulge them.

At an earlier point in the story, Lerner's capacity to recollect his own experience enables him to appear more creditable in his close identification with Stappler: 'I thought back to the moment when we had first hit the beach in Sicily, and I understood what he meant. For I, too, had known fear and even panic. But I was in the company of friends and comrades, and we had drawn strength and sustenance from each other's fear and so had conquered our fear. But he was utterly alone, dependent solely on himself' (86). Even in these two parallel tests of bravery, Lerner is, as always, more securely placed within a society that supports him, and Stappler is the alienated individual. In a sudden burst of imaginative identification, Lerner anticipates and compassionately judges Stappler's cowardice before Stappler himself confesses it:

> I looked at him as he sat there, in my comfortable apartment, his face now almost ashen-white, drawn in remembered pain, and I knew all at once that he had failed to rise there in that station, that his fear had conquered him, and that it was this knowledge he had had to live with since that day. I knew and my heart went out to him, and I leaned forward and touched his knee lightly with my hand. . . .
> "I was also afraid once," I said. (86)

As the immediately preceding quotations and others previously cited indicate, Lerner can produce a wide variety of reactions to the bewildering events to which he is exposed (it must be remembered) in a very concentrated period of time. He can be both sensitive and insensitive, both dignified and unintentionally comic, both moved and remote, both penetrating and shallow in his judgments. His character seems midway between the deep humanity of Marlow, so much admired by critics, and the well-meaning inadequacy usually attributed to the narrator of *Under Western Eyes.* Perhaps it is more accurate to say that he is like **both** of the other two characters, at one time or another.

A judgment of Lerner would not be complete without a consideration of his sense of identification with the setting he has adopted. Born in Toronto, he has been living in Edmonton for two years when the story opens. Though his family has recent ties to Europe, though he reproaches his parents for their tendency 'to play down the past' (9), and though he himself is a professional historian, Lerner absorbs the Edmonton spirit of considering itself a brave new world to such a degree that he finds an emotional link to the past difficult to sustain: 'It is hard, for instance, to walk the streets of this growing, unself-conscious western city . . . and to realize that elsewhere the past is not merely history but something that touches sensitive nerves, evokes powerful responses' (2). Like other Torontonians before and since, Lerner quickly adopts Edmonton as his home: 'I keep telling her [his mother] that I do not intend to return to Toronto. I like it here. I like the University, I like my colleagues and, to be frank about it, I prefer to live at a distance from my close relatives' (10). At this point, loyalty to Edmonton may appear to be merely a way of rationalizing a desire to escape what Lerner characteristically regards as an excessive involvement with others. Six years and most of the novel later, Lerner is still in Edmonton, and this time his attachment to the city seems more deeply rooted, as his use of the central word *involved* indicates: 'I have watched with interest and satisfaction the growth of this city and of this university, have felt involved in it and derived some pleasure from playing a small part in it' (204). When Stappler, on his way to the North, claims a link with Lerner (' "You are alone. Like me" '), Lerner resists the identification by asserting his tie to the city: ' "At least I'm anchored to a place" ' (211).

Lerner is like the narrator of *Under Western Eyes* (an Englishman who has 'lived for a long time in Geneva' [11]) in that he has come to be associated with a city that is not his birthplace. More significantly, the values of the city give each character a context with which to evaluate the agitation of the protagonist, who has been immersed in a far different world. Here we find possibly the strongest analogy between Conrad and Kreisel: the unnamed narrator's vision of Russia through Western eyes has become Lerner's vision of Nazi Austria through Western Canadian eyes.

I have already quoted several passages in which Lerner rejoices in his Canadian detachment from European miseries. Canada, he tells us, is 'a country in which justice and law, though God knows often abused, were nevertheless very real' (46), whereas in Stappler's Austrian world he felt that he 'was wading through a moral pigsty, where all was dirt' (118). Edmonton, with 'its feeling that the world has only just begun and history is a tomb' (2), with its physical remoteness from Europe, and lack of an extended past, with its appearance (as Stappler sees it from the air at the end of the novel) as ' "a great circle of light" ' emerging ' "out of an immense darkness" ' (211) is much more appropriate than Toronto would be as a vantage point from which to regard Europe at a safe emotional distance.

The *Under Western Eyes* narrator's identification with Geneva is not as clear-cut. As Tony Tanner has pointed out, the narrator can speak 'with uncharacteristic mordancy' of Geneva's bourgeois limitations; yet, as Tanner also says, 'This is really Conrad's contempt: the narrator should be more approving of the achieved security of democratic civilisation.'[16] In essence, the spirit of the narrator and the spirit of Geneva are one, in that they both reject the violent, primitive, unpredictable element in humanity which the narrator disparagingly identifies with the Russian character.

Critics of *Under Western Eyes* have often tended to take the narrator's contemptuous judgment of Russia at face value. Tanner argues persuasively, however, that Conrad's choice of narrator should make us as skeptical of the 'Western eyes' as of what the Western eyes see:

> Marlow is one kind of narrator, the one who involves us with his dangerous material. But there is another kind in Conrad's work—the narrator who tries to impress on us the remoteness, the alienness, the regrettable primitiveness of his material. He will represent the virtues of decency, moderation, a sort of polite if bemused tolerance of what is unusual. . . . To make such a reasonable man recount to us some deeply irrational occurrence, to make the nightmarish material pass through the complacent filter, to make the western eye strive to get into focus some seemingly unwestern form of experience—this is to achieve a double irony. . . . The frame delimits and places the picture—but the picture can challenge and even ridicule the frame.[17]

These remarks make very good sense in relation to *Under Western Eyes;* it remains to be determined whether Tanner's frame can be made to fit Kreisel's picture. One must acknowledge that Lerner's character is not very different from the portrait Tanner gives of the *Under Western Eyes* narrator. Yet, though Lerner's self-congratulation is ironically treated in parts of *The Betrayal,* the Western eyes in Kreisel's novel are not exposed to the consistent irony that is found in Conrad. Kreisel uses Conrad's technique of juxtaposing opposite worlds for Conrad's purpose of underscoring a sinister atmosphere by contrast, but he presents an ordered society with more sympathy than Conrad seems to have for his Western world.

To some degree, the difference in tone between the two novels may be explained by the fact that the opposed societies are not contrasted in quite the same way. Though Conrad's image of Russia is certainly grim, it is not quite as absolutely black as Nazi Austria: in Mikulin and Sophia Antonovna, Conrad has drawn characters of intelligence and sensitivity, the one a senior bureaucrat, the other a revolutionary, who can sincerely if misguidedly defend their political choices. The Nazis, seen as a group rather than individuals, are aptly termed by Stappler ' "the devil's men" ' (83). The opposite world in Conrad is that of democratic and liberal tradition, for which the narrator is a spokesman. Canada generally, and Western Canada in particular, does not seem to represent any deeply ingrained tradition in Kreisel's novel so much as an untested innocence, a quality shared, to a considerable extent, by Lerner.[18] Stappler initially adopts a rather crude version of this idea of Canada; more detailed observation prompts him to modify, but not abandon, his conception, and in its re-stated form it is hard to deny:

> "Europeans think always that this is an unsophisticated country, incapable of producing subtle works. A country of mountains and vast spaces and Indians and the mounted police. I thought so too, at one time."
>
> "And you don't think so any more?"
>
> He began to eat slowly, thoughtfully. "Of course not. But...." He hesistated for a little while. "In a way, yes," he said then. "It is an innocent country."
>
> "How do you mean?"
>
> "I mean," he said, "that history ... has been very kind to this country. At least so it seems to someone like me. So the country hasn't had to—to corrupt itself. To betray. To murder. Unlike a good many other countries one could mention." (34-35)

Parallel scenes and descriptions serve to dramatize the contrast Stappler draws between European evil and Canadian innocence. Stappler describes in detail the atmosphere in the train station at Saarbrücken, where his mother is arrested, and also the atmosphere in the Edmonton train station when he arrives to confront Held. In both cases, Stappler feels deeply alienated, in Germany because of the agonizing events that took place, in Canada because of the guilt he still carries around with him. But the two places in themselves are quite different. The German station is in the grip of Nazi war fever, and throbs with intense evil. The Canadian station does not correspond to the mythic 'vision of a western frontier town' (55) Stappler had imagined; it is dowdy in appearance, and a girl with whom he tries to converse rebuffs him, but it is not a potential setting for tragic drama.

After Stappler leaves the Edmonton station, he finds a tawdry hotel and at his first meal encounters the province's quaint liquor laws. Although there is nothing appealing about this first glimpse of Alberta, the Canadian scene is at least not sinister as is the description of Vienna which immediately follows. Stappler says that what he remembers about his birth-place are ' "cobbled streets, little winding

streets that lead me to a dark wood" ' (65). The last phrase is
reminiscent of the *'selva oscura'* of the first canto of Dante's *Inferno,*
and the allusion becomes more prominent on the next page—at the
Schönbrunn Palace zoo, Stappler encounters the same animals as
Dante found blocking his path at the beginning of the *Inferno.*
Clearly, if Edmonton is not the earthly paradise, Vienna is hell on
earth. In another reference to the liquor laws, Stappler remarks that
Edmonton is ' "a very pure city",' making a proper celebration of
Stappler's and Lerner's ' "last supper" ' (156) impossible. This is
immediately followed by a description of another religious rite, the
Corpus Christi parade in Vienna. At first, this event seems more
attractive than Edmonton's customs, but it gives Stappler, then a
little boy, his first bitter taste of religious bigotry.

Each city's river is given a symbolic role. For Stappler, just as the
idea of Vienna as a city of ' "Wine, women and song" ' is ' "a lot of
nonsense" ' (65), so also the Danube, in which his father committed
suicide, is over-sentimentalized: ' "There are some pretty treacherous
eddies in the Danube. But people swim in the Danube, anyway. They
also drown, some of them. Every year a number of people are caught
in those whirlpools of the beautiful blue Danube, and they drown" '
(154). Lerner admits that swimming in the North Saskatchewan is
' "too dangerous" ' (154), but the main impression the Alberta river
makes, even more on Stappler than on Lerner, is of beauty and
strength. Stappler's negative view of Edmonton on first arrival is
partly offset by 'a marvelous vista of the winding, white, and frozen
river' (58). He returns to the river ' "Almost every day" ' (153), and
comes back for a final glimpse just before the Helds arrive at his
hotel: ' "I wish I could be here in the spring to see the ice on the river
go," he said. "It must be an exciting sight. . . . It must be wonderful . . .
to see all that force released. A real kind of liberation" ' (154). This
passage occurs just before Stappler's brooding remarks about the
sinister Danube whirlpools. A contrast between the destructive
pattern of European life and the potential energy of Canada (once its
frozen innocence has been transformed) seems clear. It is presumably
a mark against Lerner that he says 'to look at a frozen river' is 'not the
kind of thing I normally went in for' (153), but by the time Stappler
sees him again, Lerner has become a convert to the river's beauty: 'My
living room window overlooks the river valley, and I look down on
the magnificent river winding its way through the city, and watch the
changes of the seasons as they reflect themselves in the mirror of the
river, until I think that I could not live without the river' (205). The

passage characteristically balances Lerner's impulse towards detachment (in a high-rise apartment, he is a safe distance from the river) and his tendency to find emotional involvement nevertheless (as the final quoted words indicate). At dawn, the two friends silently observe the river which, 'calm and peaceful in the soft, grey morning light' (215) reflects the serenity that has come into their lives.

The human landscape in The Betrayal, like the physical landscape, suggests a Canada that is still unformed, but also unobjectionable. Lerner patronizingly characterizes one of his colleagues as 'exactly the man' to write about voyageurs, who were 'Uncomplicated fellow[s]' (21). Sam, the room clerk at the Victory Hotel, is warm-hearted despite his efforts to appear worldly-wise, and the hotel guests are genuine innocents. After the tense scene with Stappler and the Helds, Lerner incongruously joins a honeymoon party hosted by a rustic couple in the next room. One of the other guests, in a soliloquy prompted by intoxication, provides a summation of the unachieved national identity which unconsciously reinforces Stappler's comment about Canadian innocence: ' "What country needs is. . . . is flag. Tha's what th' country needs. Nash'nal flag. We don't want no. . . . Nothing. Flag. So we know—so we goddam well know who we're supposed—what is supposed—what— who we. . . . Can't be nobody. . . . Gotta be somebody' " (187).

It will be apparent that in outline the story of a sheltered and in some ways naive North American coming to terms with European evil sounds closer to Henry James than to Joseph Conrad. But Kreisel's spare style owes nothing to James; as I have tried to show, his characterization, plot elements, and mode of narration have strong analogies with Conrad. Even more importantly, Kreisel, like Conrad, did not hesitate to make the 'horror' of human degradation central to his fiction. Yet for all its authentic portrayal of tragic events, The Betrayal does not seem entirely to share the despairing distrust of all human institutions and societies that we often find in Conrad's fiction. Kreisel's complex picture of Mark Lerner and of Edmonton is not sentimentalized, but we can find in it some support for the eternal North American hope that in the New World human nature is given a new chance.

---

[1]'Joseph Conrad and the Dilemma of the Uprooted Man,' Tamarack Review, 7 (Spring 1958), 78.

[2]John Carroll, 'Stirring echoes of Conrad,' *Globe and Mail Magazine*, November 7, 1964, 13.

[3]Hugo McPherson, 'Betrayal, Desertion, Atonement,' *Tamarack Review*, 34 (Winter 1965), 108.

[4]*Journals of André Gide*, translated by Justin O'Brien, vol. III, 94-95. Quoted in Frederick R. Karl, *Joseph Conrad: The Three Lives* (New York: Farrar, Straus and Giroux, 1979), p. 709.

[5]'Joseph Conrad and the Dilemma of the Uprooted Man,' 84.

[6]Joseph Conrad, *Lord Jim*, edited by Thomas C. Moser (New York: Norton, 1968), p. 129. All subsequent references will be identified in the text.

[7]Joseph Conrad, *Under Western Eyes* (Harmondsworth: Penguin, 1957), p. 37. All subsequent references will be identified in the text.

[8]Ian Watt, *Conrad in the Nineteenth Century* (Berkeley, Los Angeles: Univ. of California Press, 1979), p. 320.

[9]*Ibid.*, p. 315.

[10]Robert A. Lecker, 'States of Mind: Henry Kreisel's Novels,' *Another Country: Writings by and about Henry Kreisel*, pp. 311, 312.

[11]McPherson, 108.

[12]F.W. Watt, 'Letters in Canada: 1964 (Fiction),' *University of Toronto Quarterly*, 34, 4 (July 1965), 378.

[13]Ian Watt, pp. 312-13.

[14]This term, central to *Lord Jim* and much of Conrad's other work, is analyzed in Ian Watt, pp. 312-16, 319-20.

[15]Joseph Conrad, *The Secret Sharer*, in *The Portable Conrad*, edited by Morton D. Zabel (New York: Viking, 1947), p. 683.

[16]Tony Tanner, 'Nightmare and Complacency: Razumov and the Western Eye,' *Critical Quarterly*, 4, 3 (Autumn 1962), 200, 201.

[17]*Ibid.*, 198.

[18]Warhaft (ix), in his 'Introduction' to *The Betrayal*, also takes the view that Lerner 'is primarily a Canadian, relatively innocent and untried.'

Neil Besner

Across Broken Globes:
The Almost Meeting

Henry Kreisel opens his well-known essay 'The Prairie: A State of Mind' with his memory of a letter in an Edmonton newspaper, from a man Kreisel imagined as 'a giant . . . , a lord of the land [who] asserted what his eyes saw, what his heart felt, and what his mind perceived' ('The Prairie,' 254)—that the earth was flat. Kreisel eventually transformed that giant's unshakeable faith in his flat prairie world into the figure at the centre of his finest story, 'The Broken Globe.' All of Kreisel's stories document the breakup of worlds and world-views; as a Jew fleeing Austria in the late 1930s, Kreisel lived his own way through one. His forced passage to the new world fissured his ties with the past, and, inevitably, with his first language—any writer's first home. Deciding to write in English, Kreisel adopted Conrad as a 'patron saint'; deciding to make a life in Canada, Kreisel looked to A.M. Klein, who showed him that he could lay claim to both halves of the immigrant's world without sacrificing either.

In the title story, appearing here for the first time, Kreisel pays Klein a warm tribute. 'The Almost Meeting' recreates Klein's personality, transforms lines of his poetry, and evokes the enigmas of his reclusion in the figure of David Lasker, 'a great poet as well as a great novelist, who had created an astonishing body of work, but had then suddenly fallen silent' (11). Lasker writes narrator Alexander Budak a congratulatory note on his first novel, an autobiographical story of old world feuds splitting up a new world marriage. The son, Budak, searches all over North America for his father, but never quite meets him. Budak's eagerly anticipated meetings with Lasker never materialize either, but Lasker's closing note explains that even almost meetings are ' "something" ': ' "It was impossible for me to see you. . . . You wanted to ask me things. I have no answers. But you are in my heart. Let me be in your heart also. We had an almost meeting. Perhaps that is not much. And yet it is something. Remember me" ' (21). Kreisel has: his heartfelt evocation of Klein, like Livesay's 'For Abe Klein: Poet,' is imaginative literary history, private and public.

'Homecoming,' revised and greatly expanded in this version, is Kreisel's bleakest evocation of the European postwar waste land. Mordecai Drimmer feels compelled to return to what remains of his home town in Poland; he is Kreisel's most tormented figure, haunted by demons real and imagined, Jew-hating peasants and leering gargoyles that threaten him from church spires. Kreisel's vision of the post-Holocaust landscape is surreal, vaporous with desolation; Drimmer's agonized descent into the past is so powerfully imagined, the devastation so utter, that in contrast his final rebirth of hope seems a fragile scene, more wished for, more strained after than fully realized.

The remaining six stories are reprinted without change. 'The Travelling Nude' is a comical, tongue-in-cheek sendup of an art instructor who loses his job teaching extension courses in outlying prairie communities because he insists that a travelling nude would be just the ticket for his students. Mahler, the artist/teacher, opens his story with a portrait of his travelling nude, travelling nude—to pose for aspiring artists in Great Fish Lake, Three Bears Hills, Pollux, Castor. . . . Kreisel gives Mahler's tantalizing obsession whimsical, lighthearted treatment.

'Annerl' and 'An Anonymous Letter' show Kreisel's sensitivity to children's rites of passage into adolescence. Annerl is an irreverent old peasant woman who sells roasted chestnuts on a Viennese street-corner. Two schoolboys make her post a regular stop; she disappears for a few days and then returns, her drunken husband dead and buried. She continues to rail at him as she had when he was alive, but fondly remembers that he was a ' "right good 'un" ' (86) in bed when he wasn't too drunk. Intrigued, the boys ask her to explain how men make love, but Annerl sends them off with free chestnuts and orders to pray for her Joseph's soul, and they walk off towards several initiations at once. 'An Anonymous Letter' follows a boy's investigation into his father's infidelity. David tracks his father to his rendezvous with his mistress and then confronts them in a restaurant. His innocence gives way to ambiguity in the space of a sentence: wondering if he is guilty of spying, and whether he should now tell his mother, he realizes that 'Everything was too tangled up and nothing could ever be simple and straightforward again' (103).

In 'Two Sisters in Geneva,' Warren Douglas, a young Canadian student of history at Oxford, is privy to two sisters' monologues in a Geneva train station; his occupation makes him an apt auditor for a debate between Old and New World sensibilities. Mrs. Miller emigrated with her husband from England to Canada; after his death, she moves from their Peace River homestead to Edmonton. Now she's come to Europe, bent on dragging her sister away from her home in Florence to the alleged comforts of the New World. Mrs. Miller is intolerant, bigoted, a blithe materialist. She can't pronounce her sister's name; she's shocked that Emily would ' "up and marry an Eyetalian" ' (126) and she's scandalized at statues of nude figures in Florence. Emily Buonarroti, also widowed, tells Douglas a very different history: her husband was a teacher of Renaissance art, and ' "when you live in Firenze—in Florence—you have to learn something. Art, religion, history—it is all preserved around you" ' (129). Nowhere is Kreisel's perception of the deep divisions between worldviews more artfully imagined. The story closes with the three boarding their train—Emilia longing for Florence, Mrs. Miller eager to show her the ' "wide-open prairie . . . and the Rocky Mountains" ' (131), and the student of history silent; the sisters' monologues have told separate stories all too well.

I've saved for last the two stories I admire most. 'Chassidic Song' sings first with the voice of a Chassid, another of Kreisel's giant, faithful figures. During a plane ride from Montreal to New York, the Chassid questions Arnold Weiss (a modern Jew, a Joyce scholar who has just presented a paper on Leopold Bloom) on the nature of his faith. Rhythmically reasoning, the Chassid answers himself with more questions, in dialectical couplets: in the mind's eye, he sways back, forth, nodding, sighing, incantatory: ' "What do you mean—I? . . . Did I start this? What did I start? Did I talk to you first or did you talk to me first? Did I tell you where I was going? Or did you ask me? Who mentioned the *Farbrengen?* Did I or did you? . . . . But even did you? Or perhaps it was Moses Drimmer speaking through you. Not the father. The grandfather" ' (30). The Chassid communicates a grandfather's faith to his grandson, a song submerged for a generation. He leaves Weiss with an invocation: ' "Remember your grandfather. He knew that the tongue is the pen of the heart, but melody is the pen of the soul. . . . He sang. Your grandfather. Oh, yes. He sang, too" ' (35).

'The Broken Globe' is simply a classic. Nick Solchuk, a young geophysicist in London, is making a name for himself with his work on the earth's curvature. He is estranged from his father: the two had quarrelled years ago when Nick came home with a toy globe to show him that the earth moved, that it was round. The father had smashed the globe and beat Nick. As in other Kreisel stories, there is an intermediary in this one, a figure poised between two worlds, looking both ways; here, the narrator accepts a teaching post at the University of Alberta and promises Nick that he'll drive out to his father's farm to bring him greetings. The broken globe still sits in the old house; when he sees the narrator examining it, the father tells him the story behind it. Like Kreisel, the narrator is fascinated with the farmer's brooding, massive figure; the closing image evokes his unbroken faith in all its stillness, size, and shadow: 'I looked back at the house, and saw him still standing there, still looking at his beloved land, a lonely, towering figure framed against the darkening evening sky' (147).

In postwar Europe, on the prairie, in the family, at the writer's desk, Kreisel's immigrants inherit and inhabit a broken globe, living the double experience that Kreisel knows so intimately. By presenting all of his stories to us in one place, *The Almost Meeting* makes one of the richest aspects of Kreisel's varied contribution to Canadian literature that much more coherent.

Michael Greenstein

Close Encounters:
Henry Kreisel's Short Stories

Geometrically, the title of Henry Kreisel's collection of short stories, *The Almost Meeting*, could refer to a hyperbola or the vanishing point of two parallel lines, an important image in his two novels. Biographically, the title can be seen as the convergence of the European and Canadian experiences in Kreisel's background. Thematically, the title points to the failure of characters to get together, as in *The Rich Man*, where Jacob Grossman meets Tassigny and his own Austrian family but fails to communicate the truth, or in *The Betrayal*, where the meeting of Held, Lerner, and Stappler has tragic consequences.

The first story, 'The Almost Meeting,' depicts a near encounter between two writers, Alexander Budak and David Lasker. Having received an encouraging letter from Lasker, whom he has greatly admired, Budak attempts to contact the elder poet and novelist on a visit to Toronto. Throughout his failed quest the *doppelgänger* motif reverberates much as in Kreisel's second novel, *The Betrayal*. Kreisel, Lasker, and Budak all explore the same theme: 'Often in his writing people of different nationalities came together and almost touched, only to find themselves pulled apart again' (12). This thematic magnet has a structural counterpart, for the external Lasker-Budak plot is interrupted by the details of Budak's first novel, in which an immigrant by the name of Lukas (an amalgam of Lasker and Budak) marries Helena against her family's wishes. Her father disowns her and her two children, but they are reconciled after Lukas abandons her. Torn between his love for his grandfather and the need to find his father, the boy, who is really David Lasker in this autobiographical novel, searches across North America for his father, but fails to meet him. After this description of the novel, the outer frame is restored by reference to Lasker's letter: ' "An almost meeting is often more important than the meeting. The quest is all" ' (17). Despite the letter, a phone call, and a visit to Lasker's house, Budak does not succeed in confronting the man who is evidently his father and whose Kafkaesque deferments frustrate his son's hopes. Indeed, the repeated description of Lasker's handwriting as 'the intricate web spun by a long-legged spider' (17) suggests the snare of an almost meeting. In Toronto, Budak has ' "the strangest feeling of déjà vu" ': ' "That store looked exactly like a little grocery store up in Yellowknife where I once waited for my father. Someone told me he always came there at a certain time, but he never showed up" ' (20). Thus, through a series of facing but not touching mirrors reflecting *ad infinitum*, and through a synecdochic inner plot that recapitulates the larger frame of the story, Kreisel succeeds in creating a *mise en abyme* for the values of opposing generations of immigrants.

The opposing values in the next story, 'Chassidic Song,' belong to a liberal Jew, Arnold Weiss, and an orthodox Jew, Joseph Shemtov, who find themselves seated side by side on a flight from Montreal to New York. They establish contact by means of the shibboleth, *Farbrengen*, a Chassidic gathering to sing. 'Arnold Weiss heard himself speak, the words shaping themselves almost involuntarily, as if it was someone else's voice that was speaking' (27). Like cadences in a writer's mind, the 'voice' of the past frequently inhabits the souls of Kreisel's protagonists, who are haunted by the Holocaust. As a child, Weiss had first heard the word from his grandfather, Moses Drimmer, so the Chassidic Shemtov interprets his use of the term as the Chassidic voice of Drimmer speaking through his secular grandson. After Weiss has finished his story, Shemtov recounts his own escape from Hitler, who had not spared the rest of his family. An embittered Shemtov rejected God: ' "For ten years, the Presence withdrew itself from me, and I withdrew myself from the Presence" ' (34). Later, in a Montreal Chassidic song of joy, this repulsion changes to a permanent attraction, and this Chassidic song shared by Shemtov and the grandfather constitutes an almost meeting between the two spheres of Weiss's existence.

Drimmer's name reappears in the third story, 'Homecoming,'[1] by far the longest story in this collection. Subtitled 'A Memory of Europe After the Holocaust,' it attempts to come to terms—through a Kafkaesque dreamscape—with the demonic aftermath of the genocide perpetrated by the Nazis. Having survived the Holocaust, Mordecai Drimmer returns to his Polish village in search of any remaining members of his family. A kind of medieval creaturalism pervades this morality play from the opening simile, 'The little dirt road wound along like a moving snake' (39), to the 'grotesque, rag-tattered' Polish peasant (45), to the lengthy description of the writhing worm that Drimmer handles and inspects. But many other elements contribute to the macabre atmosphere as the somnambulant Everyman makes his way toward Narodnowa. The first section, for example, focuses on Drimmer's encounter with a bigoted peasant who rejoices in the annihilation of Polish Jews and who believes that Drimmer answers to the descriptions of the devil figure that his priest has so often spoken about.

In the second section, the stranger (another central word in these stories) approaches the town in the rain and sees a church spire. 'It was as if he were walking through a dream, seeing things, feeling things, but perceiving them as through a gently-swaying screen of gauze, now very clear, now hazily shimmering, and never quite real' (51). During this surrealistic pilgrimage, voices and visions flash through Drimmer's waking dream, as his ghostlike mother also sleep-walks, 'tripping lightly, as if she were dancing, her feet hardly touching the ground' (53). The cemetery juts out into the road, becoming a part of it: 'No barrier divided the dead from the living' (53) in this abstract and unreal world. The church welcomes him home diabolically when the two gargoyles on its spire free themselves from their pedestal. 'From a niche in the tower two gargoyles stared down at him, their eyes screwed up curiously, their lips pursed into a scoffing pout, their bodies twisted and warped like a misshapen root' (55). Eventually he passes these gargoyles, a beggar, and a dog, and discovers that his uncle is still alive, the only other remaining member of his family. Rachel, the woman who guides him to his uncle's apartment, becomes his companion by the end of the story, and the two of them who have suffered so much will try to build a new life in a new world.

Two stories in the middle of this volume present a boy's point of view. The first-person narrator in 'Annerl,' a thirteen-year-old schoolboy, describes his education in the streets of Vienna at the hands of Annerl, a middle-aged chestnut vendor whose husband precedes her to the grave, thereby upsetting her destiny. In 'An Anonymous Letter,' the scene shifts to the New World as a boy discovers his father's relationship to his mistress. Both open-ended stories offer brief moments of insight concerning the differences between an adult's and a child's viewpoints. These two stories together with 'Two Sisters in Geneva,' which has a Jamesean trans-atlantic theme, are the most straightforward works in the volume.

'The Travelling Nude' differs markedly from the other stories both in the style and tone of its casual first-person narrator, Mahler, an artist in name and in training. For the first time, Kreisel refers to the second-person pronoun as a way of including the reader in the narrative process. Phrases like 'but you'll admit' (107), 'Oh, I forgot to tell you' (108), 'Let me assure you that I am as sane as you' (111), and 'if you know what I mean' (116) intervene in each of the four short sections as Mahler tries to establish an almost meeting with his Canadian *doppelgänger*. The outer frame of the distorted plot opens with the narrator worrying about how he is going to explain his loss of a good job to his father. 'Now when he hears about the travelling nude, he's quite likely to become momentarily deranged' (107). This introduction of madness, reiterated at the beginning of Section II, makes the reader question Mahler's fantasy about a nude model who travels from prairie town to prairie town for the benefit of Alberta's art students. After this 'painting' of the travelling nude in Section I, Mahler backtracks in the second section to present his own personal history from art student in Toronto to his eventual position as lecturer at the University of Alberta. As in the first two sections, Section III opens enigmatically: 'I resigned from this position largely because of the travelling nude' (114). There follows an explanation of this enigma: the puritanical denizens of rural Alberta reject Mahler's exaggerated idea of the travelling nude, and he is forced to resign when his boss advises him to see a doctor. The final irony occurs when Mahler informs the reader of his model's name, Valerie. Where Valerie shares the secrets of her female anatomy, the reader becomes the narrator's secret sharer in Kreisel's game of irony with artistic license challenging academic authority.

The final story, 'The Broken Globe,' examines the prairies more than any of the other stories; at the same time, it recapitulates transatlantic themes and the irreconcilable differences between an immigrant generation and its assimilated offspring. The narrator acts as a go-between for his friend Nick Solchuk, a geophysicist doing research in England, and Nick's father, a farmer in Three Bear Hills, Alberta. Although Nick solves problems related to the earth's curvature and although his room overlooking the Thames gives him a sense of distance and space, he misses the openness of the Canadian prairies: 'He referred to himself, nostalgically, as a prairie boy, and when he wanted to demonstrate what he meant by space he used to say that when a man stood and looked out across the open prairie, it was possible for him to believe that the earth was flat' (135). In contrast to his son's modern scientific outlook, Mr. Solchuk believes in the fundamental flatness of the earth: '... the shape of the world he lived in had been forever fixed for him by some medieval priest in the small Ukrainian village' (137). The narrator-mediator between these two world-views leaves England's 'nature humanized' for Canada's expanses: '. . . the land became flatter until there seemed nothing . . . to disturb the vast unbroken flow of land until in the far distance a thin, blue line marked the point where the prairie merged into the sky' (139). This narrative vanishing point, an almost meeting between two theories of the earth's shape, prepares for the interchange with Mr. Solchuk and the broken globe. As a schoolboy, Nick had received the globe, and when he tried to show his father how the earth moves, the traditionalist smashed the globe. A confirmed empiricist, Mr. Solchuk points out the prairie's earlier features at the end of the story to the narrator, who had earlier observed that 'all motion seemed suspended' (139). ' "Look . . . she is flat, and she stands still" ' (147). Geometrically, the squashed globe resembles an ellipse whose foci are Europe and the Canadian West, history and geography, Kreisel's past and present whose hemispheres almost always meet throughout his fiction.

---

[1]The title recalls Harold Pinter's play and, more importantly, the last section of Herman Broch's *The Death of Virgil*. Like Kreisel, Broch fled his native Vienna during the *Anschluss*. Kreisel's relationship to Broch and to the rest of the Jewish Viennese intellectuals—Karl Kraus, Wittgenstein, and Elias Canetti—is a fascinating topic that remains to be explored. Broch and Kreisel both employ the theme of sleep-walking in their fiction. Broch and Canetti studied crowds and mass psychology; Kreisel frequently contrasts the emptiness of Canadian space with the crowds of Europe.

W.J. Keith
Almost Meetings

Henry Kreisel is a slow, deliberate writer—this is only his third book in over thirty years; *The Rich Man,* his first novel, appeared in 1948, and *The Betrayal,* his second, in 1964. Now he has gathered together his short stories, most of which have been published before but without receiving the attention they obviously deserve. Cumulatively, as they present themselves in book-form, they are extremely impressive.

Their most noteworthy characteristic is a deceptive simplicity. Kreisel's prose is direct and spare; without imitating the self-conscious simplicity of Callaghan, he nonetheless eschews any hint of the rhetorically ornate. A spade is a spade is a spade. The plots, too, are straightforward and clear-cut. In 'Homecoming,' for instance, surely a minor masterpiece, a young Polish Jew, who has survived the Holocaust, returns to his native town in hope of finding his parents and relatives. Little happens, but the human process of painfully facing the realities of a shattered life and making an effort towards new growth is movingly presented. It is not merely the subject-matter that reminds us, without any sense of incongruity, of the great Russian writers.

I have said that little happens, but Kreisel is at the opposite extreme from so many of his contemporaries who give us detailed and elaborate slices of life to illustrate the rich but frustrating meaning-lessness—and helplessness—of everyday living. A true humanist, he is preoccupied with moral values. In 'Annerl' and 'An Anonymous Letter,' youths are prematurely confronted with—and so initiated into—the bewildering complexities of adult problems and responsibilities. In 'Chassidic Song,' a chance encounter in a plane jolts a young man into reconsidering his Jewish heritage. In 'The Broken Globe,' a story which examines a subject Kreisel later explored in an influential critical essay, 'The Prairie: A State of Mind,' a modern intellectual is shown developing a grudging respect for an obstinate, ignorant farmer who belongs in a moral world centuries older than that of his scientist son.

At the same time, Kreisel is not as morally austere as the above discussion might suggest. He is eloquent on the importance of the artistic imagination. 'The Travelling Nude,' whose title (and, to some extent, subject) depends upon a pun, is more whimsical in tone than we usually expect from him, but its presentation of the clash between artistic principle and puritan or (worse) prurient response is central to his work.

But it is in his latest story, 'The Almost Meeting' itself, that we encounter Kreisel's most absorbing and creative, albeit unostentatious, foray into artistic theory. Alexander Budak has written a novel in which a young man goes out in quest of his father, who disappeared some years previously. He almost finds him on two occasions 'only to have him vanish before he could meet him face to face' (17). Budak receives a letter of appreciation from David Lasker, a distinguished poet and novelist (whose description intriguingly recalls A.M. Klein), congratulating him on his achievement. Budak then makes a number of attempts to meet Lasker, but the older man always (and, it seems, deliberately) eludes him. As Lasker wrote about the protagonist in Budak's novel: ' "An almost meeting is often more important than the meeting. The quest is all" ' (17).

So life, in a curious way, is made to imitate art. The novelist finds himself within a situation that he has himself imagined, invented, created. Or, we might say, Kreisel has himself imagined, invented, created an 'almost meeting' between art and life. What impresses me about this story is that Kreisel has taken a decidedly 'modern' subject—the claimed autonomy of text, the artist's capacity to play with the connections and separations between his art and the world in which he lives—but has explored it in a probing yet traditional way. In other words, he displays another 'almost meeting' between conventional realistic modes and the more serious challenges of the current avant-garde.

Kreisel's stories, in my experience, have a curiously delayed effect. They are likely to impress immediately, but they go on to expand and develop within the mind. We realize that they contain depths and resonances that do not reveal themselves at once. These stories sent me back to *The Betrayal,* and I find myself even more impressed on the second reading than on the first. There is no one quite like Kreisel in Canadian fiction. If we underestimate him, we are doing ourselves an injustice.

Stephen Scobie

On the Edge of Language

Henry Kreisel has not been a prolific writer of fiction. His two novels—*The Rich Man* (1948) and *The Betrayal* (1964)—are spaced sixteen years apart, and another seventeen elapsed before this sparse collection of eight short stories, dating from 1954 to 1980. The stories have a consistency and a thematic unity which might suggest an almost obsessive return to a few central issues—the distances between generations, between the Old World and the New, between pre- and post-war—but they also have, in their very number as well as in their modest, understated technique, a reticence, a withholding, a hesitance to believe that even in the limited world of the text such distances can truly be bridged.

Almost half of the title story, 'The Almost Meeting,' is given over to a plot summary of a novel envisaged to have been written by one of the two main characters, Alexander Budak. It sounds very much like a Henry Kreisel novel: the story of a father and son divided by the deeply rooted religious prejudices of the Old World, with the son seeking but failing to find his father in the New. The story's summary of the novel's plot makes it sound fascinating—but very much in the mode of conceptual art. One is led to doubt whether one would derive all that much more, in terms of thematic suggestiveness, from a two- or three-hundred page version than one can in fact deduce from this summary. Borges used to say that he wrote short stories because he was too lazy to write novels: what Kreisel gives us here is a Borgesian text, the skeleton or (to switch metaphors and critical models) the Derridean 'trace' of another, fictional text.

Furthermore, in Kreisel's story, this text-within-a-text encounters another text-within-the-text, in this case the poems of David Lasker, the other major character. Indeed, it is only through this mode of intertextuality that the two characters 'meet' at all. Each reads and admires the other's work; each senses an affinity between their two formally different expressions. But just as Budak's text, the novel, is attenuated into Kreisel's summary, so Lasker's poems are 'enigmatic utterances . . . in which the artist seemed to want to refine himself out of existence, to separate his fleshly self from the works of his own creation until all that was bound up with the self was burned away. The poet himself would become a zero. Only the created work would glimmer and shine in its anonymity' (11-12). This is of course an extended allusion and tribute to A.M. Klein's 'Portrait of the Poet as Landscape':

> Meanwhile, he
> makes of his status as zero a rich garland,
> a halo of his anonymity,
> and lives alone, and in his secret shines
> like phosphorus. At the bottom of the sea.[1]

(Kreisel has in fact mentioned that the story is in part based on his own 'almost meeting' with Klein.)

Lasker succeeds in disappearing behind his texts, all of which are distanced from him in a manner reminiscent of the endless recession of Derrida's 'signified,' which retreats from the illusion of solidity, in any given text, towards that ideal essence (or 'meeting'), the existence of which Derrida denies. Lasker begins as a letter, written with 'the thinnest possible nib' (11), becomes a series of messages delivered at second or third hand, then a presence/absence refusing to answer the door, and finally, by letter again, a text proclaiming that an ' "almost meeting" ' is ' "not much. And yet it is something" ' (21).

The 'almost meeting,' then, takes place as intertextuality. Just as Budak and Lasker can never meet in the flesh (enacting the paradigm already textually established in Budak's novel), so the author and reader meet only in the equivocal and shifting realm of writing. Each reader is of course a kind of writer: faced with a text as attenuated as the novel's plot summary, we are invited to flesh it out in the act of reading, not just in the obvious ways of forming a mental image of the appearance of characters and setting, but here in the more fundamental way of imagining whole scenes, whole chapters of a novel which might generate the summary we are given. But every manifestation of text is undercut by its inherent equivocation as the 'trace' of a previous text which we can never track down. The other stories in the book, Kreisel's earlier stories, show a series of *meetings* which, however surrounded they are by hesitations and doubts, provide privileged moments in which the distances are bridged; but in the title story, the meeting has been reduced to an 'almost' meeting, and the hesitations and doubts, previously realized in such plot devices as chance and temporary encounters, often between travellers, have now been resituated in the very medium of the meeting itself: the text.

It was perhaps a mistake to place 'The Almost Meeting' at the beginning of Kreisel's book: both chronologically and thematically, it stands at the end. The other stories are certainly very fine, especially 'Two Sisters in Geneva' and, a classic of prairie fiction, 'The Broken Globe.' They provide a necessary thematic backdrop against which 'The Almost Meeting' may finally appear, not so much in a spotlight as in a negative, black light. But none of them has the surrounding complexity of the title story; none of them has its essentially post-modernist awareness of the problematic nature of its own textuality. The tentative and impermanent encounters of these stories tend to take place either by chance (in 'Chassidic Song') or through inter-mediaries (the academic in 'The Broken Globe,' the traveller in 'Two Sisters in Geneva'). In 'An Anonymous Letter' the question of the authority and referentiality of a text is raised, but only as a device to unsettle the confidence of the protagonist, not the narrator. These and other narrative techniques may indicate the equivocal nature of the 'meetings' within the stories; but only in 'The Almost Meeting' is the equivocation extended the final step to the text of the story itself. There it is Kreisel himself who is no longer sure of how, or if, he means what he says; the very brilliance of the first story has the effect of undermining the confident, unself-questioning narration of the subsequent stories. It remains to be seen whether Kreisel, like Lasker (his almost-anagram) will retreat into silence, or whether he can continue to perform these acts on the edge of language, affording us that ' "not much" ' which is yet, with all its reservations, decidedly ' "something".'

---

[1]*The Collected Poems of A.M. Klein*, edited by Miriam Waddington (Toronto: McGraw-Hill Ryerson, 1974), p. 335.

Bibliography of
Henry Kreisel's Writing

Collections

The Almost Meeting and Other Stories. Edmonton: NeWest Press, 1981. All citations of *The Almost Meeting* in the bibliography following are to this volume.

Another Country: Writings by and about Henry Kreisel, edited by Shirley Neuman. Edmonton: NeWest Press, 1985. All citations to *Another Country* in the bibliography following are to this volume.

Juvenilia

Henry Kreisel's early work has been published on two occasions:

white pelican, 4, 3 (Summer 1974), included a poem, 'Herschel Grynspan (Thought when hearing of his deportation to Germany)' (40) and excerpts from a novel *Miguel Amore [The Torch of Hate]* (36-39);

printed in this volume, *Another Country,* are two poems, 'The Violin' (p. 81) and 'Visit' (p. 82); excerpts from the novel, *The Torch of Hate* (pp. 73-79); and three short stories, 'Ginger' (pp. 85-90), 'Shall I Buy an Icecream?' (pp. 100-05), and 'Two Streets (pp. 93-99).

Novels

The Rich Man. Toronto: McClelland and Stewart, 1948.
[London: Heinemann, 1952; Toronto: New Canadian Library, 1961, 1971; Toronto: Simon and Schuster, 1975.]
[Condensed version: *National Home Monthly,* 51, 10-11 (October-November 1950).]
[Chapter Ten reprinted as 'Uncle Jacob' in *The Spice Box: An Anthology of Jewish Canadian Writing,* selected by Gerri Sinclair and Morris Wolfe. Toronto: Lester & Orpen Dennys, 1981. pp. 47-63.]

The Betrayal. Toronto: McClelland and Stewart, 1964.
[Toronto: New Canadian Library, 1971.]
['An episode from The Betrayal.' Edge, 1 (Autumn 1963), 49-59.]

Short Stories

'The Travelling Nude.' Prism, 1, 1 (Fall 1959), 7-17.
[Reprinted in: More Stories from Western Canada, edited by
Rudy Wiebe and Aritha van Herk. Toronto: Macmillan, 1980.
pp. 73-86;
Henry Kreisel, The Almost Meeting. pp. 107-20;
West of Fiction, edited by Leah Flater, Aritha van Herk, and
Rudy Wiebe. Edmonton: NeWest Press, 1983. pp. 156-68.]

'Homecoming.' Klanak Islands: A Collection of Short Stories.
Vancouver: Klanak Press, 1959. pp. 7-15.

'Two Sisters in Geneva.' Queen's Quarterly, 67 (Spring 1960), 67-75.
[Reprinted in: A Book of Canadian Stories, edited by Desmond
Pacey. 2nd rev. ed.; Toronto: Ryerson Press, 1962. pp. 294-303;
Modern Canadian Stories, edited by Giose Rimanelli and
Roberto Ruberto. Toronto: Ryerson Press, 1966. pp. 262-70;
Chinook Arch: A Centennial Anthology of Alberta Writing,
edited by John Patrick Gillese, W.G. Hardy and Margaret
Coleman Johnson. Edmonton: Government of Alberta, 1967.
pp. 321-29;
Tradition-Integration-Rezeption Symposium 1978, edited by
Karin R. Gürttler and Herfried Scheer. Montréal: Université de
Montréal, 1979. pp. 132-39;
Henry Kreisel, The Almost Meeting. pp. 123-32.]
[Translated as 'Zwei Schwestern in Genf,' by Armin Arnold, in
Neue Zürcher Zeitung. Zurich, Switzerland: Sonntag, 8, Januar,
1961, Blatt 6-7; reprinted in Kanadische Erzähler der Gegenwart,
selected and translated by Armin Arnold and Walter Riedel.
Zurich: Manesse Verlag, 1967. pp. 377-90.

'Annerl.' Prism, 2, 4 (Summer 1961), 35-40.
[Reprinted in: Henry Kreisel, The Almost Meeting. pp. 81-88.]

'The Broken Globe.' Literary Review, 8, 4 (Summer 1965), 484-95.
[Reprinted in: The Best American Short Stories 1966, edited by

Martha Foley and David Burnett. Boston: Houghton Mifflin Co., 1966. pp. 155-65;
Contact One: Short Stories of the 1960s, collected by F.E.S. Finn. London: John Murray, 1969. pp. 161-70;
Stories from Western Canada, edited by Rudy Wiebe. Toronto: Macmillan, 1972. pp. 92-103;
Perceptions in Literature, edited by Philip McFarlane, Allen Kirschner and Morse Peckham. Boston: Houghton Mifflin Co., 1972. pp. 98-106;
The Best Modern Canadian Short Stories, edited by Ivon Owen and Morris Wolfe. Edmonton: Hurtig Publishers, 1978. pp. 50-58;
The Alberta Diamond Jubilee Anthology, edited by John W. Chalmers, James Moir, June Bhatia, and Hugh A. Dempsey. Edmonton: Hurtig Publishers, 1979. pp. 92-101.
Henry Kreisel, *The Almost Meeting*. pp. 135-47.
The Oxford Anthology of Canadian Literature, edited by Robert Weaver and William Toye. 2nd ed.; Toronto: Oxford University Press, 1981. pp. 223-33;
An Anthology of Canadian Literature in English, edited by Donna Bennett and Russell Brown. Toronto: Oxford University Press, 1983. II, 97-105.]
[Translated as 'Der verbeulte Globus,' by Walter Riedel, in *Moderne Erzähler der Welt: Kanada*, selected and edited by Walter Riedel. Stuttgart: Horst Erdmann Verlag, 1976. pp. 252-64.]

'An Anonymous Letter.' In *Wild Rose Country: Stories from Alberta*, edited by David Carpenter. Ottawa: Oberon Press, 1977. pp. 115-28.
[Reprinted in: Henry Kreisel, *The Almost Meeting*. pp. 91-103.]

'Chassidic Song.' *Tamarack Review*, 75 (Fall 1978), 78-88.
[Reprinted in: Henry Kreisel, *The Almost Meeting*. pp. 25-35;
Mirror of a People: Canadian Jewish Experience in Poetry and Prose, edited by Sheldon Oberman and Elaine Newton (Winnipeg: Jewish Educational Publishers of Canada, 1985), pp. 212-20.]
[Translated as 'Chassidische Weise,' by Gottfried Probst, in *Gute Wanderschaft, mein Bruder: Eine Kanadische Anthologie*, edited by Gottfried Friedrich and Walter E. Riedel. Leipzig: St. Benno Verlag, 1985. pp. 163-73.]

'Homecoming: A Memory of Europe after the Holocaust' [revised and extended from its earlier version in *Klanak Islands*]. In Henry Kreisel, *The Almost Meeting*. pp. 39-77.

'The Almost Meeting.' In Henry Kreisel, *The Almost Meeting*. pp. 11-21.

'An Evening with Sholom Aleichem.' *Prism International*, 21, 3 (April 1983), 7-18.
[Reprinted in: *Another Country*. pp. 240-52.]

'To Visit Mother Rachel's Grave.' In *Another Country*. pp. 253-64.

Radio and Television Plays

He Who Sells His Shadow. Produced on CBC Wednesday Night Stage, September 1956; CBC Stage, 1960.
Published: *Another Country*. pp. 206-39.

The Betrayal. Produced on CBC-TV Bob Hope Theatre, December 1965.

Diaries, Memoirs

'Diary of an Internment' [1940-41]. *white pelican*, 4, 3 (Summer 1974), 5-35.
[Reprinted in: *Another Country*. pp. 18-44.]

'from Journal entries, December 1970 and January 1971.' In *Another Country*. pp. 65-68.

'Notes on Indian Convention at Driftpile, June 21-22 [1955].' In *Another Country*. pp. 159-61.

'Postscript to an Interview' [1980]. In *Another Country*. pp. 59-60.

'Vienna Remembered.' In *Another Country*. pp. 50-58.

'[Written on the death of my father].' In *Another Country*. pp. 62-65.

Personal Essays

'Problems of Writing in Canada' [mid-50s for CBC]. In *Another Country*. pp. 131-34.

'The "Newer" Canadians,' *Century 1867/1967, The Edmonton Journal,* Week of February 13th, 1967, pp. 49-50.

'The West—still the unknown country,' *The Edmonton Journal,* June 7, 1978, A5.

'Sheila Watson in Edmonton.' In *Figures in a Ground: Canadian Essays on Modern Literature Collected in Honor of Sheila Watson,* edited by Diane Bessai and David Jackel. Saskatoon: Western Producer Prairie Books, 1978. pp. 4-6.

'Language and Identity: A Personal Essay.' In *Tradition-Integration-Rezeption, Symposium 1978,* edited by Karin R. Gürttler and Herfried Scheer. Montréal: Université de Montréal, 1979. pp. 105-14.
[Extended version: published as 'The "Ethnic" Writer in Canada.' In *NeWest Review,* 5,3 (November 1979) 7, 16, and 5, 4, (December 1979), 7, 14; rpt. in *Identifications: Ethnicity and the Writer in Canada,* edited by Jars Balan. Edmonton: University of Alberta Press, 1982. pp. 1-13.
Another version: published as 'Language and Identity: A Personal Essay.' In *Another Country.* pp. 119-30.]

'Roy Daniells 1902-1979.' *Canadian Literature,* 81 (Summer 1979), 140-42.

'Has Anyone Here Heard of Marjorie Pickthall?: Discovering the Canadian Literary Landscape.' *Canadian Literature,* 100 (Spring 1984), 173-80.
[Reprinted in: *Another Country.* pp. 109-18.]

Critical Essays

'Bad Lands Sculptor [the Work of Wilfred Hodgson].' *1957 Encyclopedia Year Book.* [New York]: Grolier Society, 1957. pp. 35-37.

'The Arts—Useless—But Expensive.' *Bulletin of the Humanities Association of Canada* (April 1958), 7-10.

'Joseph Conrad and the Dilemma of the Uprooted Man.' *Tamarack Review,* 7 (Spring 1958), 78-85.

'Introduction' to John Heath, *Aphrodite* [edited by Henry Kreisel]. Toronto: Ryerson Press, 1958. pp. 3-4.

'Literature as Language.' *English Teacher,* 2, 2 (June 1962), 100-05.

'Are We Neglecting Modern Writers?' *English Teacher*, 4, 2 (June 1964), 34-40.

'A Place of Liberty.' *CAUT Bulletin*, 13, 1 (October 1964), 27-32.

'The Prairie: A State of Mind.' *Transactions of the Royal Society of Canada*, 6, series 4 (June 1968), 171-80.
  [Reprinted in: *Contexts of Canadian Criticism*, edited by Eli Mandel. Toronto: University of Toronto Press; Chicago, London: University of Chicago Press, 1971. pp. 254-66; *Canadian Anthology*, edited by Carl F. Klinck and Reginald E. Watters. Toronto: Gage, 1974. pp. 620-27; *Horizon: An Anthology of the Canadian Prairie*, edited by Ken Mitchell. Toronto: Oxford University Press, 1977. pp. 247-57. *An Anthology of Canadian Literature in English*, edited by Donna Bennett and Russell Brown. Toronto: Oxford University Press, 1983. II, 105-14.]

'Summing Up.' *Crossing Frontiers: Papers in American and Canadian Western Literature*, edited by Dick Harrison. Edmonton: University of Alberta Press, 1979. pp. 138-43.

In *Taking Stock: The Calgary Conference on the Canadian Novel*, edited by Charles Steele. Toronto: ECW Press, 1982. pp. 91-93; 142-44.

Reviews

Untitled review of *The Letters of Thomas Wolfe*, edited by Elizabeth Newell, and of *The Letters of D.H. Lawrence*, edited by Aldous Huxley. *Tamarack Review*, 2 (Winter 1957), 84-88.

Untitled review of *A Lattice for Momos* by R.G. Everson. *Dalhousie Review*, 39, 2 (Summer 1959), 277-79.

'The African Stories of Margaret Laurence.' *Canadian Forum*, 41 (April 1961), 8-10.
  [Reprinted in: *Margaret Laurence: Critical Views on Canadian Writers*, edited by William New. Toronto: McGraw-Hill Ryerson, 1977. pp. 105-10; *A Place to Stand On: Essays by and about Margaret Laurence*, edited by George Woodcock (Edmonton: NeWest Press, 1983) pp. 106-12.]

'Life and Letters' [review of *Edward Thomas: The Last Five Years* by Eleanor Farjeon]. *Queen's Quarterly*, 68 (Spring 1961), 193-94.

'Recent Criticism of the Novel.' *University of Toronto Quarterly,* 31, 2 (January 1962), 246-50.

Untitled review of *Masks of Fiction,* edited by A.J.M. Smith. *University of Toronto Quarterly,* 31, 4 (July 1962), 478-79.

'Dreams and Reality' [review of *Under the Ribs of Death* by John Marlyn]. *Canadian Literature,* 21 (Summer 1964), 64-66.

'A Familiar Landscape' [review of *The Tomorrow-Tamer and Other Stories* and *A Bird in the House* by Margaret Laurence]. *Tamarack Review,* 55 (1970), 91-94.
[Reprinted in *Margaret Laurence: Critical Views on Canadian Writers,* edited by William New. Toronto: McGraw-Hill Ryerson, 1977. pp. 143-45.]

'The Prairie Observed' [review of *Vertical Man/Horizontal World* by Laurie Ricou and of *Writers of the Prairies,* edited by Donald G. Stephens]. *Canadian Literature,* 61 (Summer 1974), 88-90.

Untitled review of *Bertolt Brecht's Berlin* by Wolf von Eckhardt and Sandor L. Gilman. *Modernist Studies,* 2, 1 (1976), 54-56.

'The Games of Martin Myers: Mr. Mannheim's Magical Mystery Tour' [review of *Izzy Mannheim's Reunion* by Martin Myers]. *Essays on Canadian Writing,* 11 (Summer 1978), 147-50.

'The Humanism of George Faludy' [review of *East and West: Selected Poems of George Faludy,* edited by John Robert Colombo]. *Canadian Forum,* 58 (March 1979), 27-29.

'The Poet as Radical: Dorothy Livesay in the Thirties.' *Contemporary Verse II,* 4 (Winter 1979), 19-21.

'Festschrift' [review of *A Political Art: Essays and Images in Honour of George Woodcock,* edited by W.H. New]. *Canadian Literature,* 84 (Spring 1980), 82-84.

Untitled review of *The Practical Vision: Essays in English Literature in Honour of Flora Roy,* edited by Jane Campbell and James Doyle. *Canadian Review of Comparative Literature,* 8, 4 (December 1981), 540-42.

Review of *A Voice in the Land: Essays by and about Rudy Wiebe,* edited by W.J. Keith. *Prairie Forum,* 7, 1 (Spring 1982), 131-36.

'Touching the Cultural Pulse' [review of *Division on a Ground: Essays on Canadian Culture* by Northrop Frye]. *Edmonton Journal* (July 11, 1982), C5.

Untitled review of *Masks of the Prophet: The Theatrical World of Karl Kraus* by Kari Grimstad. *Nineteenth Century Theatre Research*, 11, 1 (Summer 1983), 59-62.

Untitled review of A.M. Klein, *Short Stories*, edited by M.W. Steinberg. *Journal of Canadian Studies*, 19, 2 (Summer 1984), 160-62.

Interviews

Cherniavsky, Felix. 'Certain Worldly Experiences: An Interview with Henry Kreisel.' *Sphinx*, 2, 3 (Winter 1977), 10-22. [Excerpts reprinted in: *Another Country*. pp. 170-75.]

Butovsky, Mervin. 'Interview with Henry Kreisel.' In *Another Country*. pp. 176-201.

Name Index